I0132125

Henrietta L. (Henrietta Lee) Palmer

The Stratford Gallery, or, the Shakspeare Sisterhood

Comprising Forty-Five Ideal Portraits

Henrietta L. (Henrietta Lee) Palmer

The Stratford Gallery, or, the Shakspeare Sisterhood
Comprising Forty-Five Ideal Portraits

ISBN/EAN: 9783337032111

Printed in Europe, USA, Canada, Australia, Japan

Cover: Foto ©Thomas Meinert / pixelio.de

THE

STRATFORD GALLERY;

OR THE

SHAKSPEARE SISTERHOOD:

COMPRISING FORTY-FIVE IDEAL PORTRAITS,

DESCRIBED BY

HENRIETTA LEE PALMER.

Illustrated

WITH FINE ENGRAVINGS ON STEEL, FROM DESIGNS BY EMINENT HANDS.

"Here comes the Lady!"
ROMEO AND JULIET.

"I have no other reason but a woman's reason:
I think her so because I think her so."
TWO GENTLEMEN OF VERONA.

NEW YORK:
D. APPLETON AND COMPANY.
1867.

DEDICATION.

TO

J. W. P.

THE MOST EXACTING AND THE MOST ENCOURAGING:—

"SOMETHING BETWEEN A HINDERANCE AND A HELP."

PREFACE.

In offering the first fruits of her labor of love to the generous world of Shakspeare-lovers, the writer distinctly disclaims the intention of presumptuously identifying herself, in her unpretending task, with those whose names are honorably associated with the Master-Poet's, and who are known by their works, as his wise and faithful scholars and expounders. Yet does she confidently claim the right to speak of these, his Sisterhood, as one woman may justly speak of another—judging them, not with sophisticated research nor oracular criticism, but simply, naturally, sympathetically, as she may regard her fellow-women whom she meets from day to day.

New York, November 1, 1858.

THE PORTRAITS.

THE DESCRIPTIONS.

LADY MACBETH.

Gruoch, Lady Macbeth, was the wife of a renowned Scottish general in the royal army, of near kin to Duncan, the reigning king. Returning from victorious warfare against rebellious troops, in company with his comrade, Banquo, an officer of rank similar to his own, Macbeth was accosted by three witches, who prophesied that he should be king. This extraordinary good fortune—for witchcraft was then in high repute—he hastened to communicate to his wife, a woman of towering ambition, who immediately set about contriving the speediest plan to realize the promise of the weird sisters.

Chance rendered timely aid to her unscrupulous purpose. King Duncan, surnamed the Meek, for his amiable virtues, desiring to signally honor his faithful servant, made a visit to Macbeth's castle, accompanied by his two sons and gentlemen of the court. After the royal guest had retired for the night, his chamberlains having been drugged by Lady Macbeth, her husband, confirmed in his half-conceived treachery by the daring woman, murdered the good old king in his sleep.

The two princes fled for their lives—the one to England, the other to Ireland; and Macbeth, as next of kin, was proclaimed

King of Scotland; thus bringing to pass the witches' words, and realizing his wife's inordinate aspirations.

And now Macbeth remembered, how it had been promised to Banquo that his issue should succeed to the throne; and this thought so rankled in the minds of the guilty pair, that they determined to put to death Banquo and his son, to secure to their own posterity the honors for which they had paid so dearly. Accordingly Banquo was murdered by hired assassins, on his return from a grand feast given by his friend, King Macbeth; but his son Fleance escaped into a neighboring country; and from him eventually descended a long line of Scottish monarchs.

Thus, from one desperate crime to another the wretched king was impelled, by morbid fear of conspirators against his dignity or his life, till the people, exasperated, took violent measures to free themselves from his tyranny. Lady Macbeth died, an unpitied victim to "a mind diseased;" and her husband was killed in personal encounter with Macduff, a Scottish nobleman, whose wife and children had been inhumanly butchered by the usurper's order. Malcolm, the lawful successor of Duncan the Meek, was raised to the throne.

This is one of the many plays of Shakspeare in which the superstitious element constitutes a distinguishing feature; its supernatural effects are neither childish nor commonplace; they contribute in no small degree to the depicting of a terrible retribution, and are imbued with all the weirdness of the Black Art, in the days when the wisest believed in, and the boldest trembled before, its revelations.

Of all the Shakspearian Sisterhood, there is perhaps least unanimity of opinion as to the character of Lady Macbeth. She enjoys the distinction of being a successful puzzle to critics and commentators, who have exhausted even their ingenuity in attempting to deduce from her attributes any satisfactory conclusions. In the wide range of opinion she exists, successively: as a monstrous horror, delighting, vampire-like, in blood, for its own sake; a "pure demoniac," abstract incarnation of cruelty; a vulgar, vixenish fury; and a magnificent instance of the perversion, by one bad passion, of the rarest natural endowments—powerful intellect, marvellous force, and strong affections.

It is almost needless to say that the latter is the nearest approach to an intelligent appreciation of Lady Macbeth. Intellect and force we must all concede to her; and notwithstanding our first impulse to deny her any thing "pure womanly," her affections are as profound as may coexist with a mind exclusively masculine, and a heart fully possessed of a very devil of ambition.

It has been contended, with amiable plausibility, that this ambition was entertained only for her husband—that it was her complete identification of her own with his hopes and far-reaching aspirations which thus steeled her conscience, her woman's tenderness, her very physique, to an insane indifference to crimes, however revolting, so they but advanced his fortunes. But it is not easy to discover this absorbing passion for her husband in Lady Macbeth, or, indeed, any higher regard for him than the half-contemptuous, yet tenacious, affection almost always entertained by "strong-minded" women for men greatly inferior to themselves in force of character and intellect. On the other hand, Macbeth's implicit confidence in his wife, his boundless admiration of her courage, even in crime, his dependence upon her in every emergency to which he feels himself unequal, are but the tribute which every vacillating character, uncertain of its own powers, suspicious of its best efforts, pays to a forcible, self-asserting nature, capable of swaying it at its own grand will.

The individualization of Lady Macbeth is almost independent of her social relations, of her sex even; she is that hateful accident, a masculine heart, soul, and brain, clothed with a female humanity. Even the few touches of pathos or tenderness, introduced to remind us of her sex, as it were, would be natural to any man not positively monstrous; and her final remorse, madness, and death, we cannot regard as the repentance, or even horror, of the soul for its own deeds, but simply as the consequences of an organization physically inadequate to the demands of a too vigorous intellect.

In the same manner, the almost diabolic nerve displayed by her on the night of the king's murder, and subsequently, is plainly a mental victory over a body as frail as becomes her sex; the moment her vigilance is relaxed, or the immediate necessity for its exercise is removed, the fragile structure gives way, and drags down to its pitiful level all the splendors which have glorified its weakness.

What we mean to say is: that a *man*, having had the wickedness to plan, the courage to dare, the nerve to execute, so revolting a crime as the murder of an anointed king, who was moreover an illustrious kinsman and a condescending guest, would have lived on to the end with as little remorse as Lady Macbeth really felt, and with none of the physical demonstrations which may easily be mistaken for it. Separate Lady Macbeth the individual, from Lady Macbeth the woman, and the mystery of her character is at once cleared—she is woman in her incarnation only.

The text, oddly enough, supports our theory, in not affording a single hint of her person, whether tall or short, dark or fair.

We are told by Mrs. Jameson that Mrs. Siddons "had an idea that she was a small, fair, blue-eyed woman, from her Celtic origin;" she adds, however, that she cannot help fancying Lady Macbeth dark, like Black Agnes of Douglas, which we imagine must agree with the popular notion of her person.

We take our leave of Lady Macbeth with the following soliloquies—both well known, and most characteristic. The first occurs on the receipt of her husband's letter, announcing the prophetic salutations of the three witches; the second on hearing that the king will sleep that night at the Castle:

Lady M. * * * * * *
* * * * * * * *
Glamis thou art, and Cawdor; and shalt be
What thou art promis'd:—Yet do I fear thy nature;
It is too full o' the milk of human kindness,
To catch the nearest way. Thou would'st be great,
Art not without ambition; but without
The illness should attend it. What thou would'st highly,
That would'st thou holily; would'st not play false,
And yet would'st wrongly win. Thou'dst have, great Glamis,
That which cries, *Thus thou must do, if thou have it;*
And that which rather thou dost fear to do,
Than wishest should be undone. Hie thee hither,
That I may pour my spirits in thine ear,
And chastise with the valor of my tongue
All that impedes thee from the golden round
Which fate and metaphysical aid doth seem
To have thee crown'd withal.

* * * * * * The raven himself is hoarse
That croaks the fatal entrance of Duncan
Under my battlements. Come, come, you spirits
That tend on mortal thoughts! unsex me here,
And fill me, from the crown to the toe, top-full
Of direst cruelty! make thick my blood!
Stop up the access and passage to remorse,

That no compunctious visitings of nature
Shake my fell purpose, nor keep peace between
The effect and it! Come to my woman's breasts,
And take my milk for gall, you murd'ring ministers,
Wherever in your sightless substances
You wait on nature's mischief! Come, thick Night,
And pall thee in the dunnest smoke of hell!
That my keen knife see not the wound it makes,
Nor Heaven peep through the blanket of the dark,
To cry, *Hold, hold!*

For the somnambulic scene, that master-piece of physiological effect, which would suffer by mutilation, we refer our readers to the text.

JULIET.

Juliet was the only daughter, and heiress, of the Capulets, one of the proudest families of Verona, conspicuous for the deadly enmity existing between them and the equally influential Montagues. When Juliet had arrived at marriageable age, her father gave a grand masque at his palace, to which all the beauty and nobility of Verona were bid—among whom was Rosaline, niece to old Capulet, a fair but disdainful beauty, beloved by young Romeo Montague. To cure him of a hopeless passion, his friend, Benvolio, persuaded him to go to the entertainment, strictly disguised, and there compare his fair Rosaline with the excelling beauties who would be present.

Accordingly, Romeo and Benvolio, masked with studious precaution, for discovery would have been perilous, took part in the gay revel; and the young Montague no sooner beheld the beautiful Juliet than he forgot his Rosaline, and became passionately enamored of the fair Capulet. It was in his recklessly enthusiastic praise of her charms to Benvolio, that he was overheard by Tybalt, a hot-headed young kinsman of the Capulets, and recognized by his voice; Tybalt would have laid violent hands on him at once, but old Capulet interfered. That very night, after the guests had departed, and the inmates of the Capulet mansion had retired to their chambers, Romeo, spurred on by this new and irresistible passion, climbed the garden wall, and beheld the lady of his love seated on a balcony, indulging in the delicious reveries consequent upon her interview, in the ball-room, with Romeo. Overhearing her rapturous soliloquy, in which she called his name, he replied to it; and they parted only after exchanging vows of everlasting constancy, and a promise to meet at Friar Laurence's cell the next day, for the solemnization of their nuptials. On the morrow, accordingly, Romeo and Juliet were married by the holy Friar, who thought by this union to cancel forever the bitter feud between their houses; but that very day, Tybalt, still intent upon avenging the insolent intrusion of Romeo, met him in the street, provoked a quarrel, fought with him, and was killed.

For this fatal broil, the Prince of Verona banished Romeo, who, after taking a brief farewell of his few hours' bride, betook himself to Mantua. Juliet's tears and lamentations were attributed to her grief for the loss of her cousin Tybalt—the sooner to dissipate which, her father insisted upon marrying her almost immediately to the county Paris, "a gentleman of princely parentage and fair demesnes;" the wedding-day was set, and every preparation made.

Poor Juliet, finding remonstrance unavailing, hastened in her sorrow to the good Friar, who bade her feign obedience to her father's will, and gave her a potent drug which should cause her to appear as if dead—telling her that, while in this state, she should be borne to the burial vault of the Capulets, whence he and Romeo, for whom he would send, would rescue her. Juliet fulfilled his instructions; in the morning, when young Paris came with music to awaken his bride, she was found "dead," and the joyful festivities were changed into a doleful funeral service.

The Friar then despatched a special messenger to Romeo, with a letter informing him of the true case; but by some accident he was detained, and Romeo received intelligence through another source of his wife's death, which so distracted him with grief that he procured a deadly poison, and repaired forthwith to Juliet's tomb, determined to die on her beloved corse. Having reached the vault of the Capulets, he broke open the gloomy portal, and beheld the still beautiful body of his adored lady; with one kiss he drained the fatal bowl, and breathed his last, just as Juliet awoke, and the Friar, warned of the detention of his envoy, arrived in the hope of preventing the impending disaster.

This fatal catastrophe was productive, however, of one beneficial result: the Capulets and the Montagues were ever after united in bonds of friendship and interest—freely joining to do honor to the memory of those hapless victims to their accursed feud.

Of Juliet, Mrs. Jameson says: "Such beautiful things have already been said of her, only to be exceeded in beauty by the subject that inspired them, it is impossible to say any thing better—but it is possible to say something more." Alas for our task! this latter clause was true only before Mrs. Jameson wrote: not a detail of the subject has been neglected by her sympathetic pen; at the best, we can hope but to repeat her.

The loves of Romeo and Juliet, though physiologically, mentally, and morally, possible only to their traditional birth-place, Italy, have in them that "touch of nature which makes the whole world kin;" and it is to this element that we must attribute the universal popularity of the tragedy which commemorates them. To even the most lymphatic blood, the least susceptible fancy, there come those few, brief, "perfect days," when Passion, for the first time, asserts its boundless sway over the brain and the pulses —filling the one with ecstatic dreams of a future as blissful as it is infinite, kindling in the other a tormenting yet delicious tumult; and in proportion to the intensity with which we are capable of conceiving these emotions, is our sympathy with this story of two lovers, whose very names may stand for personifications of the passion to which they were beautiful martyrs.

At first it is the ingenuousness, the almost infantine simplicity, of Juliet's character, which endears her to our hearts. Her ex treme youth, her rare beauty, which has been perfected in jealous seclusion; her warm affections, repulsed by her austere parents, running to waste on her old nurse,—the only familiar object about which they may twine their eager tendrils; and finally, her love for Romeo, born of a glance, a sigh, a touch—yet, from the moment of its birth, a Titan which shakes to the centre her tender soul: all these constitute a picture, of which the interest and romance are almost too intense.

Yet it is not thus—in the first, happy delirium of her love—that Juliet engages our profoundest sympathy, our liveliest admiration. Not until Fate seems to have executed its most pitiless freaks upon her solitary heart; not until, her husband banished, she loses her sole friend and confidante, by the discovery of her time-serving baseness—the only mother, in familiar affection, she has ever known—and she, for the first time in her young life, asserts her own individuality, invincible through the force of her love, does she command that absorbing interest which would never have been awakened by mere self-abandonment to passion.

To use the words of Hazlitt, Juliet is, indeed, "a pure effusion of Nature"—a woman whose emotions and manifestations are of primeval innocence and vigor—in whom Love is the outward expression of an instinct as beautiful and holy as it is vehement—who is "Love itself—the passion which is her state of being, and out of which she has no existence." In nothing has Shakspeare proved his wondrous skill more clearly than in this creation of a human being in whom sense asserts itself paramount over reason—indeed, whose only manifestations of intellect are the inspirations of exalted sentiment, a sensuously excited eloquence; and yet who is endowed with such exquisite purity, as distinguished from the false teachings of a conventional modesty, that Eve herself is not more sacred from an imputation of grossness.

It is in this view of her character, and of the idea which Shakspeare expressed through her, that we propose to exceed, by a little, our privileges, to consider a question which properly belongs to the province of legitimate criticism.

A woman and a wife, to whom the hymeneal mysteries are the solemnest of rites, at whose altar she presides with veiled eyes, a jealous priestess, could almost reproach this awful Master, that he has entered the nuptial chamber of Juliet's soul, and exposed its beautiful secrets in words well-nigh too sacred to be pronounced, even to herself; but, since he has done so, she must bow before him as one unto whom, indeed, all hearts were open!

Jul. Gallop apace, you fiery-footed steeds,
Towards Phœbus' mansion! such a waggoner
As Phaeton would whip you to the west,
And bring in cloudy night immediately.
Spread thy close curtain, love-performing Night,
That run-away's eyes may wink—and Romeo
Leap to these arms, untalk'd of, and unseen!

* * * * * *

Come, Night! Come, Romeo! Come, thou day in night!
For thou wilt lie upon the wings of night
Whiter than new snow on a raven's back!

* * * * * *

O! I have bought the mansion of a love,
But not possess'd it; and, though I am sold,
Not yet enjoy'd. So tedious is this day,
As is the night before some festival
To an impatient child, that hath new robes
And may not wear them.

In this adjuration to Night, which is imbued with all the dim, ecstatic fervor of an epithalamium, the one word "run-away's" has given cause, perhaps, for more learned disputation and ingenious invention, to arrive at a satisfactory substitute, than any other in all of Shakspeare's much-abused text. And as to be his "scholar" is a position which "the humblest may with humility assume," may we not offer, with all becoming diffidence, a suggestion, which can be valuable only because it is the fruit of long pondering with our heart?

It will be remembered that Juliet, with the quick susceptibility of an Italian woman, having seen Romeo but once, *loves* him —with such absorbing love as, in a colder clime, would have required months, or even years, to mature; the very difficulties which surround them—the feudal enmity between their houses, which is fatal to their hopes—serve but to augment the enthusiastic fervor with which she abandons herself to her newly found delight. They exchange love-vows on the night of their very first meeting, and the next day they are joined by Holy Church in wedlock.

It is evidently late in the afternoon of a long, long, weary day of anxious hope and fear, and all the delirious ebbing and flowing of her heart's full tide, that Juliet gives utterance to this passionate longing, as, trembling with the reaction of her excited alarms, she sees almost within her reach the blessed darkness which shall again bring her lover to her—this time a husband;

so that in blest security her eyes, *run-away's eyes*—wide open the livelong day, on the look-out lest the very flowers may have blabbed her cherished secret—may *wink:* that is, may close in grateful repose, in exquisite peace, at last; and that, shut in from all the world, as with curtains, ("Spread thy close curtain, *love-performing* Night,") Romeo may leap to her arms, "untalk'd of, and unseen."

The term "run-away," in her application of it to herself, affects us with peculiar tenderness; could any thing be more touching in its pretty playfulness, more Juliet-like, than for her thus to liken herself unto a naughty child, which has stolen away from its parents to do the very thing, of all others in the world, that would most anger them? And she pursues the image, in again comparing herself to an "impatient child, that hath new robes and may not wear them." If the original word be "run-aways," plural, the same idea will apply equally to Romeo and herself; it would be even more natural for her to couple, and name alike, their identical transgressions.

> Spread thy close curtain, love-performing Night,
> That run-away's eyes may wink; and Romeo
> Leap to these arms, *untalk'd of, and unseen!*

The formidable stumbling-block to emendators has consisted in the supposed necessity of substituting for "run-away's" a metaphorical word to which these two participles can equally apply; but when we consider the fact that the discovery by her cousin Tybalt, of Romeo's audacious intrusion on their revel the night before, must have constituted the absorbing topic of conversation all day among the members of Juliet's own family—every word of which has blanched her cheek and filled her soul with quick alarms—does it not seem reasonable that the immediate reference for the "untalk'd of" should exist only in her mind? Is not a critically sustained figure even unnatural to the excited state of imagination which inspires the whole passage—and very un-Shakspearian besides?

As for the "unseen," why should that refer to the shutting of somebody's or something's eyes, when Romeo's invisibility depends only on what she is praying for, the coming of night? Is it not far more probable that the direct allusions of both participles should be "understood," than that in a soliloquy, under the influence of such emotions, Juliet would have employed a figure so elaborate, or so remote, that its discovery has baffled the learning and ingenuity of patient students from that time to this?

The word *Rumoure's* has been advanced with confidence, to take the place of "run-away's;" but—granting that Juliet could have maintained a figure of speech unimpaired, amid a chasing whirl of thoughts which found their only relief in fantastic extravagances without rule or order—in a highly figurative sense how can it be said that Rumor (meaning scandal) ever shuts her eyes? How could Juliet feel assured that the simple coming of night would close the eyes of this she-Argus, when it is then that she is most awake, and finds the choicest morsels for her flippant tongue?

An accomplished scholar and critic, Mr. Richard Grant White, has declared: "To correct a single passage in Shakspeare's text is glory enough for one man. He who discovers the needful word for the misprint, 'run-away's eyes,' will secure the honorable mention of his name as long as the English language is read and spoken."

To rescue the same passage from unnecessary "correction," and keep out "needful words" where no misprint is, should be glory enough for one woman; and without presuming to believe that the writer of this has succeeded where so many abler have failed, she may still venture to hope that the promised honor may yet fall to her sex. Where learning and research have been tried in vain, much faith should be reposed in the intuitive poetry, the quick, sympathetic understanding of a woman's heart, on a subject wherein her instincts are directly involved; and such an interpreter will not appeal in vain to the pure bridal mind of the Juliets of to-day, for whose sympathetic understanding the passionate outburst of their Shakspearian sister has utterances, almost unutterably true.

For a picture of superlative delicacy, the boldness of conscious innocence, and the delicious flutterings of a young heart wherein Love has but commenced the erection of his airy throne, Juliet in the balcony scene is unapproached. Hazlitt says of this scene, and that where the lovers part, the morning after their marriage: "Both are like a heaven upon earth—the blissful bowers of Paradise let down upon this lower world."

From the first, which we all know by heart—where "the whole of the dialogue appropriated to Juliet is one rich stream of imagery"—the following extract, alone, will suffice to prove that Juliet's character is the union of "passionate violence" with the rarest refinement and most delicate purity:

> *Jul.* Thou know'st the mask of night is on my face;
> Else would a maiden blush bepaint my cheek,
> For that which thou hast heard me speak to-night.
> Fain would I dwell on form—fain, fain deny
> What I have spoke; But farewell, compliment!
> Dost thou love me? I know thou wilt say—Ay;
> And I will take thy word. Yet, if thou swear'st,
> Thou may'st prove false; at lovers' perjuries
> They say Jove laughs. O gentle Romeo,
> If thou dost love, pronounce it faithfully;
> Or if thou think'st I am too quickly won,
> I'll frown, and be perverse, and say thee nay—

So thou wilt woo; but, else, not for the world.
In truth, fair Montague, I am too fond;
And therefore thou may'st think my haviour light:
But trust me, gentleman, I'll prove more true
Than those that have more cunning to be strange.
I should have been more strange, I must confess,
But that thou overheard'st, ere I was ware,
My true love's passion. Therefore pardon me,
And not impute this yielding to light love,
Which the dark night hath so discovered.

* * * * * * * *

Well, do not swear. Although I joy in thee,
I have no joy of this contract to-night:
It is too rash, too unadvis'd, too sudden—
Too like the lightning, which doth cease to be,
Ere one can say—It lightens. Sweet, good night!
This bud of love, by summer's ripening breath,
May prove a beauteous flower when next we meet.
Good night, good night! as sweet repose and rest
Come to thy heart, as that within my breast!

Without vain preface of admiration, here is the other:

Jul. Wilt thou be gone? it is not yet near day:
It was the nightingale, and not the lark,
That pierc'd the fearful hollow of thine ear;
Nightly she sings on yon pomegranate tree—
Believe me, love, it was the nightingale.
Rom. It was the lark, the herald of the morn,
No nightingale. Look, love, what envious streaks
Do lace the severing clouds in yonder east!
Night's candles are burnt out, and jocund Day
Stands tiptoe on the misty mountain tops;
I must be gone and live, or stay and die.
Jul. Yon light is not day-light—I know it, I:
It is some meteor that the sun exhales,
To be to thee this night a torch-bearer,
And light thee on thy way to Mantua.
Therefore stay yet, thou need'st not to be gone.

Rom. Let me be ta'en, let me be put to death;
I am content, so thou wilt have it so.
I'll say yon gray is not the morning's eye—
'Tis but the pale reflex of Cynthia's brow;
Nor that is not the lark, whose notes do beat
The vaulty heaven so high above our heads.
I have more care to stay than will to go;—
Come, Death, and welcome! Juliet wills it so.—
How is't, my soul? Let's talk, it is not day.
Jul. It is, it is! Hie hence, be gone, away!
It is the lark that sings so out of tune,
Straining harsh discords, and unpleasing sharps.
Some say the lark makes sweet division;
This doth not so, for she divideth us.
Some say the lark and loathed toad change eyes;
O, now I would they had changed voices too!
Since arm from arm that voice doth us affray,
Hunting thee hence with hunts-up to the day.
O, now be gone! more light and light it grows.
Rom. More light and light?—more dark and dark our woes.

Instead of ignoring the personal charms of Juliet in the superior interest which attaches to the tragic events of her story—as is true of almost every other woman in this fair company—there is no situation in the whole play of such dramatic intensity that it compels us to lose sight of them, so completely is the whole picture imbued with their excelling richness.

The single description by Romeo, as he gazes for the first time on her who will be his wife ere another night rolls round, is sufficient, of itself, to set her forever in our mind's eye, a thing of beauty and "a joy forever."

O, she doth teach the torches to burn bright!
Her beauty hangs upon the cheek of Night
Like a rich jewel in an Ethiop's ear—
Beauty too rich for use, for earth too dear!
So shows a snowy dove trooping with crows,
As yonder lady o'er her fellows shows.

And not less to this effect is his address to her, as she lies on her bier in the tomb of the Capulets:

> Here lies Juliet; and her beauty makes
> This vault a feasting presence full of light.
>
> * * * * * * * * *
> * * * * O, my love! my wife!
> Death, that hath suck'd the honey of thy breath,
> Hath had no power yet upon thy beauty.
> Thou art not conquer'd; Beauty's ensign yet
> Is crimson in thy lips and in thy cheeks,
> And Death's pale flag is not advanced there.
>
> * * * * * * * *
> * * * * Ah, dear Juliet,
> Why art thou yet so fair? Shall I believe
> That unsubstantial Death is amorous,
> And that the lean abhorred monster keeps
> Thee here in dark to be his paramour?

OPHELIA.

Ophelia, daughter of Polonius, lord-chamberlain to Claudius, King of Denmark, was beloved by Prince Hamlet, son of the previous, and nephew of the then reigning sovereign; for Queen Gertrude, Hamlet's mother, had with indecent haste married her deceased husband's brother. The shame of this unseemly conduct in his mother, added to grief for the death of his revered father, had so preyed on the mind of Hamlet, that a morbid melancholy took possession of him, and, it would seem, endowed him with supernatural prescience to suspect that his father had been murdered by his uncle, who had crowned his wicked ambition by marrying the queen-widow. While in this state of distracting doubt, he was informed, by some gentlemen of the court, that as they were on guard before the palace, the ghost of the late king, his noble father, had appeared to them three successive nights; whereupon, Hamlet watched with them, to test the truth of their words. At midnight the ghost appeared, and beckoned to Hamlet to follow it to a retired spot, where to his amazed ears it revealed the story of its murder by the treacherous brother, and commanded Hamlet to avenge the foul deed, but to leave the punishment of the guilty queen to Heaven and her own conscience: and then, as the cock crew, the poor ghost vanished.

Henceforth, self-dedicated to retribution, Hamlet counterfeited a harmless insanity, with fantastic tricks and "wild and whirling" words, calculated to distract attention from his secret purpose.

The king and queen, believing that the death of his father had occasioned this deplorable result, devised amusements to divert his mind: a company of players having been summoned to court, Hamlet seized the opportunity, and made use of them to prove to his own satisfaction the truth of the ghost's communication. He contrived for their representation a play, to be performed before the king, which should reproduce to the life the scene of his father's murder, as described by the ghost—the wife marrying with the poisoner of her husband.

The snare was successful; the guilty fears of the king betrayed him; with incoherent exclamations he interrupted the play, and retreated, all aghast, from the apartment.

Immediately after this scene of confusion, Queen Gertrude summoned Hamlet to her closet, intending to remonstrate with him upon his indecorous behavior; and during the somewhat violent altercation between them, he heard a noise behind the hangings of the room. Suspecting that the king was concealed there, he exclaimed, in an assumed frenzy, "A rat! a rat!" and pierced the arras with his sword, thereby killing the wily old statesman, Polonius, who had been posted to take note of the interview.

This fatal mistake served as a pretext for sending Hamlet out of the country—there being much disaffection among the people consequent upon the unwarrantable murder of Polonius; and the king despatched him to England, with secret papers providing for his assassination immediately on his arrival. The ship being attacked by pirates on the voyage, Hamlet boarded their vessel during the fight, and the king's creatures put off at once, leaving him to his fate. The pirates, on learning the rank of their captive, treated him with singular respect, and in consideration of his promise to exert a merciful influence in their behalf, landed him, unharmed, on the shores of Denmark.

In the meanwhile, however, the gentle lady Ophelia, overwhelmed with grief for the madness of her lover, and horror of her father's murder by his hand, had languished and "pined in thought," till her mind became hopelessly imbecile. She wandered about at her own lost will, bedecked with fantastic finery, chanting snatches of old ballads, her modest tongue now babbling coarse jests; and one day, climbing a willow that grew on the margin of a brook, to hang a garland on its far-reaching bough, the slender limb broke, and she was precipitated into the stream:

Her clothes spread wide,
And, mermaid like, a while they bore her up:
Which time, she chanted snatches of old tunes,
As one incapable of her own distress,
Or like a creature native and indu'd
Unto that element. But long it could not be,
Till that her garments, heavy with their drink,
Pull d the poor wretch from her melodious lay
To muddy death.

The funeral of the hapless lady was celebrated with all affection and honorable ceremony, the king and queen in person taking part in her obsequies; and it was this sad spectacle which greeted Hamlet on his return home—the procession entering the churchyard while he was loitering there, in conversation with his friend Horatio. Frantic with grief, cruelly augmented by such sudden intelligence of Ophelia's death, and the manner of it, he leaped into her grave, vowing to be buried alive with her whom he had loved so fondly, till the horrible purpose of his life had driven every other emotion from his harassed mind.

Hamlet, shortly after this sad event, met his death at the hands of Laertes, with whom he was engaged in a fencing match in the presence of the court. The king had easily won over Laertes to play treacherously with Hamlet, and had prepared a poisoned draught for the prince, in case he should escape the envenomed blade of his adversary. The queen, not privy to the king's plot, drank of the fatal bowl, from the effects of which she died on the spot. Laertes and Hamlet wounded each other mortally with the poisoned foil, which changed hands in the scuffle. In his dying agonies Laertes confessed his vile plot with the king, and Hamlet, with his last remaining strength, stabbed the royal parricide to the heart with the same weapon which had dealt his own death-blow.

We shrink from the task of dissecting the sensitive beauties of Ophelia's character, as we should from the necessity of tearing apart the blushing bosom of a rose to count its stamens, or of impaling a butterfly to ascertain its "family;" we prefer to have a not too sharply defined idea of this most delicate embodiment, to accept her as a beautiful article of faith, which it is neither necessary nor desirable to thoroughly understand.

Ophelia is a more ideal, a more purely imaginative creation than Juliet or Desdemona; with the story of her youth, her tender beauty, her hapless love which leads to insanity and a tragic death, we sympathize less painfully than with the sorrows of those more vividly depicted heroines; indeed the very tints, pale yet enduring, in which her shadowy outline is traced, constitute a touching appeal to the hand of a would-be "restorer;" one should be content to spare her retiring delicacy any sentiment of pity more impertinently familiar than a tender pathos.

The childlike nature of Ophelia, innocent of even the knowledge of evil, impresses us from the first with the conviction that she is foredoomed a victim—a beautiful but inevitable sacrifice to relentless Destiny. Amid the bad passions, the subtle plottings, the tasteless criminality of the Danish court, she alights, a dove of gentleness and love, a very snowflake of virginity; she must die, or suffer contamination—and she fulfils the only alternative possible to her. In contradistinction to our almost resentful contemplation of the sad fates which befall Juliet and Desdemona, we are perfectly reconciled to the melancholy consummation of Ophelia's woes. We feel that, to her, reaction from so blasting a shock would be impossible—that after the first rude jarring of her delicately attuned sensibilities, which leaves them shattered and discordant, their sweet harmony can never again be restored.

It is pitiful to note how this young creature, whose love is so exquisitely sensitive that she scarce confesses it to herself, is tortured by the tactless catechizing of her hot-headed brother, and her garrulous, worldly-wise old father—of all men the two least fitted to probe the tender depths of her heart, and having found its secret, to advise her of her danger without corrupting her angelic purity.

The very faith she reposes in their words, accepting them as oracles, however her instinctive belief in her lover's honor may cry out against the outrage, renders their lessons the more cruel; she has no wit with which to confound them, no words to uphold her in ever so gentle an argument; she has no choice but to believe and obey—a mere puppet in their hands. At first, allowed the full bent of her inclination in giving audience "most free and bounteous" unto the lord Hamlet; then forbidden to see or speak with him; and still again, given up to him, as it were, as an unfeeling test of his alleged madness for her love: when we consider the alternations of hope, fear, and final despair which must have attended each experiment, we cannot be surprised that they result in a total overthrow of her "most ingenious sense," "dividing her from her fair judgment."

The interviews between Ophelia and Laertes, or Polonius, are inexpressibly touching:

Laer. For Hamlet, and the trifling of his favor,
Hold it a fashion, and a toy in blood—
A violet in the youth of primy nature,
Forward, not permanent, sweet, not lasting,
The perfume and suppliance of a minute;
No more.
Oph. No more but so?
Laer. Think it no more.
* * * * * * * * *
Pol. What is't, Ophelia, he said to you?
Oph. So please you, something touching the lord Hamlet.
Pol. Marry, well bethought:
'Tis told me, he hath very oft of late
Given private time to you; and you yourself
Have of your audience been most free and bounteous.
* * * * * * * * * *
What is between you? Give me up the truth.
Oph. He hath, my lord, of late, made many tenders
Of his affection to me.
Pol. Affection? puh! you speak like a green girl,
Unsifted in such perilous circumstance.
Do you believe his tenders, as you call them?
Oph. I do not know, my lord, what I should think.
Pol. Marry, I'll teach you: think yourself a baby,
That you have ta'en these tenders for true pay
Which are not sterling.
Oph. My lord, he hath importun'd me with love,
In honorable fashion.
Pol. Ay, fashion you may call it; go to, go to!
Oph. And hath given countenance to his speech, my lord,
With almost all the holy vows of heaven.

Pol. Ay! springes, to catch woodcocks.
From this time,
Be somewhat scanter of your maiden presence;
Set your entreatments at a higher rate
Than a command to parley. For lord Hamlet,
Believe so much in him—that he is young;
And with a larger tether may he walk
Than may be given you; In few, Ophelia,
Do not believe his vows. * * *
* * * * This is for all:—
I would not, in plain terms, from this time forth,
Have you so slander any moment's leisure,
As to give words or talk with the lord Hamlet.
Look to 't, I charge you; come your ways.
Oph. I shall obey, my lord.

But if these exhibitions of Ophelia's pitiable helplessness are sad, what shall be thought of her permitted interview with her lover, to whom, in two short, simple sentences, she tells the story of all she has suffered, and must die for?—and what shall be said of Hamlet, thus to flay alive the innocent soul which had given itself so unreservedly into his keeping? But we are magnifying our office; not ours, thank heaven, the task to justify that myth of myths:

Ham. * * * * * * *
* * * * * Soft you, now!
The fair Ophelia:—Nymph, in thy orisons
Be all my sins remember'd.
Oph. Good my lord,
How does your honor for this many a day?
Ham. I humbly thank you—well.
Oph. My lord, I have remembrances of yours
That I have longed long to re-deliver;
I pray you, now receive them.
Ham. No, not I;
I never gave you aught.
Oph. My honor'd lord, you know right well you did;
And, with them, words of so sweet breath compos'd

As made the things more rich. Their perfume lost,
Take these again; for to the noble mind
Rich gifts wax poor when givers prove unkind.
There, my lord!

* * * * * * * * *

Ham. * * * * * * *

I did love you once.

Oph. Indeed, my lord, you made me believe so.

Ham. You should not have believed me; for virtue cannot so inoculate our old stock but we shall relish of it. I lov'd you not.

Oph. I was the more deceived.

* * * * * * * * * *

Ham. If thou dost marry, I'll give thee this plague for thy dowry: Be thou as chaste as ice, as pure as snow, thou shalt not escape calumny. Get thee to a nunnery; farewell! Or, if thou wilt needs marry, marry a fool; for wise men know well enough what monsters you make of them. To a nunnery, go! and quickly too. Farewell!

Oph. Heavenly powers, restore him!

Ham. I have heard of your paintings, too, well enough; God hath given you one face, and you make yourselves another; you jig, you amble, and you lisp, and nickname God's creatures, and make your wantonness your ignorance: Go to, I'll no more of 't; it hath made me mad. I say, we will have no more marriages: those that are married already, all but one, shall live; the rest shall keep as they are. To a nunnery, go!

Oph. O, what a noble mind is here o'erthrown!
The courtier's, soldier's, scholar's eye, tongue, sword,
The expectancy and rose of the fair state,
The glass of fashion and the mould of form,
The observed of all observers—quite, quite down!
And I, of ladies most deject and wretched,
That suck'd the honey of his music vows,
Now see that noble and most sovereign reason,
Like sweet bells jangled, out of tune and harsh—
That unmatch'd form and feature of blown youth,
Blasted with ecstasy. O, woe is me!
To have seen what I have seen, see what I see!

IMOGEN.

The princess Imogen, daughter of Cymbeline, King of Britain, had secretly married Posthumus, an orphan, who had been in a manner adopted by the king, and educated as his own son. Cymbeline, by his first queen, had three children—Imogen, and two sons, who were stolen in infancy by a revengeful courtier: his second queen had one son by a former marriage, named Cloten, for whom she employed every means to secure the hand of Imogen, sole heiress to the British throne. The discovery of Imogen's secret marriage frustrated these ambitious plans, and so incensed the king, her father, that he banished Posthumus from the kingdom. Posthumus left with his bride, for their mutual service, his faithful gentleman Pisanio; and so they parted, after having exchanged love-pledges—Imogen giving her husband a rare diamond ring, and he bestowing in return a curious bracelet.

Arrived in Rome, Posthumus fell in company with a party of gay young fellows, who were descanting on the charms and superior excellencies of their respective mistresses; and he, joining the good-humored wranglers, boasted his blessed possession of the faultless Imogen. Whereupon Iachimo, a Roman, laid a wager—

the half of his estates against the diamond ring which Posthumus wore—that he would repair to Britain and bring back abundant proof that he had won Imogen's love, and accomplished her dishonor. The wager was accepted; and Iachimo arrived at the British court with a letter from Posthumus to his wife, recommending his honored friend to her courteous attention.

Iachimo, after insinuating doubts of her husband's fidelity into the chaste mind of the princess, told her of his shameless relations with some Roman woman, and ended by inciting her to revenge herself upon her recreant lord by accepting his own infamous proposals. Imogen's indignation at this gratuitous insult to her virtue, left Iachimo no chance of success; but he quickly obtained her forgiveness by confessing it a ruse to test her chastity. Before he took his leave he received permission from Imogen to allow a chest of valuables, in which he said her husband was interested, to be conveyed to her bed-chamber for safe-keeping. In this trunk he concealed himself; and when the princess was asleep, he emerged from his hiding-place, took careful note of the furnishings of the apartment, as well as of a secret mark on her person, and possessed himself of the precious bracelet, that he might take back to Rome plausible proofs of his having succeeded in his extraordinary adventure.

Provided with these, he had little difficulty in deceiving Posthumus, who, distracted with grief, sent orders to Pisanio to kill Imogen. At the same time, Posthumus despatched a letter to his wife, instructing her to meet him at a Welch town. Pisanio, convinced of his mistress's innocence, revealed to her her husband's suspicions, and assured her that, so far from obeying his master's cruel orders, he had accompanied her thus far only to set her on the way to Posthumus, whom she must disabuse of his false impressions; for her better protection, he disguised her as a page, and, in case she should be ill, gave her a powerful drug, which the queen had bestowed upon him as a valuable restorative.

Exhausted with fatigue and hunger, Imogen entered a cave, in the forest through which she was journeying, which was inhabited by an old man and his two sons, who led the lives of hunters. They made her welcome to their rude comforts; but she fell ill, and bethinking her of Pisanio's drug, swallowed a portion of it, and was thrown into a trance, which so resembled death that the youths laid her in the forest, making her a grave of leaves and flowers.

Awaking from this deep slumber, she was found by Lucius, the Roman general, who took her into his service as a page; and thus she travelled with the grand Roman army, which had then invaded England, and was marching towards the capital. Posthumus also was following this army, to join the British host so soon as it should reach its destination.

In an engagement between the opposing forces, Posthumus, and the two hunter-lads who had entertained Imogen, by their desperate valor saved King Cymbeline from defeat and death. Lucius, together with his page Fidele, and Iachimo, were taken prisoners and brought before the king—Posthumus being summoned likewise, to receive sentence of death for having, unbidden, returned from banishment. Whereupon all mystery was cleared away: the two youths proved to be Cymbeline's lost sons, who had been brought up by Belarius; Imogen discovered herself, to the great joy of her father; Iachimo confessed his treachery; and Posthumus, freely pardoned by his king and wife, was restored to her faithful love.

To Imogen has been awarded, almost without a dissenting voice, the high distinction of being the most admirable of her immortal company—a woman in whom all perfections meet in rare harmony—who never cloys, never disappoints.

Of all Shakspeare's *wives*—and he delighted in shaping models of conjugal fidelity—she is the master-piece; chaste, ardent, brave, devoted, and beautiful, she is indeed "best of wives, most delightful of women." The secret charm of Imogen's character is that she comes within the range of popular sympathy more successfully than her equally excellent married sisters: we never recognize Juliet as a wife—in fact, she never assumes that position; at the best, we offer but cold tribute of admiration to the classic virtues of Hermione and the Roman Portia; Desdemona we pity, tenderly, though with a degree of half-conscious contempt. But our sweet princess of Britain commands our exalted respect, while she elicits a sympathy which can never degenerate into commiseration.

With all her softness, her "fear and niceness"—a "lady so tender of rebukes that words are strokes, and strokes death to her"—she is not, like Desdemona, passive under injustice, even to painful self-humiliation; or, like Hermione, statuesquely heroic. Her dignity is never more proudly asserted than in her very subjection to her husband's will, even when he is no longer entitled to her duty.

An excellent exemplification of this trait of her character is afforded by the scene in which Pisanio detains her, when midway on her rapturous journey to meet her banished lord, to confess that Posthumus has ordered him to kill her, on an accusation of infidelity.

She receives the astounding intelligence, at first, with all the indignation natural to a woman whose purity is equalled by her spirit:

False to his bed! What is it to be false?
To lie in watch there, and to think on him?
To weep 'twixt clock and clock? if sleep charge nature,
To break it with a fearful dream of him,
And cry myself awake? That's false to his bed,
Is it?

Yet her despair, her shocking disappointment in one who, to her fond eyes, had "sat 'mongst men like a descended god," even a half malicious desire to die, in order that her husband's remorse may be complete when he discovers his mistake, influence her to pray for death at Pisanio's hands:

Imo. * * * * * * * *
Come, fellow, be thou honest:
Do thou thy master's bidding. When thou see'st him,
A little witness my obedience. Look!
I draw the sword myself! take it; and hit
The innocent mansion of my love, my heart!
Fear not; 'tis empty of all things, but grief.
Thy master is not there, who was, indeed,
The riches of it. Do his bidding; strike!

How similar, and yet how unlike, too, is the following remonstrance to Hermione's words to her husband under almost the same circumstances:

* * * * * * * * * * * *
And thou, Posthumus, thou that didst set up
My disobedience 'gainst the king my father,
And make me put into contempt the suits
Of princely fellows, shalt hereafter find
It is no act of common passage, but
A strain of rareness; and I grieve myself
To think, when thou shalt be disedg'd by her
That now thou tir'st on, how thy memory
Will then be pang'd by me.

With what a pretty acknowledgment of dependence on her love, does she answer Pisanio's plans for her future disposition:

> Why, good fellow,
> What shall I do the while? Where bide? How live,
> Or in my life what comfort, when I am
> Dead to my husband?

—which is paralleled, in sentiment and construction, by her reply to Iachimo, in that grandly characteristic scene where he attempts her dishonor by poisoning her ear with foul suspicions of her lord's loyalty:

> Reveng'd!
> How should I be reveng'd? If this be true,
> (As I have such a heart that both mine ears
> Must not in haste abuse,)—if it be true,
> How should I be reveng'd?

We cannot agree with those who deny the possession of jealousy to Imogen; nor can we regard as a blemish in her the possession of just so much as is natural to a woman of sensitive imagination and ardent emotions. To be grandly superior to this most feminine weakness would argue, either that she was endowed with self-esteem so overweening as to preclude to her mind the possibility of a rival, or that she was passionless to indifference—either supposition being absurd in its application to her. We detect a pretty trace of this element in the parting scene with Posthumus:

> *Imo.* Nay, stay a little:
> Were you but riding forth to air yourself,
> Such parting were too petty. Look here, love!
> This diamond was my mother's; take it, heart!
> But keep it till you woo another wife,
> When Imogen is dead.

Post. How! how! another?—
You gentle gods, give me but this I have,
And sear up my embracements from a next
With bonds of death!

—which is plainly but a tender trick to catch his amorous protestations in reply. But she repeats it, and this time with more passionate meaning:

I did not take my leave of him, but had
Most pretty things to say. Ere I could tell him
How I would think on him at certain hours,
Such thoughts, and such; *or I could make him swear*
The shes of Italy should not betray
Mine interest and his honor; or have charg'd him,
At the sixth hour of morn, at noon, at midnight,
To encounter me with orisons—for then
I am in heaven for him; or ere I could
Give him that parting kiss which I had set
Betwixt two charming words—comes in my father,
And, like the tyrannous breathing of the north,
Shakes all our buds from growing.

This last conceit is superfinely delicate; indeed, the scene throughout shows Imogen almost Juliet-like in her extravagant fancies and highly wrought imaginings.

And again, in her vehement talk with Pisanio, she at once seizes upon the abhorred conclusion to solve the horrible mystery of her lord's injustice:

* * * * * * * * *
* * * * * Some jay of Italy,
Whose mother was her painting, hath betray'd him.
Poor I am stale, a garment out of fashion;
And, for I am richer than to hang by the walls,
I must be ripp'd:—to pieces with me!

Pisanio essays to comfort her:

It cannot be,
But that my master is abus'd:
Some villain—ay, and singular in his art—
Hath done you both this cursed injury.
Imo. Some Roman courtezan.

She persistently rejects every other supposition for this one, which is of all the least probable, except to her self-tortured heart.

Imogen, with the single exception of Juliet, must be considered the most beautiful of her sisterhood; throughout the text much pains is taken to scatter passages tending to the establishment of this charming impression. We cannot see her "clothed on" with that "bewildering plenitude of loveliness" with which a more gallant admirer endows her; our idea of her person, photographically fixed, is that of extreme but enchanting delicacy; and this is satisfactorily supported by a careful study of the effect her beauty produces on the beholder. Belarius says of her when, famished, she has entered his cave:

Stay! come not in!—
But that it eats our victuals, I should think
Here were a fairy.
* * * * * * * *
By Jupiter, an angel! or if not,
An earthly paragon!—Behold divineness
No elder than a boy!

And of like character are several descriptions in the exquisite burial scene:

Gui. Oh sweetest, fairest lily!
My brother wears thee not one half so well
As when thou grew'st thyself.

* * * * * * * * *
* * * * * Why, he but sleeps:
If he be gone, he'll make his grave a bed;
With female fairies will his tomb be haunted,
And worms will not come to thee.
Arv. With fairest flowers—
Whilst summer lasts, and I live here, Fidele—
I'll sweeten thy sad grave: Thou shalt not lack
The flower that's like thy face, pale primrose; nor
The azur'd hare-bell, like thy veins; no, nor
The leaf of eglantine, whom not to slander,
Out-sweeten'd not thy breath; the ruddock would,
With charitable bill, (O bill, sore-shaming
Those rich-left heirs that let their fathers lie
Without a monument!) bring thee all this;
Yea, and furr'd moss besides, when flowers are none,
To winter-ground thy corse.

And in Iachimo's description it is noticeable that, although its luxurious imagery is even oppressive, there is none of the grossness which might be expected from so unscrupulous a libertine; it would seem that the chaste, almost supernatural, loveliness of the sleeping lady had refined him for the time:

* * * * * * * * * *
* * * * * * Cytherea,
How bravely thou becom'st thy bed! fresh lily—
And whiter than the sheets! That I might touch!
But kiss! one kiss!—Rubies unparagon'd,
How dearly they do 't—'Tis her breathing that
Perfumes the chamber thus. The flame o' the taper
Bows toward her, and would underpeep her lids,
To see the enclosed lights, now canopied
Under these windows: White and azure, lac'd
With blue of heaven's own tinct!
* * * * * * * * *
* * * * * On her left breast
A mole cinque-spotted, like the crimson drops

I' the bottom of a cowslip. Here's a voucher,
Stronger than ever law could make!

As to the *ways* of Imogen, there is a pretty suggestiveness in the circumstance of her reading late in bed, and in the matter of her reading:

Imo. What hour is it?
Lady. About midnight, madam.
Imo. I have read three hours then; mine eyes are weak;
Fold down the leaf where I have left. To bed!
* * * * * * * * *
* * * * * * * * *
Iach. * * * She hath been reading late,
The tale of Tereus; here, the leaf's turned down
Where Philomel gave up.

MIRANDA.

ONCE upon a time, the fair kingdom of Milan was governed by Duke Prospero, an honorable prince, beloved by his subjects, but given much more to the pursuit of art and science, and the "bettering of his mind," than to the management of the state. All his worldly affairs, the cares and ceremonies devolving upon his position, he confided to Antonio, his younger brother, who, being an ambitious, unscrupulous man, so turned the flattering trust to his own advantage, that, with the assistance of the king of Naples, he usurped the throne

Antonio feared the people's displeasure if he should put his brother to death; so he sent Prospero out to sea, with Miranda, his only child, as yet an infant—giving orders to Gonzalo, one of his lords, to set them adrift in a wretched boat with no provision, and leave them thus to perish.

Gonzalo, however, took pity on the good duke and his pretty babe: he was forced to obey, in part, his new master's orders; but he filled the boat with food, clothing-stuffs, and a few volumes from the royal library, of which Prospero had been only too fond.

By and by the boat, tossed hither and thither by the waves, was cast upon an enchanted island, uninhabited save by spirits.

Here Prospero fitted up a cave to be his dwelling-place, and here he tenderly nurtured his child, and studied his books of magic, of which pet science of that day, he was a master. By virtue of this knowledge he released many beautiful spirits, confined in the bodies of trees by a cruel witch who had held dominion over the island; and they, in gratitude, were his faithful servants ever after.

Thus lived the duke and his daughter, seeing no other human being, pursuing together their studies and innocent amusements, till Miranda had become a beautiful young maiden. About this time it happened that the king of Naples, with his son, Prince Ferdinand, and Antonio, duke of Milan, accompanied by Gonzalo, Prospero's kind friend, and many attendant courtiers, took voyage together in a stately ship; and as she approached the island, Prospero, informed by his art of her passengers, commanded his attendant elves to raise a great storm about the vessel, which cast the travellers, shipwrecked, on his shores.

Ariel, chief of the aerial sprites, instructed by his master, led Prince Ferdinand at once, by his supernatural song, into the presence of the duke and his daughter; for Prospero had conceived the fine plan of revenging himself on the treacherous king of Naples, by causing his son to fall in love with Miranda, and make her his wife and future queen. His project succeeded: the young prince became enamored at first sight of the enchanting maiden, and invited her to be the partner of his throne. The rest of the shipwrecked party were not permitted to interrupt their love-making till their preferences were firmly established; then Ariel was commanded to conduct the king of Naples and Antonio, with their servants, to the shelter and refreshment of Prospero's cave, where every thing was quickly explained: Antonio implored the forgiveness of his brother Prospero; the Neapolitan king sanctioned the union of his son with Miranda; and finally, the delicate Ariel accomplished his last task—that of accompanying the ship with gentle gales, which should waft her noble passengers to home and happiness.

Miranda, the Admirable, as her name denotes, is a purely ideal creation of the poet's mind—Titania herself not more imbued with the essence of fairy-land.

So spiritual, so ethereal is her organization, that it baffles all merely practical attempts to analyze or classify it; to her most material beholder she is scarce more than an exquisite, magical illusion, which, if too boldly approached, a wave of some mystic wand will instantly dispel.

In body, mind, and spirit, Miranda is essentially virgin; her grace, her beauty, her self, are as guiltless of any meretricious suggestion as in the hour when she was born: "society" is a sealed book to her innocent eyes—the world, a myth. Her quick susceptibility to a love as pure as it is passionate seems the one only quality she possesses in common with her sisters; she is the child of Nature and super-Nature—belonging to humanity, but a humanity so free from base alloy that it is but a step removed from the pure spiritual.

The fact that she is a duke's daughter, and the affianced bride of a prince, does nothing toward humanizing Miranda: the duke is the legitimate magician-duke of fairy romance; the prince, the invariable Prince Charming, whose intrepid devotion is rewarded by the hand of the enchanted beauty.

Surrounded by all the witchery of a spell-bound home, ministered to by invisible spirits who rejoice to acknowledge her their mistress, charmed by strains of supernatural melody, isolated from association or sympathy with all human beings save her father, who is, himself, less a man than a weird, powerful necromancer, Miranda exists apart, in our imagination—something less than goddess, yet more than woman.

There is no attempt to depict a beauty so ethereal that in the very process of description it would become materialized, and thus lose half its charm. But its effect upon all beholders is carefully reproduced; and that alone sets one's fancy dreaming of all most beautiful "things of beauty," in heaven or on earth, to make up this ideal "joy forever." We perfectly sympathize with Ferdinand's salutation on first meeting her; that which, addressed to any other woman, would have passed but as an amorous hyperbole, or a courtly phrase of the time, becomes, in its application to her, the expression of a bewitched conviction:

> Most sure, the goddess
> On whom these airs attend! * * * *
> * * * * * My prime request,
> Which I do last pronounce, is, O you wonder!
> If you be maid or no?
> *Mir.* No wonder, sir;
> But certainly a maid.

And this is not simply the illusion of young and ardent eyes. Alonzo, king of Naples, exclaims on first seeing her at chess with his son:

> What is this maid, with whom thou wast at play?
> Is she the goddess that hath severed us,
> And brought us thus together?

The dainty delicacy of the love-making scene, between Miranda and her lover, cannot be surpassed; under her chaste influence, Ferdinand, the young gallant of a gay court, confessing himself to have kept no fast at Pleasure's board, becomes, for the time at least, almost as pure in heart as she, and their love, resolved into a beautiful instinct, loses every gross attribute of passion.

Ferdinand, by command of Prospero, is bearing logs—he "must remove some thousands of these logs, and pile them up, upon a sore injunction:"

> *Mir.* You look wearily.
> *Fer.* No, noble mistress; 'tis fresh morning with me,
> When you are by, at night. I do beseech you,
> (Chiefly that I might set it in my prayers,)
> What is your name?
> *Mir.* Miranda:—O my father
> I have broke your 'hest to say so!
> *Fer.* Admired Miranda!
> Indeed, the top of admiration—worth
> What's dearest to the world! Full many a lady
> I have eyed with best regard, and many a time
> The harmony of their tongues hath into bondage
> Brought my too diligent ear; for several virtues
> Have I liked several women—never any
> With so full soul but some defect in her
> Did quarrel with the noblest grace she owed,
> And put it to the foil. But you, O you,
> So perfect and so peerless, are created
> Of every creature's best!
> *Mir.* I do not know
> One of my sex! no woman's face remember,
> Save from my glass mine own; nor have I seen
> More that I may call men, than you, good friend,
> And my dear father; how features are abroad
> I am skill-less of. But, by my modesty,
> (The jewel in my dower,) I would not wish
> Any companion in the world but you!
> Nor can imagination form a shape,
> Beside yourself, to like of.—But I prattle
> Something too wildly, and my father's precepts
> Therein forget.

Fer. I am, in my condition,
A prince, Miranda—I do think, a king
(I would not so !) ; and would no more endure
This wooden slavery than I would suffer
The flesh-fly blow my mouth.—Hear my soul speak :
The very instant that I saw you, did
My heart fly to your service ; there resides,
To make me slave to it ; and for your sake
Am I this patient log-man.
Mir. Do you love me ?
Fer. O heaven, O earth ! bear witness to this sound,
And crown what I profess with kind event
If I speak true ; if hollowly, invert
What best is boded me to mischief ! I,
Beyond all limit of what else i' the world,
Do love, prize, honor you !
Mir. I am a fool,
To weep at what I am glad of.
Fer. Wherefore weep you ?
Mir. At mine unworthiness, that dare not offer
What I desire to give ; and much less take
What I shall die to want.—But this is trifling ,
And all the more it seeks to hide itself,
The bigger bulk it shows. Hence, bashful Cunning !
And prompt me, plain and holy Innocence !
I am your wife, if you will marry me ;
If not, I'll die your maid : to be your fellow
You may deny me ; but I'll be your servant
Whether you will or no.
Fer. My mistress, dearest,
And I thus humble ever.
Mir. My husband then ?
Fer. Ay, with a heart as willing
As bondage e'er of freedom : here's my hand !
Mir. And mine, with my heart in 't. And now, farewell
Till half an hour hence.
Fer. A thousand ! thousand !

DESDEMONA.

Desdemona was the daughter and heiress of Brabantio, a Venetian senator. Othello, a famous Moorish general, being a friend of Brabantio, made frequent visits to his house; and with no more studious wooing than the relation of his adventures and "hair-breadth 'scapes" in strange lands, did he win the love of the senator's beautiful daughter.

Desdemona, fearing the opposition of her father, who naturally wished to marry his child to some one of the many young nobles of Venice who were suitors for her hand, fled from her home by night, and became the Moor's wife.

On that same night, Othello was ordered by the reigning duke to set out at once to war against the Turks in the isle of Cyprus, whither his bride was permitted to follow him. On this expedition Othello had selected Cassio, a young Florentine nobleman, true friend to himself and Desdemona, to be his lieutenant, a post greatly desired by Iago, an old follower of Othello, who had received the appointment of "ancient" instead. Iago accompanied Othello in this capacity, while his wife, Emilia, attended upon the lady Desdemona as waiting-gentlewoman.

From the first, Iago had conceived the diabolic idea of prompting Othello to suspect his wife's intimacy with young Cassio, as well to avenge his disappointed ambition, as from a suspicion of the Moor's previous relations with Emilia—but above all, to gratify the taste for treacherous plotting which was part of his detestable temper. His stratagems were admirably contrived for the victim they were intended to ensnare, though too transparent for a less generous and more suspicious nature than that of the passionate Othello. On the first night of the Moor's arrival in the island of Cyprus, Iago artfully prevailed upon Cassio to drink to excess—whence a brawl, ending in Cassio's disgraceful suspension from his military office. Nothing could be more natural, nor, as it proved, more fatal, to the tender Desdemona than to exert her influence with her newly-wedded lord to procure the pardon and reinstatement of their mutual friend, "Michael Cassio, that came a-wooing with him"—on which artless importunity the wily Iago ingeniously led Othello to put the vilest construction.

Desdemona possessed a curiously wrought handkerchief, most precious to her as the first gift of her husband, and which she superstitiously believed to be endowed with magic virtue. Iago bribed his wife to steal this dainty trifle from her mistress; and, having dropped it in Cassio's bed-chamber, he persuaded Othello that Desdemona had presented it to the young lieutenant as a token of her guilty preference. Such innocent trifles did this malignant spirit construe to his own vile meaning, till the Moor, maddened with jealous doubts of his wife's chastity, smothered her in her bed.

After the dreadful deed had been done, Othello received abundant proof of Desdemona's innocence from Emilia—whom Iago killed on the spot for betraying him; and, stabbing himself, the Moor, so miserably deceived, died on the body of his lovely victim.

The type of all gentle and refined beauty—"O, the world hath not a sweeter creature!"—Desdemona by her rare simplicity, her childlike artlessness of character, wins her way to the hearts of all who have conned the story of her woes and mourned her cruel fate.

In our own mind we class her naturally with Miranda and Ophelia; but she is less purely ideal than either of these; her dramatic condition differs from theirs in being simply domestic; though highly picturesque, it is dependent for its interest on no more romantic accessories than are afforded by the privacy of a sumptuous household, to the skilful management of which—notwithstanding that she was "an admirable musician," and of "high and plenteous wit and invention"—she does not scorn to devote a considerable portion of her time. With whatsoever of intense effects her married life is produced," herself is never part of them—she, indeed, constitutes their principal figure, but she is never involved in them, never understands them; her identity is preserved intact throughout.

Subordination, in thought and word and act, is the prominent feature of Desdemona's character: not simply the non-resisting humility of a weak, spiritless nature, but that honorable submission to one having authority (whether God, king, father, or husband) which, then, as in the later day of English Margaret More, formed an essential part of the education of the gently bred, only less important than religion itself, or, rather, included in that.

That Desdemona is not necessarily tame because her "spirit, so still and quiet," has been chastened by a graceful discipline, is proved by the boldness with which she takes her fate into her own hands when the occasion demands prompt action.

Disdainful of the "wealthy, curled darlings of her nation," she hearkens to and loves the gallant Moor, to whom "the flinty and steel couch of war" was "thrice-driven bed of down;" and with the courageous delicacy of a true woman, she discovers her love to him who, last of all, would dream of winning it:

> She thanked me;
> And bade me, if I had a friend that lov'd her,
> I should but teach him how to tell my story,
> And that would woo her;

and they elope and are married.

Again, no woman of meagre intellectual endowments—and as such Desdemona is too often regarded—or without sufficient of what we term *character*, could, with such force and graceful logic, have defended the step she had taken, in the presence of an august senate, which, of itself, would have overwhelmed the soft, timorous Desdemona as she exists in the popular imagination.

The reader will recollect that, on their wedding-night, Othello is brought before the Senate to answer the charge of Brabantio, of having procured the affections of his daughter by some unlawful means; Desdemona being summoned, her father appeals to her:

> * * * * * * * * * *
> Come hither, gentle mistress;
> Do you perceive, in all this noble company,
> Where most you owe obedience?
> *Des.* My noble father,
> I do perceive here a divided duty:
> To you I am bound for life and education;
> My life and education both do learn me
> How to respect you; you are the lord of duty—
> I am hitherto your daughter: But here's my husband;
> And so much duty as my mother show'd
> To you, preferring you before her father,
> So much I challenge that I may profess
> Due to the Moor, my lord.

And how full of eloquence, of the unfaltering pride of an honor able wife, is her petition to the duke to be allowed to follow her husband to Cyprus:

That I did love the Moor, to live with him,
My downright violence and scorn of fortunes
May trumpet to the world: my heart's subdued
Even to the very quality of my lord:
I saw Othello's visage in his mind;
And to his honors, and his valiant parts,
Did I my soul and fortunes consecrate.
So that, dear lords, if I be left behind,
A moth of peace, and he go to the war,
The rites for which I love him are bereft me,
And I a heavy interim shall support
By his dear absence: Let me go with him.

In Desdemona's passion for Othello we have a fair example ot the proverbial tenacity of an Italian woman's love, however suddenly, or for whatever freak of fancy, it may have been conceived. No wrong, no outrage to her tender devotion, can for a moment alienate her loyal heart; while their honeymoon is yet high in the heavens, Othello treats her with "strange unquietness," with petulant impatience; but her generous fondness readily finds ex cuse for him:

Nay, we must think, men are not gods;
Nor of them look for such observances
As fit the bridal.—Beshrew me much, Emilia,
I was (unhandsome warrior as I am,)
Arraigning his unkindness with my soul;
But now I find I had suborn'd the witness,
And he's indited falsely.

He tries upon her unoffending head all the fantastic tricks of his half-crazed wits; he even strikes her—her of such tender beauty, such careful nurture; yet no more bitter reproach escapes her injured heart than these patient words to Iago, to whom she has recourse in her afflicted strait:

> Those that do teach young babes
> Do it with gentle means, and easy tasks:
> He might have chid me so; for, in good faith,
> I am a child to chiding;

—concluding the interview with an appeal so touching as to move any but a fiend, or an Iago·

> O good Iago,
> What shall I do to win my lord again?
> Good friend, go to him; for, by this light of heaven,
> I know not how I lost him. Here I kneel:—
> If e'er my will did trespass 'gainst his love,
> Either in discourse, or thought, or actual deed,
> Or that mine eyes, mine ears, or any sense,
> Delighted them in any other form;
> Or that I do not yet, and ever did,
> And ever will,—though he do shake me off
> To beggarly divorcement,—love him dearly,
> Comfort forswear me! Unkindness may do much;
> And his unkindness may defeat my life,
> But never taint my love.

There is nothing in all Shakspeare, to our mind, more affecting than the final night-scenes in this moving tragedy: the half-prescient sadness of the victim; her request, full of poetic pathos, to Emilia, to lay on her bed her wedding sheets, and, if she should die, to shroud her in one of them; the chanting of an old song which she had heard, long back in her childhood, sung by her mother's maid, who died of love—are all, from their sweet tinge of superstition, most touchingly effective. In her conversation with Emilia, while disrobing for bed—that bed which is so soon to be her bier—the extreme delicacy of Desdemona's mind, the spotless chastity, which cannot be persuaded of the existence of a grossness so foreign to itself, is strikingly contrasted with the loose opinions, the coarse good sense, and the easy virtue of Iago's wife; it is the crowning beauty of her blameless life.

ROSALIND.

Rosalind was the only child of the reigning Duke of a French province; while she was yet almost an infant, Frederick, a younger brother of her father, usurped his throne, and drove him and his followers into exile. Duke Frederick had also a young daughter, Celia; and that she might not pine in her new home, he detained his niece, Rosalind, to be her playmate. In Celia's own beautiful words: they

> * * * * "Slept together,
> Rose at an instant, learn'd, play'd, eat together;
> And wheresoe'er they went, like Juno's swans,
> Still they went coupled and inseparable."

Thus were they reared in the ducal palace as sisters; till one day, grown to be lovely maidens, they witnessed in company the then favorite pastime at court, of wrestling, and Rosalind fell in love with one of the competitors,—a tall, elegant young stripling, who came off victor from the contest. But unhappily for the princess Rosalind, the handsome stranger proved to be Orlando, son of Sir Rowland de Bois, who had been in his lifetime a fast adherent to the deposed Duke; and this so aroused the anger of Duke Frederick, that he not only dismissed the young man, but ordered Rosalind, who had displeased him by her fearless expressions of sympathy with the son of her father's best friend, to quit the palace at once, and seek the exiled Duke's retreat—the forest of Arden.

Celia's prayers to her father in behalf of her cousin were in vain; so, true to her sisterly affection for Rosalind, she determined to share her banishment. The better to conceal their flight, they set out on their journey disguised as peasants; and to insure themselves against annoyance, Rosalind, who was the taller and more courageous of the two, assumed the attire of a country lad, calling herself *Ganymede;* while Celia, the pretty shepherdess, took the name of *Aliena*, sister to *Ganymede.*

With but few adventures they came to the forest of Arden, wherein Orlando had also taken refuge from a cruel, jealous brother, who sought his life. Orlando, ardent and romantic, had by no means received unmoved the delicate sympathy of the fair Rosalind; on the contrary, he had cherished the memory of it so tenderly, that before long his love for her became as absorbing as it was hopeless. To the great marvel of our princesses, as they continued their journey through the forest, they found the bushes hung with amorous sonnets in praise of Rosalind's beauty, and the young trees eloquent with her name, cut in their tender bark; but after a while the mystery was joyfully explained, to one at least, by the appearance of Orlando.

With the coquetry of a true woman, certain that she was beloved, Rosalind, still disguised, amused herself by teasing her lover into a frenzy of passion, "piquing and soothing him by turns."

The gentle Celia also found a lover in the now repentant Oliver, Orlando's brother; and finally the nuptials of the two couples, sanctioned and blessed by the good Duke, were celebrated in the grand old forest.

As if nothing should be withheld, necessary to complete the happiness of their wedding-day, a messenger arrived with the news that Duke Frederick had been brought suddenly to repent of his injustice to his elder brother, and that, converted from wickedness and the world, he had put on a religious life—relinquishing the crown to the brows that should wear it of right, and restoring all their lands to them that were exiled.

Rosalind, of all her "infinitely various" sisterhood, is most universally the pet, as combining in her single person qualities which appeal to all classes of men and women. She has wit to charm the intellectual; a fund of lively romance for the sympathetic; fresh beauty, and a hearty, ringing vitality, for the merely material; and store of tender, graceful, womanly virtues to delight the popular heart—which, certainly, on such a subject, must be esteemed infallible.

Notwithstanding that the princess Rosalind was born and bred among the formal etiquettes of a court, and accustomed to the sumptuous luxury of ducal palaces, it is plain that she has pined and wilted in so artificial an atmosphere, till, casting it like a tiresome garment, she bounds, full of ardent, exuberant life, into the green midst of Arden. We cannot easily recognize our Rosalind in the languid court-lady of legitimate caprices and vapors, who "shows more mirth than she is mistress of;" nor ever in the meek victim of whom her uncle, the duke, draws this melancholy picture, impossible to a true conception of such a very madcap of animal spirits:

> * * * * Her smoothness,
> Her very silence, and her patience,
> Speak to the people, and they pity her.

Rosalind smooth, and silent, and patient—above all, pitied!

Is there, in that, a trace of her spirited, self-reliant, voluble self? Could we not far more readily believe, of our gallant little *Ganymede*, that she had restored his lawful throne to her father by sheer dint of her wits, and her sure trick of reaching the hearts of "the people," than that they had simply looked on and pitied her?

Rosalind's character is made up of apparently irreconcilable attributes: she is endowed with exquisite sensibility, yet with ready, dazzling wit; she is intensely romantic, but without a sigh of sentimentalism; her heart is brimful of tenderness, while she conceals its dearest passion beneath a saucy, playful raillery, which would be giddy, were it not for its good sense, and acute insight into human nature. The more Orlando mopes, and grows "deject and wretched," under the teasing treatment of the fascinating *Ganymede*, the more ingenious is she in the contrivance of her pretty tortures, which every now and then reveal charming glimpses of the love-full heart under all.

The dialogues between Orlando and *Ganymede*, wherein she personates his lady-love, sparkle throughout, replete with playful coquetry, arch libels on "the fair Rosalind," and flashes of humor so keen that they have become proverbial—"familiar in our mouths as household words:"

> *Ros.* Now tell me how long you would have her after you have possessed her.
>
> *Orl.* Forever, and a day.
>
> *Ros.* Say a day without the ever. No, no, Orlando; men are April when they woo, December when they wed. Maids are May, when they are maids; but the sky changes when they are wives. I will be more jealous of thee than a Barbary cock-pigeon over his hen; more clamorous than a parrot against rain; more new-fangled than an ape; more giddy in my desires than a monkey.

Drummond — Wm Edwards

Shepherdess

I will weep for nothing, like Diana in the fountain; and I will do that when you are disposed to be merry. I will laugh like a hyen, and that when thou art inclined to sleep.

Orl. But will my Rosalind do so?

Ros. By my life, she will do as I do!

Ros. There is none of my uncle's marks upon you: he taught me how to know a man in love. * * * *

Orl. What were his marks?

Ros. A lean cheek—which you have not; a blue eye and sunken—which you have not; an unquestionable spirit—which you have not. * * * * * * Then your hose should be ungarter'd, your bonnet unbanded, your sleeve unbuttoned, your shoe untied, and every thing about you demonstrating a careless desolation.

Love is merely a madness; and, I tell you, deserves as well a dark house and a whip as madmen do; and the reason why they are not so punished and cured is, that the lunacy is so ordinary that the whippers are in love too.

* * * * * Men have died from time to time, and worms have eaten them—but not for love.

Break an hour's promise in love! He that will divide a minute into a thousand parts, and break but a part of the thousandth part of a minute in the affairs of love, it may be said of him that Cupid hath clapp'd him o' the shoulder, but I warrant him heart-whole.

Farewell, monsieur traveller! Look you lisp, and wear strange suits; disable all the benefits of your own country; be out of love with your nativity, and almost chide God for making you that countenance you are; or I will scarce think you have swam in a gondola.

But to do her wit and ready repartee full justice, we should be compelled to transcribe half the play; let us pass then from what Rosalind says, to what is said of her.

Of her person no descriptive passages are given, save as she appears in the character of *Ganymede;* of these, that of Phebe, a shepherdess, who becomes enamored of the sprightly boy, is best known:

> Think not I love him, though I ask for him;
> 'Tis but a peevish boy—yet he talks well.
> But what care I for words?—Yet words do well,
> When he that speaks them pleases those that hear.
> It is a pretty youth—not very pretty;
> But sure he's proud;—and yet his pride becomes him.
> He'll make a proper man. The best thing in him
> Is his complexion: and faster than his tongue
> Did make offence, his eye did heal it up.
> He is not tall—yet for his years he's tall.
> His leg is but so-so;—and yet 'tis well.
> There was a pretty redness in his lip—
> A little riper and more lusty red
> Than that mix'd in his cheek; 'twas just the difference
> Betwixt the constant red and mingled damask.

And Oliver says of her:

> The boy is fair,
> Of female favor; and bestows himself
> Like a ripe sister. * * *

There is nothing of Rosalind more Rosalindy than her "Conjuration" in the Epilogue:

> * * * * My way is to conjure you; and I'll begin with the women.—I charge you, O Women, for the love you bear to men, to like as much of this play as pleases them. And so I charge you, O Men, for the love you bear to women (as I perceive by your simpering,

> none of you hate them), that between you and the women the play may please. If I were a woman, I would kiss as many of you as had beards that pleased me, complexions that liked me, and breaths that I defied not; and, I am sure, as many as have good beards, or good faces, or sweet breaths, will, for my kind offer, when I make curt'sy, bid me Farewell.

Though, properly, it is the actor, speaking for himself (the women being played by boys in Shakspeare's time), who says, "If I were a woman," Rosalind, speaking for *Ganymede*, could say nothing more characteristic.

CELIA.

The pensive sweetness of Celia's character is too apt to pass unappreciated, outshone as it is by the brilliancy of her gifted cousin, Rosalind. Yet she is, in fact, scarcely inferior in personal or mental endowments—she is only more quiet; her wit would be distinguished, were it not in direct juxtaposition with the pyrotechnic displays of the rattling Rosalind; and that her heart is equally full of tender susceptibility, is proved by her almost instantaneous love for Oliver, of which her cousin says:

> * * * * * * * * * *
> There was never any thing so sudden. * * *
> For your brother and my sister no sooner met, but they looked; no sooner looked, but they loved; no sooner loved, but they sighed; no sooner sighed, but they asked one another the reason; no sooner knew the reason, but they sought the remedy: and in these degrees have they made a pair of stairs to marriage.

The heroic devotion of her nature is beautifully manifest in her friendship for her cousin, "dearer than the natural bond of sisters"—a friendship so complete that it ignores all selfish considerations, to be true to its own high ideal. Even before Rosalind is banished the court, Celia has resolved, if it should ever be in her power, to restore the throne to its rightful heir, her cousin:

> You know my father hath no child but I, nor none is like to have; and, truly, when he dies, thou shalt be his heir: for what he hath taken away from thy father perforce, I will render thee again in affection—by mine honor, I will! and when I break that oath, let me turn monster. Therefore, my sweet Rose, my dear Rose, be merry.

And her pleading to the duke is unsurpassed for simple, natural tenderness:

> * * * * * * *
> If she be a traitor,
> Why so am I: we still have slept together,
> Rose at an instant, learn'd, play'd, eat together;
> And wheresoe'er we went, like Juno's swans,
> Still we went coupled, and inseparable.
> *Duke F.* * * * * * *
> Thou art a fool: she robs thee of thy name;
> And thou wilt show more bright, and seem more virtuous,
> When she is gone. Then open not thy lips;
> Firm and irrevocable is my doom
> Which I have pass'd upon her; she is banish'd.
> *Cel.* Pronounce that sentence then on me, my liege;
> I cannot live out of her company.

Celia's friendship for Rosalind exceeds that which she receives in return, from the very difference in their characters. Celia has far less vitality; she yields to the potent influence of Rosalind as a matter of course, confessing herself absolutely dependent upon her companion.

Rosalind calmly contemplates the necessity of leaving Celia forever; Celia tells her father, after he has pronounced his cruel sentence, that she "cannot live out of her company;" and left alone with her cousin, having at once resolved to share her exile, she says to her:

*   *   *   *   *   *   *   *   *   *

Pr'ythee, be cheerful: know'st thou not the duke
Hath banish'd me, his daughter?
Ros. That he hath not.
Cel. No? hath not? Rosalind lacks then the love
Which teacheth thee that thou and I am one.
Shall we be sunder'd? shall we part, sweet girl?
No; let my father seek another heir.
Therefore devise with me, how we may fly,
Whither to go, and what to bear with us;
And do not seek to take your change upon you,
To bear your griefs yourself, and leave me out;
For, by this heaven, now at our sorrows pale,
Say what thou canst, I'll go along with thee!

The text affords no description of Celia's person except as *Aliena*, and contrasted with *Ganymede:*

*   *   *   *   *   *The woman low,*
And browner than her brother.   *   *   *

BEATRICE.

Beatrice was the niece of Leonato, Governor of Messina, and the beloved companion of his daughter Hero, with whom she lived in her uncle's palace. Certain gentlemen of rank, on their way home from a war in which their valor had shone conspicuously, tarried a while in Messina, as guests of the worthy governor. Among these were Don Pedro, Prince of Arragon; Claudio, a Florentine nobleman, friend to the prince; and Benedick of Padua, a wild, light-hearted lord, as brave as he was witty.

These gentlemen had visited Messina before the war began; and during their sojourn at the palace, the governor's sharp-witted niece had amused herself with not very amiable raillery at Benedick's expense, while Hero and Claudio had been forced to part just as they discovered that they were almost necessary to each other's happiness. Now their several "occupations" were renewed: Don Pedro procured the governor's consent to Claudio's marriage with the gentle Hero, and Benedick and Beatrice laughed at love, and waged a fiercer war of words than ever.

As a merry mode of passing the time which must elapse before the day fixed for the nuptials, Don Pedro suggested to his gentlemen the practical joke of making Beatrice and Benedick—the two sworn foes—fall in love with each other; and at once they contrived a plan, which soon succeeded to perfection.

Meanwhile, however, a less amiable plot was hatching, to overthrow the fond hopes of Hero and her affianced husband. Don John, a bastard brother of Don Pedro, and full of malignant spite against him, hired Borachio, a low fellow, to put aside, by a scandalous proceeding, this marriage, in which Don Pedro's honor and interest were so deeply engaged.

Borachio, being a suitor to Margaret, the lady Hero's waiting-woman, persuaded her to listen to his wooing from her mistress's bed-chamber at midnight; and the night before the wedding-day, Claudio and Don Pedro were brought by Don John to witness this assignation, which convinced them of Hero's infidelity.

Next morning, in the church, before the friar who would have married them, before all the noble company assembled, Claudio publicly repudiated his bride—Don Pedro bearing testimony to her unworthiness—and so left the unhappy lady in a deadly swoon at his feet. Following the friar's advice, Leonato proclaimed his daughter dead, meaning to avenge the insult if she should prove to have been slandered, or to immure her in a convent, if it should indeed be as the two gentlemen had declared. That very day, however, a watchman brought Borachio before the governor, charging that he had overheard the fellow talking to a comrade of the vile plot against the lady Hero. The confession of Borachio at once cleared the fair fame of the injured bride from all suspicion; her lover, Lord Claudio, was inconsolable for her loss, nor could he forgive himself the rashness which had ruined his dearest hopes. Leonato demanded of him, as a reparation to the lady's family, that he should take to wife his young niece, "almost the copy of her that was dead;" and Claudio, indifferent now as to his fate, consented. What was his amazement, his joy, to find in the masked lady who awaited him at the altar his own beloved Hero, on whose grave he had wept so many heart-wrung tears. Too happy to ask for more, he was content with the explanation vouchsafed him by Leonato:

> She died, my lord, but whiles her slander lived.

They were married; and at the same time the formidable Beatrice gave her hand to Benedick, on which occasion there was such rejoicing and festivity in celebration of the two weddings as had never before been known in Messina.

If this sharp-tongued young lady serve no better purpose to the humanity of this day and generation, at least she saves it from one graceless distinction, by proving in her own person that the "fast" woman is by no means a modern "institution:" not that we would detract from the perfected specimens of our own time, by comparison with this rudimentary example; but we contend that she possesses all the qualities necessary to a successful assumption of the character—her education, and the manners of the time, alone impede her.

Beatrice, like many another woman before and since, is the slave of a pert tongue; her intellect, though quick, is not strong enough to keep her vanity in subjection, and the consciousness of possessing in a ready wit the power of discomfiting others, proves a successful snare for her good taste and all the graceful effects of her gentle breeding. It is only in situations so inspiring as to compel her for the moment to forget her flippant affectations, that she appears as Nature made her—a spirited, generous, clever woman.

One is apt to liken Beatrice to Rosalind; yet their only points of resemblance consist of dramatic situations somewhat similar, and the distinguishing endowment of wit. As to the quality of this gift, however, the two ladies so differ that it can scarcely constitute a characteristic in common between them. The wit of Beatrice, brilliant as it is, is but the dazzle of words—it has no imaginative element, none of the half-playful pathos which renders that of Rosalind so charming; the two compare as the cold, artificial glitter of a diamond with the cordial warmth of sunshine. To use Benedick's own words—and he, as chief sufferer, should be excellent authority—Beatrice "speaks poignards, and every word stabs;" while, in the poetic simile of Mrs. Jameson, "the wit of Rosalind bubbles up and sparkles like the living fountain, refreshing all around."

Beatrice has none of Rosalind's romantic susceptibility, no passion; her love for Benedick we can never regard as more than an experimental freak; though, to do her justice, her soliloquy in the garden, where, concealed, she has overheard that Benedick loves her, is creditable alike to her heart and her good sense:

> What fire is in mine ears? Can this be true?
> Stand I condemn'd for pride and scorn so much?
> Contempt, farewell! and maiden pride, adieu!
> No glory lives behind the back of such.
> And, Benedick, love on; I will requite thee—
> Taming my wild heart to thy loving hand;
> If thou dost love, my kindness shall incite thee
> To bind our loves up in a holy band:
> For others say thou dost deserve; and I
> Believe it better than reportingly.

It seems scarcely fair to select purposely exaggerated descriptions of Beatrice, by her cousin Hero; but as caricatures are often the best portraits, so we cannot fail to draw from these severe reports a correct impression of their subject:

*   *   *   *   *   *   *   *

Nature never framed a woman's heart
Of prouder stuff than that of Beatrice:
Disdain and scorn ride sparkling in her eyes,
Misprising what they look on; and her wit
Values itself so highly, that to her
All matter else seems weak. She cannot love,
Nor take no shape nor project of affection—
She is so self-endear'd.

*   *   *   *   *   *   *   *

*   *   *   *   I never yet saw man,
How wise, how noble, young, how rarely featured,
But she would spell him backward: if fair-faced,
She'd swear the gentleman should be her sister;
If black, why, Nature, drawing of an antic,
Made a foul blot; if tall, a lance ill-headed;
If low, an agate very vilely cut;
If speaking, why, a vane blown with all winds;
If silent, why, a block moved with none.
So turns she every man the wrong side out,
And never gives to truth and virtue that
Which simpleness and merit purchaseth.
Urs. Sure, sure, such carping is not commendable.
Hero. No: not to be so odd, and from all fashions,
As Beatrice is, cannot be commendable.
But who dare tell her so? If I should speak,
She'd mock me into air; oh, she would laugh me
Out of myself, press me to death with wit.

It would appear that Don Pedro's plot found her in a happy hour, more than half-prepared for its consummation, if we may judge from a little scene where Hero is bestowed upon Claudio by her father, after which ceremony the loud vivacity of Beatrice is for the first time, slightly overcast by genuine emotion:

Beat. Good Lord, for alliance!—Thus goes every one to the world* but I, and I am sun-burned; I may sit in a corner, and cry—Heigh-ho! for a husband.

* * * * * * * *

D. Pedro. Will you have me, lady?

Beat. No, my lord—unless I might have another for working-days: your grace is too costly to wear every day. But, I beseech your grace, pardon me; I was born to speak all mirth, and no matter.

D. Pedro. Your silence most offends me, and to be merry best becomes you; for, out of question, you were born in a merry hour.

Beat. No, sure, my lord—my mother cry'd; but then there was a star danced, and under that was I born.—Cousins, God give you joy!

But however the gratuitous impertinence and unseemly forwardness of Beatrice may jar with one's fine ideas of a lady, she nobly redeems herself by her chivalrous defence of her cousin Hero, on the occasion of her cruel disgrace; her hearty, clear-headed

Oh, on my soul, my cousin is belied!

in the face of her uncle's conviction of his daughter's shame, and Benedick's amazed suspicion, is worth whole volleys of her murderous wit.

The love-scene, immediately succeeding the "scene" in the chapel, is as characteristic as it is comic; and though we may question the sincerity of Beatrice's love, in that she demands a test so fraught with danger for her lover, we cannot deny our admiration to such valiant championship in the cause of maligned innocence:

Bene. I do love nothing in the world so well as you;
Is not that strange?

Beat. As strange as the thing I know not. It were as possible for me to say I loved nothing so well as you.

* *To go to the world*—a cant phrase, meaning to get married.

But believe me not; and yet I lie not; I confess nothing, nor I deny nothing.—I am sorry for my cousin.

Bene. By my sword, Beatrice, thou lovest me!

* * * * * * * *

Beat. Why then, God forgive me!

Bene. What offence, sweet Beatrice?

Beat. You have staid me in a happy hour; I was about to protest I loved you.

Bene. And do it, with all thy heart.

Beat. I love you with so much of my heart that none is left to protest.

Bene. Come, bid me do any thing for thee.

Beat. Kill Claudio.

Bene. Ha! not for the wide world.

Beat. You kill me to deny it: Farewell.

* * * * * * * *

Bene. Is Claudio thine enemy?

Beat. Is he not approved in the height a villain, that hath slandered, scorned, dishonored my kinswoman?—O, that I were a man!—What! bear her in hand until they come to take hands; and then, with public accusation, uncovered slander, unmitigated rancor—O God, that I were a man! I would eat his heart in the market-place.

Bene. Hear me, Beatrice;—

Beat. Talk with a man out at a window?—a proper saying.

Bene. Nay but, Beatrice;—

Beat. Sweet Hero!—she is wronged, she is slandered, she is undone.

Bene. Beat—

Beat. Princes, and counties? Surely, a princely testimony, a goodly count-confect, a sweet gallant, surely! O that I were a man for his sake! or that I had any friend would be a man for my sake! But manhood is melted into courtesies, valor into compliment, and men are only turned into tongue, and trim ones too: he is now as valiant as Hercules that only tells a lie, and swears it.—I cannot be a man with wishing, therefore I will die a woman with grieving.

HERO.

In point of romantic interest and dramatic situation, Hero is undoubtedly the leading character in *Much Ado about Nothing*, although, adopting the popular appreciation, we have conferred the distinction of "first lady" on her cousin Beatrice—not the first time, by the by, that loud and persistent vanity has succeeded in usurping the honorable place belonging to modest, graceful excellence.

A rare chasteness of thought and person is plainly the trait in Hero's character which expresses itself most distinctly in the affairs of her daily life; and in this particular she affords a lively contrast to her cousin's inherent vulgarity. Her emotions are as still as they are deep—her words few; yet, that she can express herself well on occasion, is attested by her conversation with Ursula, designed to be overheard by Beatrice, in which her caustic description of that flippant young woman is quite equal to many of *her* renowned sallies; no wonder that Beatrice issues from her concealment with "fire in her ears."

The readiness with which this "maiden, never bold" enters into the plot for catching her cousin's heart—"if so be that she have such a thing about her"—as well as the admirable manner in which she plays her part, proves that Hero, with all her quiet dignity, entertains no small relish for fun, and that she is far from lacking in the healthy vivacity befitting her youth and happy circumstance. Her reply to Don Pedro, when he proposes her share in the merry conspiracy, is as characteristic as it is unhesitating:

> I will do any modest office, my lord, to help my cousin to a good husband.

It is noticeable that in the repartee—coarse even for the women of Shakspeare's time—bandied by the less fastidious tongues of her rattle-brain cousin and her gentlewoman, she never takes part, unless to repel some direct attack upon herself, with a

> Fye upon thee! Art not ashamed?

—and that, too, with no affectation of prudery; her delicacy is as virgin as Desdemona's, that very snow-drop among women.

This quality is beautifully displayed in the church, also, whither she has been led by her "new-trothed lord"—to be made a wife, she fondly believes; but finds herself, instead, suddenly forsworn, and charged with that of which her pure mind has no conception. The simple words of incredulous amazement with which she at first receives her lover's violent accusations, remind one of the majestic Hermione on an occasion somewhat similar:

> *Claud.* Out on thy seeming! I will write against it:
> You seem to me as Dian in her orb,
> As chaste as is the bud ere it be blown;

But you are more intemperate in your blood
Than Venus, or those pamper'd animals
That rage in savage sensuality.
Hero. Is my lord well, that he doth speak so wide?

We can far more easily forgive Claudio, in the full tide of youth and passion, his suspicions of his mistress—particularly as he had "assisted" at the chamber-window scene—than Leonato his ready conviction of his daughter's guilt; but we accord a grateful memorial, for this fair lady's sake, to the good priest, whose words of wisdom befit the sanctity of his calling and the purity of his heart:

Friar. Hear me a little—
For I have only been silent so long,
And given way unto this course of fortune,
By noting of the lady; I have mark'd
A thousand blushing apparitions start
Into her face, a thousand innocent shames
In angel whiteness bear away those blushes;
And in her eye there hath appear'd a fire,
To burn the errors that these princes hold
Against her maiden truth:—Call me a fool,
Trust not my reading, nor my observations,
Which with experimental zeal doth warrant
The tenor of my book; trust not my age,
My reverence, calling, nor divinity,
If this sweet lady lie not guiltless here
Under some biting error.

* * * * * * * *
Your daughter here the princes left for dead;
Let her awhile be secretly kept in,
And publish it that she is dead indeed;

* * * * * * * * *
So will it fare with Claudio:
When he shall hear she died upon his words,
The idea of her life shall sweetly creep

Into his study of imagination;
And every lovely organ of her life
Shall come apparell'd in more precious habit,
More moving-delicate, and full of life,
Into the eye and prospect of his soul,
Than when she liv'd indeed.

Of Hero's person we have only a few hints: she was certainly of low stature, much less tall than her cousin Beatrice, for Benedick styles her "Leonato's short daughter;" and if it be not hazardous to take this merry lord's word on so grave an issue, we may gather from him a more distinct personification—always remembering that he is already half in love, in his madcap way, with Beatrice, and would be therefore likely, in comparing them, to disparage Hero:

Claud. Benedick, didst thou note the daughter of Signior Leonato?

Bene. I noted her not; but I looked on her.

Claud. Is she not a modest young lady?

Bene. Do you question me, as an honest man should do, for my simple true judgment? or would you have me speak after my custom, as being a professed tyrant to their sex?

Claud. No, I pray thee speak in sober judgment.

Bene. Why, i' faith, methinks she is too low for a high praise, too brown for a fair praise, and too little for a great praise. Only this commendation I can afford her: that were she other than she is, she were unhandsome; and being no other but as she is, I do not like her.

* * * * * * * * * * *

Claud. In mine eye, she is the sweetest lady that ever I looked on.

Bene. I can see yet without spectacles, and I see no such matter; there's her cousin, an she were not possessed with a fury, exceeds her as much in beauty as the first of May doth the last of December.

Be this as it may, we feel bound to attribute no inconsiderable amount of beauty to a woman who could inspire her lover with such a delicate declaration of his perception of it, as is contained in these words of Claudio to Don Pedro, his patron:

> O my lord,
> When you went onward on this ended action,
> I look'd upon her with a soldier's eye,
> That lik'd, but had a rougher task in hand
> Than to drive liking to the name of love;
> But now I am return'd, and that war-thoughts
> Have left their places vacant, in their rooms
> Come thronging soft and delicate desires,
> All prompting me how fair young Hero is,
> Saying I lik'd her ere I went to wars.

JULIA.

The fair Julia of Verona was the beloved but coy mistress of Proteus. This gallant had a bosom friend, named Valentine—a gay young fellow, who laughed at Love and its victims, and who, persuaded that

> Home-keeping youths have ever homely wits,

had just set out on a journey to Milan, where he was to engage in the service of the emperor. A short time after his departure, Antonio, the father of Proteus, determined that his son should join his friend in his honorable position at court, and forthwith notified that young gentleman to prepare for the journey. Proteus had but one sweet drop in his bitter cup of trial: his cruel mistress, full of remorse and sorrow, confessed her love for him. At parting they exchanged rings, after the fashion of true lovers; and Proteus took a last agonizing farewell of his Julia in the following high-flown speech:

> Here is my hand for my true constancy;
> And when that hour o'erslips me in the day
> Wherein I sigh not, Julia, for thy sake,
> The next ensuing hour some foul mischance
> Torment me for my love's forgetfulness!

—while poor Julia was too much overcome to utter a single word.

Arrived at Milan, Proteus found Valentine violently enamoured of Silvia, the beautiful daughter of the Duke of Milan, to whom Proteus had no sooner been presented by his friend than he forgot the lady of his vows, and set his wits to work to win this new love at all hazards.

The Duke of Milan desired to marry his daughter to a nobleman of his court, Thurio by name, who was "by her very soul abhorred;" for she reciprocated Valentine's passion, and longed for nothing more than to reward it by the gift of her hand in marriage. Feeling sure that the duke would never consent to this, they had made all their arrangements to elope, but were discovered through the treachery of Proteus, who, maddened at the thought of losing Silvia forever, had betrayed Valentine to her father.

Valentine was at once banished the kingdom, and Thurio, reanimated, urged anew his suit, through Proteus, to the hapless Silvia; Proteus played a treacherous game with Thurio, also—pretending to advance his interests with the lady, while he spoke only for his own.

Meanwhile, Julia, grown impatient to behold her plighted lover, conceived the romantic idea of following him to Milan; and with no attendant or protection, save her disguise as a "well-reputed page," she accomplished her "sentimental journey" to that city. Having reached there safely, the host of the inn where she lodged, in pity for the loneliness of his young guest, led her at night to where she should hear music—but alas! what should the music be, but a serenade given by her faithless Proteus to the Lady Silvia, to whom he was pressing his suit as she leaned from her window. Apparently but little daunted, Julia contrived to enter her lover's service as a page; and like Viola—and yet *not* like Viola—she became the martyred Mercury between her own beloved and the lady of his new passion. But little success attended this thankless office: Silvia scorned the thrice-perjured Proteus—for she knew of his faithlessness to a lady in Verona; and finally, to rid herself of his abhorred proposals, and her father's importunities in behalf of Thurio, she formed the hazardous project of escaping to join Valentine, who, she had heard, had taken refuge in Mantua.

But Valentine, on his way to Mantua, had been waylaid in a forest not far from Milan, and by his gallant bearing had so pleased the bandits that they made him their captain. Silvia, with a gentleman who had volunteered to accompany her, on entering the forest was seized by one of this band of ruffians, but rescued by Proteus, who, followed by his page, had pursued her in hot haste. Proteus took advantage of her lonely condition—her companion having been separated from her in the *melée*—to urge his suit in no very gentle terms; but Valentine arrived just in time to thwart his ungracious purpose. Finally, the duke and Thurio, likewise in pursuit of Silvia, were captured by the robbers, and brought in triumph before their captain; whereupon full explanations were afforded to all concerned: Thurio relinquished his claim to Silvia's hand, and the duke, at last assured of Valentine's worth, bestowed his daughter where she had given her affections. Proteus confessed his baseness to his friend, who was so generous in his forgiveness as to offer him even his share in Silvia's love; at which prospect the pretty page swooned at his master's feet. On recovering, he exhibited two rings, and uttered mysterious words which established his identity with a certain lady of Verona. Proteus, seized with remorse and re-awakened love for his faithful Julia, vowed perpetual constancy thenceforth; and if she was content to take him at his word, in the face of all she had been privy to in his double dealings, it is not for us to demur.

An intense, and somewhat fantastic, romance influences every thought and action of this spoiled coquette and beauty; yet in her case, as in that of many passionate natures, it is but the superficial expression of deep and genuine emotions. We have proof of this in the persistent coyness with which she receives her lover's suit—an artful affectation of indifference, which is cast aside at once when she learns that he is going away from her—as well as in her after relations with him.

The scene in which her maid Lucetta brings her a love-letter from Proteus, is considered inimitable for its coquetry:

Jul. Say, say! who gave it thee?
Luc. Sir Valentine's page; and sent, I think, from Proteus.
He would have given it you; but I, being in the way,
Did in your name receive it—pardon the fault, I pray.
Jul. Now, by my modesty, a goodly broker!
Dare you presume to harbor wanton lines?
To whisper and conspire against my youth?
Now, trust me, 'tis an office of great worth,
And you an officer fit for the place.
There, take the paper! see it be return'd;
Or else return no more into my sight.
* * * * * * * * *
Jul. And yet, I would I had o'erlook'd the letter.
It were a shame to call her back again,
And pray her to a fault for which I chid her.
What fool is she, that knows I am a maid,
And would not force the letter to my view!
Since maids, in modesty, say *No* to that
Which they would have the profferer construe *Ay*.
Fie, fie! how wayward is this foolish love

That, like a testy babe, will scratch the nurse,
And presently, all humbled, kiss the rod!
How churlishly I chid Lucetta hence,
When willingly I would have had her here!
How angrily I taught my brow to frown,
When inward joy enforc'd my heart to smile!
* * * * * * * * *

Jul. This babble shall not henceforth trouble me.
Here is a coil, with protestation!
Go, get you gone! and let the papers lie:
You would be fingering them to anger me.

Jul. * * * * * * *
O hateful hands, to tear such loving words!
Injurious wasps! to feed on such sweet honey,
And kill the bees, that yield it, with your stings!
I'll kiss each several paper for amends.
And here is writ—*kind Julia*;—unkind Julia!
As in revenge of thy ingratitude,
I throw thy name against the bruising stones,
Trampling contemptuously on thy disdain.
Look! here is writ—*love-wounded Proteus*:—
Poor wounded name! my bosom, as a bed,
Shall lodge thee, till thy wound be th'roughly heal'd;
And thus I search it with a sovereign kiss.

To Julia's lips Shakspeare has given one of the most admired of his love-poems:

Didst thou but know the inly touch of love,
Thou would'st as soon go kindle fire with snow,
As seek to quench the fire of love with words.
* * * * * * * * *
The more thou dam'st it up, the more it burns;
The current that with gentle murmur glides,
Thou know'st, being stopp'd, impatiently doth rage;
But when his fair course is not hindered,
He makes sweet music with the enamel'd stones,
Giving a gentle kiss to every sedge
He overtaketh in his pilgrimage;
And so, by many winding nooks he strays,

With willing sport, to the wild ocean.
Then let me go, and hinder not my course:
I'll be as patient as a gentle stream,
And make a pastime of each weary step,
Till the last step have brought me to my love;
And there I'll rest, as, after much turmoil,
A blessed soul doth in Elysium.

And there is a charming touch of feminity in the choice of a costume for her disguise, which relieves her pilgrimage of its ultra-heroic quality, and which a less subtile creator would have omitted, as unworthy the consideration of so grandiloquent a heroine:

Luc. But in what habit will you go along?
Jul. Not like a woman; for I would prevent
The loose encounters of lascivious men:
Gentle Lucetta, fit me with such weeds
As may beseem some well-reputed page.
Luc. Why then your ladyship must cut your hair.
Jul. No, girl; I'll knit it up in silken strings,
With twenty odd-conceited true-love knots:
To be fantastic may become a youth
Of greater time than I shall show to be.
Luc. What fashion, madam, shall I make your breeches?
Jul. That fits as well as—"Tell me, good my lord,
"What compass will you wear your farthingale?"
Why, even that fashion thou best lik'st, Lucetta.

Once fairly in Milan, and shocked with the sad intelligence of her lover's disloyalty—that lover for whom she has dared so much—her proud romance is quelled; the lofty ideal, which she has clothed with all the fanciful imaginings of a sentimental enthusiast, is torn down; and in its place the honorable possibilities of a very faulty man, and her own steadfast love, are all that remain to solace her disappointed heart. Yet with only these she becomes his page, to enter upon the most painful service he could allot her —the wooing of another.

It is now that Julia's true character is brought to light, stripped of the idle fantasies which waited on her happy love: she is brought face to face with that pitiless fact, the assurance of unworthiness in one beloved; and she endures the spectacle patiently, quietly, the least in the world like those heroines of romance who probably served her as models during her capricious bellehood in Verona.

Her tender remonstrance with Proteus is surpassed only by a somewhat similar scene in *Twelfth Night*, between Viola and the duke, which indeed exceeds it but little in poetic beauty and gentle pathos:

> *Pro.* * * * * * * * *
> Go presently, and take this ring with thee;
> Deliver it to Madam Silvia:
> She loved me well deliver'd it to me.
> *Jul.* It seems you loved not her, to leave her token;
> She's dead, belike.
> *Pro.* Not so; I think she lives.
> *Jul.* Alas!
> *Pro.* Why dost thou cry Alas!
> *Jul.* I cannot choose but pity her.
> *Pro.* Wherefore shouldst thou pity her?
> *Jul.* Because methinks that she loved you as well
> As you do love your Lady Silvia:
> She dreams on him that has forgot her love;
> You dote on her that cares not for your love.
> 'Tis pity Love should be so contrary;
> And thinking on it makes me cry Alas!
> *Pro.* Well, give her that ring, and therewithal
> This letter;—that's her chamber.—Tell my lady
> I claim the promise for her heavenly picture.

When Proteus has retired, Julia, taking her pride to task, gives expression to that pity wherewith she would justify her infatuation—as if she could not find it in her heart to deny her love to one so wretchedly unlovable:

> How many women would do such a message?
> Alas, poor Proteus! thou hast entertain'd
> A fox to be the shepherd of thy lambs.
> Alas, poor fool! why do I pity him
> That with his very heart despiseth me?
> Because he loves her he despiseth me;
> Because I love him, I must pity him.

—which is only any Julia's way of saying, "Because I pity, I must love him—"

> This ring I gave him, when he parted from me,
> To bind him to remember my good will;
> And now am I (unhappy messenger)
> To plead for that which I would not obtain,
> To carry that which I would have refused,
> To praise his faith which I would have dispraised.
> I am my master's true confirmed love;
> But cannot be true servant to my master,
> Unless I prove false traitor to myself.
> Yet will I woo for him.

The scene in which she first pays her duty to Silvia, as Proteus' love-messenger, is admirably conceived; and it affords our curiosity the only personal description of Julia:

> *Jul.* Madam, he sends your ladyship this ring.
> *Sil.* The more shame for him that he sends it me·
> For I have heard him say, a thousand times,
> His Julia gave it him at his departure.
> Though his false finger have profan'd the ring,
> Mine shall not do his Julia so much wrong.
> * * * * * * *
> Dost thou know her?

Jul. Almost as well as I do know myself.
* * * * * * *

Sil. Is she not passing fair?
Jul. She hath been fairer, madam, than she is:
When she did think my master lov'd her well,
She, in my judgment, was as fair as you;
But since she did neglect her looking-glass,
And threw her sun-expelling mask away,
The air hath starv'd the roses in her cheeks,
And pinch'd the lily-tincture of her face,
That now she is become as black as I.

Silvia, whose interest is as honest as it is amiable, desires to know how tall she is:

Jul. About my stature; for at Pentecost,
When all our pageants of delight were play'd,
Our youth got me to play the woman's part,
And I was trimm'd in Madam Julia's gown,
Which served me as fit, by all men's judgment,
As if the garment had been made for me;
Therefore, I know she is about my height.
* * * * * * * * *

Here is her picture: Let me see! I think
If I had such a tire, this face of mine
Were full as lovely as is this of hers;
And yet the painter flatter'd her a little,
Unless I flatter with myself too much.
Her hair is auburn—mine is perfect yellow:
If that be all the difference in his love,
I'll get me such a color'd periwig.
Her eyes are grey as glass—and so are mine;
Ay, but her forehead's low—and mine's as high
What should it be that he respects in her
But I can make respective in myself,
If this fond Love were not a blinded god?

We can but rejoice that Julia's fidelity is rewarded at last by the restored allegiance of her recreant lover; though we must confess to but little faith in a repentance which seems forced upon him. That he is a treacherous, weak, thoroughly contemptible character, however, should affect our admiration of Julia's devotion to him as little as it did her love—or in fact that of any woman since time began.

SILVIA.

The bare facts of Silvia's story, which are almost identical with those of Julia's, would to a certain extent warrant one in imagining a like identity of character; yet there is a clear difference between the gracious, well-disciplined Lady Silvia—a court beauty, whose lightest act is governed by prescribed etiquette, and whose lofty dignity despises all tricks to attract admiration, all coquettish displays of wit or person—and the Veronese belle, whose caprices are as countless as her lovers, and whose pretty head is at one time almost hopelessly turned by their fine speeches and the delightful contemplation of her own perfections. Both are in love; but how different is its expression in the two women: Silvia, incapable of indulging her vanity at the expense of her lover's peace, condescends to a pretty ruse to assure him of her favor; Julia, in the hey-day of successful coquetry, alternately blesses Proteus and drives him to despair, twenty times a day, as her fantastic humor may dictate—consenting to make him happy, by a confession of her preference, only when her genuine sorrow at parting from him gets the better of her caprice.

In devotion and fidelity they assimilate more closely—but only in degree, not in kind: we feel sure that Silvia could never have continued to love a man whom she had found treacherous; with her passion would always be subordinate to principle; a shock to her sense of honor, from the object beloved, would prove its death-blow. She is less loving, in a general application of the expression, less impulsive, less vain, less *womanly*, than Julia;—or rather, she is a higher type of woman: Silvia derives her strength from her intellect; Julia is strong only in her affections.

As for their amorous pilgrimages: Julia's is undertaken in obedience to an impulse of wild, adventurous romance, having no authorities to consult but her waiting-maid and her own accommodating will—a delicious indulgence of high-wrought passion in picturesque disguise, in mystery, in possible danger. That of Silvia, on the other hand, is forced upon her by cruel necessity: suffering the impertinent and pertinacious espionage of her father, and the suits of two detested aspirants for her hand, while her betrothed husband is banished the country, she has no choice but to comply with her father's wishes and marry Thurio, or to follow at all hazards him to whom her faith is plighted. Having once resolved on the latter course, she pursues it with her characteristic dignity and careful deliberation; and she escapes from her father's custody under the protection of a gentleman of the court, who is "vow'd to pure chastity" on the grave of his lady-love. We are convinced that nothing short of violence could have turned Silvia from her purpose; but we can readily believe that some necessary disfigurement in her page's costume might have rendered Julia's proposed freak distasteful, or even have deterred her from it altogether.

Her beauty is, with Julia, a consideration of the first importance; she has made it the study of her dainty life; in a coquettish engagement she knows to a hair of her pencilled eyebrows how much each weapon is worth, and when the time to employ it; her first thought, on seeing the woman who has caused her lover to forget her, is: In what is she more beautiful than I, that he should love her better? Silvia is not less informed of her rare charms of person—perhaps no less happy in that knowledge; but she is seemingly devoid of even a trace of vanity; her serene brows are as guiltless of the blushes of a vulgar consciousness as those, crescent-crowned, of Dian.

We may scarcely accept lovers' words as evidence, in a case requiring such nice impartiality; yet even their hyperbolical rhapsodies may assist us in establishing a theory concerning the source of their inspiration:

Pro. * * * * *
Was this the idol that you worship so?
Val. Even she; and is she not a heavenly saint?
Pro. No; but she is an earthly paragon.
Val. Call her divine.
Pro. I will not flatter her.
* * * * * * *
Val. Then speak the truth by her; if not divine,
Yet let her be a principality,
Sovereign to all the creatures on the earth.
Pro. Except my mistress.
Val. Sweet, except not any—
Except thou wilt accept against my love.
Pro. Have I not reason to prefer mine own?
Val. And I will help thee to prefer her too:
She shall be dignified with this high honor—
To bear my lady's train; lest the base earth
Should from her vesture chance to steal a kiss,
And, of so great a favor growing proud,
Disdain to root the summer-swelling flower,
And make rough winter everlastingly.
Pro. Why, Valentine, what braggardism is this?
Val. Pardon me, Proteus: all I can is nothing,
To her whose worth makes other worthies nothing;
She is alone.

Pro. Then let her alone.
Val. Not for the world. Why, man, she is mine own;
And I as rich in having such a jewel
As twenty seas, if all their sand were pearl,
The water nectar, and the rocks pure gold.

Proteus, alone:

* * * * * * *
Is it mine eye, or Valentinus' praise,
Her true perfection, or my false transgression,
That makes me reasonless, to reason thus?
* * * * * * * *
How shall I dote on her with more advice
That thus, without advice, begin to love her?
'Tis but her picture I have yet beheld,
And that hath dazzled my reason's light;
But when I look on her perfections,
There is no reason but I shall be blind.
* * * * * * * *
And Silvia—witness Heaven, that made her fair!—
Shows Julia but a swarthy Ethiope.

A few passages, here and there, will serve to illustrate Silvia's character. The following soliloquy of Proteus, touching his perfidious suit, does her honor, even from lips so unworthy:

* * * * * * * *
But Silvia is too fair, too true, too holy,
To be corrupted with my worthless gifts.
When I protest true loyalty to her,
She twits me with my falsehood to my friend;
When to her beauty I commend my vows,
She bids me think how I have been forsworn
In breaking faith with Julia whom I lov'd;
And, notwithstanding all her sudden quips,
The least whereof would quell a lover's hope,
Yet, spaniel-like, the more she spurns my love,
The more it grows and fawneth on her still.

And her own words to him, in Julia's hearing, on the night of the serenade, afford still more conclusive evidence of her incorruptible purity:

* * * * * * * *

Thou subtle, perjur'd, false, disloyal man!
Think'st thou I am so shallow, so conceitless,
To be seduced by thy flattery,
That hast deceiv'd so many with thy vows?
Return, return, and make thy love amends!
For me,—by this pale queen of night I swear!—
I am so far from granting thy request,
That I despise thee for thy wrongful suit;
And by and by intend to chide myself,
Even for this time I spend in talking to thee.

VIOLA.

Viola was the daughter of one Sebastian, a Messalinian, and of gentle blood. Voyaging with her twin-brother Sebastian, near the coast of Illyria, a terrible storm arose, which wrecked the vessel, only a few of her crew reaching the shore. Viola was among the saved; but her brother's fate for a time remained unknown. A young and beautiful woman, without protection, in a strange land, she conceived the familiar idea of attiring herself as a page, to engage service in some noble family; and thus, through the influence of the captain of the wrecked vessel, she obtained admission, under the name of *Cesario*, into the household of Orsino, duke of Illyria.

This young nobleman had long been enamoured of the Countess Olivia, a noble and wealthy lady, who did not in the least reciprocate his preference. Orsino, prepossessed with his pretty page, made Viola his confidant in his unhappy love affair, and constituted it her chief duty to deliver his tender messages to the inaccessible countess.

Olivia, denying herself to all others, received the handsome boy, with whom, despite their unequal rank, she promptly fell in love, and, after a few interviews, confessed her passion for him.

Viola, dismayed by the false position into which her disguise had betrayed her, herself in love with the gallant duke, assured the countess, in reply, that *no woman* did, or ever should, possess her heart, and that she would never again approach her, even on her master's errand.

Sebastian, Viola's brother, had happily been saved from the wreck, by his friend Antonio. Walking one day past Olivia's house, he was violently assailed by that lady's uncle, Sir Toby Belch, who, from Sebastian's exact resemblance to his sister Viola, mistook him for *Cesario*, and accused him of a previous insult. The countess, informed of the altercation, hastened to the rescue of her beloved *Cesario*, and was deceived equally with her uncle. She conducted Sebastian into the house, and bestowed her hospitality with such fascinating grace that the lucky youth, though amazed at his reception, was charmed with her elegance and beauty. Olivia, delighted to find the disdainful *Cesario* suddenly metamorphosed into a lover, at once proposed that they should seal their vows before a priest who was then at hand; to which Sebastian, now deep in love, consented—and they were married.

The marvellous resemblance between Viola and Sebastian—

> One face, one voice, one habit, and two persons—

was shortly the occasion of another *contre-temps:* Antonio, Sebastian's preserver, mistook Viola for her brother, and, in the presence of the duke, accused her of base ingratitude, in ignoring him who had saved her life. But even while he was speaking, Olivia entered, and claimed Viola as her husband; this aroused the jealous rage of Orsino, who naturally inferred that his page had been playing him false; but the *éclaircissement* and the crowning mystification were simultaneously achieved by the entrance of Sebastian.

Hereupon, explanations, satisfactory to all: Olivia was nothing loth to retain the bridegroom she had chosen so hastily; and Orsino, always tenderly attached to his faithful page, found it by no means difficult, now that Olivia was forever lost to him, to transfer his affections to Viola, when she appeared before him in her proper character—a young and beautiful woman who adored him. And thus their misfortune proved indeed a "most happy wreck" to the twins—the one gaining thereby a gallant and noble husband, the other a beautiful and wealthy wife.

Viola, without possessing any of those brilliant qualities that compel our admiration in Portia, Rosalind, or Beatrice, endears herself to us by the ingenuousness, modesty, and tenderness of her character. Like Rosalind, Viola disguises herself as a page; but instead of assuming that "swashing and martial outside" which Rosalind affects, as part of her masculine attire, she is most discreetly disposed, permitting herself no word or gesture inconsistent with the nicest propriety; she changes nothing but her dress—she is Viola throughout. Each is in daily intercourse with the man she loves. With Orlando, Rosalind is saucy and coquettish; Viola manifests her self-sacrificing devotion to Orsino, by becoming his love-herald to the proud Olivia—wooing for her master from another the bliss which she longed to bestow only through herself.

Like Rosalind again, Viola is beloved by a woman; but the Countess Olivia differs as widely from the capricious shepherdess, Phebe, as the treatment which their infatuations severally receive: Rosalind mocks, and plays with, Phebe's preference, even while she repulses it; Viola's feminine reserve is shocked at the unwooed confession of Olivia's love. Yet how full of tender pity are her words, when first she suspects the hapless truth:

> What means this lady?
> Fortune forbid my outside have not charm'd her!
> She made good view of me—indeed, so much
> That sure, methought, her eyes had lost her tongue;
> For she did speak in starts, distractedly.
> She loves me, sure;
> * * * * * * * *
> If it be so, (as 'tis,)
> Poor lady, she were better love a dream.
> Disguise, I see, thou art a-wickedness,
> Wherein the pregnant enemy does much.
> How easy is it for the proper-false
> In women's waxen hearts to set their forms!
> Alas, our frailty is the cause, not we;
> For such as we are made of, such we be.
> How will this fadge? My master loves her dearly;
> And I, poor monster, fond as much on him;
> And she, mistaken, seems to dote on me:
> What will become of this! As I am man,
> My state is desperate for my master's love;
> As I am woman—now alas the day!
> What thriftless sighs shall poor Olivia breathe?
> O Time, thou must untangle this, not I;
> It is too hard a knot for me to untie.

Of her person, her brother Sebastian says:

> A lady, sir, though it was said she much resembled me, was yet of many accounted beautiful; but though I could not, with such estimable wonder, over far believe that, yet thus far I will boldly publish her—she bore a mind that envy could not but call fair.

The description by Malvolio, Olivia's steward, is characteristic

> Not yet old enough for a man, nor young enough for a boy; as a squash is before 'tis a peascod, or a codling

> when 'tis almost an apple: 'tis with him e'en standing water, between boy and man. He is very well-favored, and he speaks very shrewishly; one would think his mother's milk were scarce out of him.

We have abundant evidence of the high-bred grace of her bearing, in the rapturous soliloquy of the Lady Olivia, even after due allowance has been made for the exaggeration of love:

> What is your parentage?
> *Above my fortunes; yet my state is well—*
> *I am a gentleman.*——I'll be sworn thou art;
> Thy tongue, thy face, thy limbs, actions, and spirit,
> Do give thee five-fold blazon.—Not too fast:—soft! soft!—
> Unless the master were the man.—How now?
> Even so quickly may one catch the plague?
> Methinks I feel this youth's perfections,
> With an invisible and subtle stealth,
> To creep in at mine eyes. Well, let it be.

A dialogue between Viola and the Duke Orsino affords us the clearest insight into the sweet pensiveness of her mind, intensified somewhat by hopeless devotion to her master:

> *Vio.* But if she cannot love you, sir?
> *Duke.* I cannot be so answer'd.
> *Vio.* 'Sooth, but you must.
> Say that some lady, as perhaps there is,
> Hath for your love as great a pang of heart
> As you have for Olivia: you cannot love her;
> You tell her so. Must she not then be answer'd?
> *Duke.* There is no woman's sides
> Can bide the beating of so strong a passion
> As love doth give my heart—no woman's heart
> So big, to hold so much; they lack retention.
> Alas! their love may be called appetite,—
> No motion of the liver, but the palate,—
> That suffer surfeit, cloyment, and revolt;

But mine is all as hungry as the sea,
And can digest as much. Make no compare
Between that love a woman can bear me
And that I owe Olivia.

Vio. Ay, but I know—

Duke. What dost thou know?

Vio. Too well what love women to men may owe:
In faith, they are as true of heart as we.
My father had a daughter lov'd a man—
As it might be, perhaps, were I a woman,
I should your lordship.

Duke. And what's her history?

Vio. A blank, my lord: She never told her love;
But let concealment, like a worm i' the bud,
Feed on her damask cheek. She pin'd in thought;
And, with a green and yellow melancholy,
She sat, like Patience on a monument,
Smiling at grief. Was not this love, indeed?
We men may say more, swear more; but, indeed,
Our shows are more than will; for still we prove
Much in our vows, but little in our love.

Duke. But died thy sister of her love, my boy?

Vio. I am all the daughters of my father's house,
And all the brothers too;—and yet I know not.—
Sir, shall I to this lady?

Duke. Ay! that's the theme.
To her in haste; give her this jewel; say
My love can give no place, bide no denay.

OLIVIA.

The prominent events in the history of the Countess Olivia have already been noted in the chapter devoted to Viola. Celebrated for beauty—the charm of which is doubtless enhanced by the "quantity of dirty lands" whereof she is mistress—of a "smooth, discreet, and stable bearing," "swaying her house, commanding her followers," with the innate dignity of a lady accustomed from birth to princely surroundings, she has nevertheless all the legitimate caprices of an imperious belle.

Olivia persistently rejects the violent suit of an accomplished, elegant nobleman—a *parti* exactly suited in every particular to her station in life—to bestow her coveted favors on the obscure little page of her princely lover; and the very condescension implied in this eccentricity acquits her love for Viola of the charge of indelicacy. We regard her sudden fancy for the pretty boy as the unchecked whim of the moment; to use her own words, it was "that time of moon" with her to be so impressed; it has by no means attained the dignity of passion in our minds, nor do we ever propose to try it by the rules and regulations applicable to cases of orthodox love-making.

Yet, for all that, it is serious enough; Juliet, herself, is not more tenderly impatient, nor more suddenly involved, than our wilful countess.

In a propitious moment she imagines she finds *Cesario* responsive to her suit, and with a woman's quick appropriation of opportunity thus addresses him:

Blame not this haste of mine: If you mean well,
Now go with me, and with this holy man,
Into the chantry by. There, before him,
And underneath that consecrated roof,
Plight me the full assurance of your faith,
That my most jealous and too doubtful soul
May live at peace.

And with what reckless abandon does she confess her love for the page:

O, what a deal of scorn looks beautiful
In the contempt and anger of his lip!
A murd'rous guilt shows not itself more soon
Than love that would seem hid. Love's night is noon.
Cesario, by the roses of the spring,
By maidhood, honor, truth, and every thing,
I love thee so, that, maugre all thy pride,
Nor wit, nor reason, can my passion hide.

She continues to urge her hopeless suit with no less ardor and self-forgetfulness; thus prettily she puts aside the duke's love-making, to advance her own:

O, by your leave, I pray you:
I bade you never speak again of him;
But, would you undertake another suit,
I had rather hear you to solicit that
Than music from the spheres.
Vio. Dear lady,——
Oli. Give me leave, I beseech you: I did send,
After the last enchantment you did here,

A ring in chase of you; so did I abuse
Myself, my servant—and, I fear me, you.
Under your hard construction must I sit,
To force that on you, in a shameful cunning,
Which you knew none of yours. What might you think?
Have you not set mine honor at the stake,
And baited it with all the unmuzzled thoughts
That tyrannous heart can think? To one of your receiving
Enough is shown; a cypress, not a bosom,
Hides my poor heart.
* * * * * * * * *
Here! wear this jewel for me; 'tis my picture.
Refuse it not; it hath no tongue to vex you;
And, I beseech you, come again to-morrow.
What shall you ask of me that I'll deny—
That honor, sav'd, may upon asking give?

As to her personal charms, Viola addresses her as "Most radiant, exquisite, and unmatchable beauty," and says of her face:

'Tis beauty truly blent, whose red and white
Nature's own sweet and cunning hand laid on.
* * * * * * * * *
I see you what you are: you are too proud;
But, if you were the devil, you are fair.

Olivia acknowledges to *Cesario* her fault of unwomanly boldness; but the confession is plainly neither preceded nor followed by even a pretence of penitence; it is but one of the thousand coquettish tricks of a spoiled beauty to win back the respect which she feels she has justly forfeited:

I have said too much unto a heart of stone,
And laid my honor too unchary out;
There's something in me that reproves my fault;
But such a headstrong, potent fault it is,
That it but mocks reproof.

MARIA.

MARIA, waiting-woman to the Countess Olivia, is a true type of the mischief-making heroine of life below-stairs--the stage *soubrette*. Arch, coquettish, full of genuine humor, her ready resources of fun are liberally diffused throughout this charming comedy, with a bewildering succession of ludicrous situations, and merry mishaps deduced from them.

Malvolio, steward of Olivia's household, having presumed to take exception to the noisy and not over-nice carousals of Sir Toby Belch, for whom Maria entertains a saucy sort of preference, she, to be quits with him—but more, perhaps, for love of a practical jest—resolves to make him ridiculous. This she accomplishes effectually; but the following groundwork of her plot affords but an incomplete idea of its laughable consequences:

> *Mar.* The devil a Puritan that he is, or any thing constantly but a time-pleaser—an affection'd ass, that cons state without book, and utters it by great swarths; the best persuaded of himself; so crammed, as he thinks, with excellences, that it is his ground of faith that all that look on him love him; and on that vice in him will my revenge find notable cause to work.
>
> *Sir To.* What wilt thou do?

Mar. I will drop in his way some obscure epistles of love, wherein, by the color of his beard, the shape of his leg, the manner of his gait, the expressure of his eye, forehead, and complexion, he shall find himself most feelingly personated: I can write very like my lady, your niece; on a forgotten matter we can hardly make distinction of our hands.

* * * * * * * * * *

Sir To. He shall think, by the letters that thou wilt drop, that they come from my niece, and that she is in love with him.

Mar. My purpose is, indeed, a horse of that color.

A sketch, only, of the garden scene, and we have done with this merry episode:

Sir To. Here comes the little villain:—How now, my metal of India?

Mar. Get ye all three into the box-tree; Malvolio's coming down this walk; he has been yonder i' the sun, practising behavior to his own shadow, this half hour: observe him, for the love of mockery; for I know this letter will make a contemplative idiot of him. Close, in the name of jesting! [*The men hide themselves.*] Lie thou there! [*throws down a letter*] for here comes the trout that must be caught with tickling.

* * * * * * * * * * *

Mal. By my life, this is my lady's hand! These be her very *C*'s, her *U*'s, and her *T*'s; and thus makes she her great *P*'s. It is, in contempt of question, her hand.

* * * * * * * * * *

* * * * * * * * * *

I do not now fool myself, to let imagination jade me; for every reason excites to this,—that my lady loves me. She did commend my yellow stockings of late; she did praise my leg being cross-gartered; and in this she manifests herself to my love. * * * * *

I thank my stars I am happy. I will be strange, stout, in yellow stockings and cross-gartered, even with the swiftness of putting on.

* * * * * * * *

Sir To. I could marry this wench for this device.

Sir And. So could I too.

Sir To. And ask no other dowry with her but such another jest.

* * * * * * * * * *

Mar. If you will then see the fruits of the sport, mark his first approach before my lady: he will come to her in yellow stockings—and 'tis a color she abhors; and cross-gartered—a fashion she detests; and he will smile upon her—which will now be so unsuitable to her disposition, being addicted to a melancholy as she is, that it cannot but turn him into a notable contempt; if you will see it, follow me.

Sir To. To the gates of Tartar, thou most excellent devil of wit!

It will be seen that Sir Toby Belch was as good as his word, for once at least; he did marry the merry Maria, whose power of amusing him had taken him captive. Yet we will hope for gallantry even from so coarse a lover; Fabian tells the Lady Olivia, in final explanation, that

> * . * * * Maria writ
> The letter at Sir Toby's great importance—
> In recompense whereof, he hath married her;

and we will amiably believe him capable of thus liberating Maria from a position of much embarrassment toward her mistress, with whose dignity she had indeed made something too free—in order that the Lady Olivia might find it easy to forgive a jest from her *aunt* which would be insufferable from her waiting-woman.

PORTIA.

Portia, mistress of "Belmont," her hereditary estate, was a wealthy heiress and an orphan, who, by her father's will, was to be bestowed in marriage according to an odd conceit, by which, before his death, she had vowed to abide. Three caskets—of gold, silver, and lead, respectively—were to be submitted to the choice of the suitor, who must previously have sworn never to marry should he fail; and the selection of the one which contained a portrait of the lady would constitute him her husband. The wealthiest and most noble gentlemen of the land, and many from afar, hastened to woo the fair Portia, the fame of whose beauty, virtues, and rich inheritance had gone abroad.

Among these romantic competitors was Bassanio, a young Venetian of high rank but fallen fortunes, for whom, in times past, Portia had entertained a preference. In order to fit himself out for his journey as became a suitor to so renowned a lady, he had been beholden to his friend Antonio, a wealthy merchant of Venice, for a loan of three thousand ducats; and Antonio, in his turn, had been compelled to borrow the money from Shylock, a Jew, and a notorious usurer. For this loan Antonio gave his bond, to the effect that, in case of his failing to pay back the money at the appointed time, he should forfeit a pound of his own flesh, to be cut from whichever part of his body Shylock should prefer — the money-lender having himself dictated this extraordinary stipulation, with a malignant motive.

Bassanio, having made himself acceptable to Portia, determined finally to decide his fate by the ordeal of the caskets; and, to their mutual joy, he chose the one which contained her picture. But, even as they were receiving the congratulations of their friends, a letter arrived from Antonio, announcing that his ships, on the safe return of which he had counted for the means of paying his debt to the Jew, had been wrecked, and that he was therefore about to submit to the cruel alternative prescribed in the bond. The high-spirited Portia, thus learning that a friend of her affianced husband was like to die for having assisted him, married Bassanio at once, to give him legal control over her possessions, and despatched him in all haste to pay the Jew and release Antonio.

No sooner, however, had Bassanio departed, than she sent a messenger to Bellario, her cousin and a counsellor, for advice, and his robes—on receiving which, she and her waiting-woman, Nerissa, disguised as a lawyer and his clerk, set out forthwith for Venice, where this extraordinary suit was already "all the talk."

Portia arrived just in time for the trial; and having presented her credentials from Bellario, introducing to the duke the young Doctor Balthazar, she took her seat in court, as counsel for Antonio.

When it was her turn to speak, she began by offering Shylock the money, even thrice the sum; but he triumphantly refused. Then she appealed in eloquent terms to his mercy; and when that failed, she bade him help himself to his pound of flesh, but to take heed that he shed not a single drop of blood, for by so doing he would forfeit all his estates and goods to the State of Venice

This timely hit of the young doctor was received with unanimous applause. Not only was Shylock thus baffled in his murderous plot for personal revenge, but for having conspired against the life of a citizen he was condemned to transfer half his possessions to Antonio, the other half to be confiscated to the State. But Antonio generously relinquished his share, on condition that Shylock, at his death, should bequeath it to his daughter Jessica, whom he had disinherited for having married Lorenzo, a Christian, and friend of Bassanio.

Portia returned home in time to welcome Bassanio and Antonio; there, in the midst of the general rejoicing, she confessed her part in the happy result, and there were no bounds to the "tender joy that filled the hearts of those who went to rest in Belmont!"

Portia is distinguished by a patrician elegance of person and presence, which is so innately her own that it depends but little for its effect on the aristocratic pretension of her surroundings. Although far from popular—her reputation for extraordinary mental endowments being sufficient to constitute a formidable obstacle to public favor—she is one of the most delightful of Shakspeare's women. Her intellectual quality is indeed marked; but that can never render a woman less lovable, when, as in Portia's case, it is subordinate to the affections. Schlegel, regarding her from a purely critical point of view, pronounces her "clever;" and although Mrs. Jameson protests against the application of so dubious an epithet to this "heavenly compound of talent, feeling, wisdom, beauty, and gentleness," we must confess that to us it seems well chosen. "Clever" does not, indeed, imply the possession of illustrious powers; but it does signify that nice "dexterity in the adaptation of certain faculties to a certain end or aim" which is eminently graceful and feminine, and exactly describes the mental characteristics of Portia, as most conspicuously displayed in the trial scene, wherein her success is achieved, not by the exercise of inherent wisdom, or an educated judgment, but by the merely clever discovery of a legal quibble. That the word has fallen into disrepute, from unworthy associations, should not impair its legitimate value. True, it does "suggest the idea of something we should distrust and shrink from, if not allied to a higher nature;" but we contend that, in Portia, cleverness *is* allied to a higher nature—to qualities which are, indeed, scarcely less perfect than her fair panegyrist has portrayed them—in a woman whose "plenteous wit" and excelling accomplishments are more than equalled by her tenderness, her magnanimity, her graceful dignity, and her lofty honor

The scene wherein the happy consummation of her love depends on the perilous chance of her lover's choosing the casket which contains her picture, is full of eloquent touches. We may almost count the heart-throbs of Portia, as she pleads to Bassanio, in such candid confusion of fear, to "pause a day or two before he hazards:"

> I pray you, tarry; pause a day or two
> Before you hazard; for, in choosing wrong,
> I lose your company; therefore, forbear a while.
> There's something tells me, (but it is not love,)
> I would not lose you; and you know, yourself,
> Hate counsels not in such a quality;
> But lest you should not understand me well,
> (And yet a maiden hath no tongue but thought,)
> I would detain you here some month or two,
> Before you venture for me. I could teach you
> How to choose right—but then I am forsworn;
> So will I never be: so may you miss me;

But if you do, you'll make me wish a sin—
That I had been forsworn. Beshrow your eyes!
They have o'erlook'd me, and divided me;
One half of me is yours, the other half yours,—
Mine own, I would say; but if mine, then yours—
And so all yours:
* * * * * * * *
Away then! I am lock'd in one of them;
If you do love me, you will find me out.

Her chaste passion, which she has studiously repressed while threatened with the possibility of disappointment, bursts forth in this exuberance of joy when her lover has indeed won her:

How all the other passions fleet to air—
As doubtful thoughts, and rash-embrac'd despair,
And shudd'ring fear, and green-ey'd jealousy!
O Love, be moderate, allay thy ecstasy,
In measure rain thy joy, scant this excess;
I feel too much thy blessing; make it less,
For fear I surfeit!

But Portia is surrounded by guests and attendants; this is no time for Love's transports, even if she were less accustomed to self-command; it is necessary that she should formally acknowledge her future husband; and with what rare tact, excelling dignity, and love disdaining all affectation of diffidence, is her acceptance of him clothed. We wonder how any one, after having read this most womanly speech, dictated by the simplest emotions of a loving and modest heart, can accuse Portia of affectation or pedantry:

You see me, lord Bassanio, where I stand,
Such as I am. Though, for myself alone,
I would not be ambitious in my wish,
To wish myself much better; yet, for you,
I would be trebled twenty times myself—
A thousand times more fair, ten thousand times
More rich;

That only to stand high on your account,
I might in virtues, beauties, livings, friends,
Exceed account. But the full sum of me
Is sum of something; which, to term in gross,
Is an unlesson'd girl, unschool'd, unpractis'd:
Happy in this—she is not yet so old
But she may learn; and happier than this—
She is not bred so dull but she can learn;
Happiest of all is, that her gentle spirit
Commits itself to yours to be directed,
As from her lord, her governor, her king.
Myself, and what is mine, to you and yours
Is now converted; but now I was the lord
Of this fair mansion, master of my servants,
Queen o'er myself; and even now, but now,
This house, these servants, and this same myself,
Are yours, my lord; I give them with this ring.

For the trial scene, that "master-piece of dramatic skill," as so much of its effect depends upon the by-play, we resign our reader to the text—except for Portia's famous appeal to Shylock, which, apart from its circumstantial force, stands alone, one of the most beautiful of the "beauties of Shakspeare:"

Por. The quality of mercy is not strain'd;
It droppeth, as the gentle rain from heaven
Upon the place beneath; it is twice bless'd:
It blesseth him that gives, and him that takes.
'Tis mightiest in the mightiest; it becomes
The throned monarch better than his crown;
His sceptre shows the force of temporal power,
The attribute to awe and majesty,
Wherein doth sit the dread and fear of kings;
But mercy is above this sceptred sway—
It is enthroned in the hearts of kings—
It is an attribute to God himself;
And earthly power doth then show likest God's
When mercy seasons justice. Therefore, Jew,
Though justice be thy plea, consider this—

That in the course of justice none of us
Should see salvation. We do pray for mercy;
And that same prayer doth teach us all to render
The deeds of mercy.

Portia's wit, guiltless of malice, irreverence, or vulgar effort at display, is as fresh, hopeful, and light-hearted as her own elastic spirit. Her conversation with her maid, Nerissa, about the lovers who have come a-wooing, is incomparably lively and satirical, yet perfectly good-humored; and not a few of her happy sallies have become proverbial. Of these we give but two: the first a portrait, as true of the subject to-day as when Portia sketched it; the second a titbit of moral philosophy, that will continue to be relished as long as a moral finger-post is left in the land:

* * * * * * * * * *
* * * * I'll hold thee any wager,
When we are both accouter'd like young men,
I'll prove the prettier fellow of the two,
And wear my dagger with the braver grace;
And speak, between the change of man and boy,
With a reed voice; and turn two mincing steps
Into a manly stride; and speak of frays,
Like a fine bragging youth; and tell quaint lies—
How honorable ladies sought my love,
Which I denying, they fell sick and died;
I could not do with all. Then I'll repent,
And wish, for all that, that I had not kill'd them;
And twenty of these puny lies I'll tell,
That men should swear I have discontinued school
Above a twelvemonth:—I have within my mind
A thousand raw tricks of these bragging Jacks,
Which I will practise.

If to do were as easy as to know what were good to do, chapels had been churches, and poor men's cottages princes' palaces. It is a good divine that follows his own instructions: I can easier teach twenty what were good to be done, than be one of the twenty to follow mine own teaching.

As to her beauty, her goodness, and the fame of both—could any one doubt—we find abundant testimony in the following passages:

In Belmont is a lady richly left;
And she is fair, and, fairer than that word,
Of wondrous virtues;
* * * * * * * *
Her name is Portia—nothing undervalued
To Cato's daughter, Brutus' Portia.
Nor is the wide world ignorant of her worth;
For the four winds blow in from every coast
Renowned suitors; and her sunny locks
Hang on her temples like a golden fleece—
Which makes her seat of Belmont Colchos' strand,
And many Jasons come in quest of her.
* * * * * * * *
* * * * All the world desires her:
From the four corners of the earth they come,
To kiss this shrine, this mortal breathing saint.
The Hyrcanian deserts, and the vasty wilds
Of wide Arabia, are as through-fares now,
For princes to come view fair Portia;
The wat'ry kingdom, whose ambitious head
Spits in the face of heaven, is no bar
To stop the foreign spirits; but they come,
As o'er a brook, to see fair Portia.
* * * * * * * *
Why, if two gods should play some heavenly match,
And on the wager lay two earthly women,
And Portia one, there must be something else
Pawn'd with the other; for the poor rude world
Hath not her fellow.

JESSICA.

To our mind, Jessica, Shylock's "one fair daughter," is, in her filial aspect, neither a pleasing nor a truthful picture; though it must be acknowledged that her derelictions from duty are committed under extenuating circumstances.

It is not for deceiving her father, so far as her love-affair with Lorenzo is concerned, that we dislike her; nor for eloping from a home which, by his graceless parsimony, and cold, forbidding harshness, he had made a "hell" to her; but for the stealing of the ducats and the jewels—above all, the trading of a turquoise ring, her mother's love-gift to her father, for a monkey—we can find no excuse, no palliation, in the best-natured virtue; theft is too mean a crime to be easily forgiven, especially in a heroine.

Mrs. Jameson says of Jessica, that she has "a rich tinge of Orientalism shed over her, worthy her Eastern origin:" to us she betrays her race only in her characteristic love of gold, to which, amorous and romantic as she is, she can give careful heed, even in the very act of eloping with her lover, by night and in disguise:

> Here, catch this casket; *it is worth the pains.*
> * * * * * * * *
> I will make fast the doors, *and gild myself*
> *With some more ducats*, and be with you straight.

> *Lor.* * * * * She hath directed
> How I shall take her from her father's house—
> What gold, and jewels, she is furnish'd with.

Fancy Juliet, Silvia, or even little Anne Page, the two latter veritable "run-aways" from the paternal roof, damaging their father's coffers as well as his authority!

As for Jessica's conversion to the Christian religion, we put no faith in it: it is plain that she is as indifferent to the faith of her husband as she was to that of her father; she would just as readily have become a Mohammedan, if her Lorenzo had sworn by Allah and the Prophet.

Once married, however, Jessica assumes a more amiable aspect—her conjugal tenderness is very beautiful; and the garden scene at Belmont, during the honeymoon of the young couple, is soulful enough to cover a multitude of meannesses; Lorenzo is the most poetic of lovers, and for his sake we can almost pardon the episode of the ducats:

> *Lor.* The moon shines bright:—In such a night as this,
> When the sweet wind did gently kiss the trees,
> And they did make no noise—in such a night,
> Troilus, methinks, mounted the Trojan walls,
> And sigh'd his soul toward the Grecian tents,
> Where Cressid lay that night.
> *Jes.* In such a night,
> Did Thisbe fearfully o'ertrip the dew;
> And saw the lion's shadow ere himself,
> And ran dismay'd away.
> *Lor.* In such a night,
> Stood Dido with a willow in her hand
> Upon the wild sea-banks, and wav'd her love
> To come again to Carthage.
> *Jes.* In such a night,
> Medea gather'd the enchanted herbs
> That did renew old Æson.

Lor. In such a night,
Did Jessica steal from the wealthy Jew;
And with an unthrift love did run from Venice,
As far as Belmont.
Jes. And in such a night,
Did young Lorenzo swear he lov'd her well—
Stealing her soul with many vows of faith,
And ne'er a true one.
Lor. And in such a night,
Did pretty Jessica, like a little shrew,
Slander her love, and he forgave it her.
* * * * * * * *
How sweet the moon-light sleeps upon this bank!
Here will we sit, and let the sounds of music
Creep in our ears; soft stillness, and the night,
Become the touches of sweet harmony.
Sit, Jessica: Look how the floor of heaven
Is thick inlaid with patines of bright gold!
There's not the smallest orb which thou behold'st
But in his motion like an angel sings,
Still quiring to the young-ey'd cherubins:
Such harmony is in immortal souls;
But whilst this muddy vesture of decay
Doth grossly close it in, we cannot hear it.

PERDITA.

Perdita, daughter of Leontes, king of Sicily, and his queen, the beautiful and excellent Hermione, was born in a prison, wherein her cruel father, in a fit of jealous rage, had confined his wife some time before the birth of Perdita.

Leontes, suspecting Hermione of infidelity with his guest Polixenes, king of Bohemia, ordered Camillo, one of his lords, to poison the latter. Camillo, however, believing his royal mistress to be most foully slandered, pretended to acquiesce in her husband's treacherous plot, only to disclose it to Polixenes; whereupon they took flight together to Bohemia. It was at this juncture that Hermione was cast into prison, where she eventually gave birth to a princess.

Paulina, a brave friend of the queen's, bore the babe to its father, hoping thus to touch his heart, and avert his displeasure from the unhappy mother. But her devoted mission failed miserably; the king commanded Antigonus, another of his lords, to take the child out to sea, and leave it to perish on some desolate shore.

This time his orders were fulfilled: Antigonus left the babe, all swaddled in rich robes and bedecked with jewels, on a lonely "fishing coast" of Bohemia, whither a storm had driven the ship—

taking the precaution, however, of pinning a paper to the baby's mantle, with the name, *Perdita*, written thereon, and a line or two dimly significant of its illustrious birth. A humane shepherd found the poor little innocent, and took it home to his wife, who nursed it tenderly; his extreme poverty, dazzled by the rare jewels, induced him to keep secret the manner in which he found the child, and she was reared in every respect as his own daughter.

Shakspeare gives proof of his loyal belief in "blood," in the sequel of this pretty tale. The royal foundling, reared in a shepherd's hut, receiving almost none of the graces of education, queen only over flocks and herds, lived and moved a princess.

The young Prince Florizel, only son of Polixenes, hunting one day near the shepherd's dwelling, saw the charming Perdita, and became desperately, but in all honor, enamoured of her high-born beauty. Under an assumed name, and in the guise of a simple gentleman, he paid court to her at once.

Polixenes, remarking Florizel's frequent absence from court, set spies on the prince, who soon apprised him of his son's love for the fair shepherdess. Forthwith, he and Camillo visited in disguise the house of the old shepherd during the merry-making of sheep-shearing. Here the king discovered himself to his son, loaded him with reproaches, and commanded Perdita never again to receive him, on pain of her own and her father's death.

Camillo, anxious to return to his native land, rescued the lovers from the wrath of Polixenes, and accompanied them to the Sicilian court, to solicit Leontes' influence and protection till Polixenes should consent to their union.

Leontes, full of remorse for the cruelty which, he supposed, had caused the death of his well-beloved queen, joyfully received Camillo back again to his favor, and made the young people welcome. The marvellous resemblance of Perdita to Hermione caused his heart to bleed afresh; and his self-accusing ejaculations aroused the suspicions of the old shepherd, who produced the proofs of Perdita's identity with the deserted babe.

Paulina, convinced of Leontes' repentance, invited him to her house to see a cunning statue from the hand of a great master. The statue was Hermione herself, whom, to protect her, Paulina had declared dead. Thus, a faithful wife was restored to the arms of her penitent husband, and the shepherd's foundling found a tender mother in the virtuous queen.

Polixenes followed the fugitives to Sicily; but there no longer existed any objection, personal or political, to the marriage of the Bohemian prince to the heiress of the throne of Sicily, and their union crowned the general rejoicing.

Though the character of Perdita is quite subordinate to that of Hermione, the heroine proper of "The Winter's Tale," it is, nevertheless, a carefully finished picture in every detail. Its delicate coloring is suggestive rather than simply descriptive, its subtile poetry conveyed to the beholder by master touches; beside the glowing, life-size portraits of Juliet, Portia, and Lady Macbeth, this unique miniature gem sparkles half concealed, yet full of exquisite beauties. Perdita, perhaps, of all Shakspeare's heroines, is the completest exemplification of the intuitive lady, whose inbred daintiness no accident of life can affect.

Frequent mention is made of her rare personal beauty, and not by her lover only. Florizel says to her, touching her gay holiday attire at the sheep-shearing:

> These, your unusual weeds, to each part of you
> Do give a life—no shepherdess, but Flora

Peering in April's front; this, your sheep-shearing,
Is as a meeting of the petty gods,
And you the queen on't.

This rhapsody, too, is plainly something more than the mere extravagance of an ardent lover:

What you do
Still betters what is done. When you speak, sweet,
I'd have you do it ever. When you sing,
I'd have you buy and sell so, so give alms,
Pray so, and for the ordering of your affairs
To sing them too. When you do dance, I wish you
A wave o' the sea, that you might ever do
Nothing but that—move still, still so, and own
No other function.

* * * Were I crown'd the most imperial monarch,
* * * Were I the fairest youth
That ever made eye swerve, had force and knowledge
More than was ever man's, I would not prize them
Without her love: for her employ them all,
Commend them, and condemn them to her service,
Or to their own perdition!

Polixenes himself pays an involuntary tribute to her charms.

This is the prettiest low-born lass that ever
Ran on the greensward; nothing she does, or seems,
But smacks of something greater than herself,
Too noble for this place.

To which Camillo replies:

* * * * Good sooth, she is
The queen of curds and cream.

Arrived with Florizel at the Sicilian court, one of the gentlemen says of her:

* * * The most peerless piece of earth, I think,
That e'er the sun shone bright on.

And another:

* * * * This is such a creature,
Would she begin a sect, might quench the zeal
Of all professors else—make proselytes
Of who she but bid follow.

Women will love her, that she is a woman
More worth than any man; men, that she is
The rarest of all women.

In Perdita's well known and oft-quoted greeting to the stranger-guests at the sheep-shearing, we have a fine example of her innate courtesy, as well as of the poetic delicacy of her fancy:

* * * * * Reverend sirs,
For you there's rosemary and rue; these keep
Seeming and savor, all the winter long;
Grace and remembrance be to you both,
And welcome to our shearing!

Here's flowers for you:
Hot lavender, mints, savory, marjoram,
The marigold, that goes to bed with the sun,
And with him rises, weeping: these are flowers
Of middle summer, and I think they are given
To men of middle age. You are very welcome!

* * * Now, my fairest friend,
I would I had some flowers o' the spring that might
Become your time of day. * * * * * *
* * * * * O Proserpina!
For the flowers now that, frighted, thou let'st fall
From Dis's wagon! daffodils,
That come before the swallow dares, and take
The winds of March with beauty; violets dim,
But sweeter than the lids of Juno's eyes,
Or Cytherea's breath; pale primroses,

That die unmarried, ere they can behold
Bright Phœbus in his strength—a malady
Most incident to maids; bold oxlips, and
The crown imperial; lilies of all kinds,
The flower-de-luce being one! O, these I lack,
To make you garlands of—and, my sweet friend,
To strew him o'er and o'er.
Flor. What? like a corse?
Perd. No, like a bank, for love to lie and play on;
Not like a corse—or if, not to be buried,
But quick, and in mine arms!

The simple dignity and exquisite tenderness of Perdita are beautifully portrayed in one or two addresses to Florizel after his royal father has commanded them to part forever:

Even here undone!
I was not much afeard; for once or twice
I was about to speak, and tell him plainly,
The self-same sun that shines upon his court
Hides not his visage from our cottage, but
Looks on alike. Wilt please you, sir, begone?
I told you what would come of this. 'Beseech you,
Of your own state take care: this dream of mine—
Being now awake, I'll queen it no inch further,
But milk my ewes, and weep.

HERMIONE.

Critically (though not popularly) considered, Hermione must ever occupy a position superior to Perdita in the charming story to which both contribute so much beauty.

Endowed with every virtue that helps to complete the perfect woman, Hermione is distinguished by her illustrious resignation under the most grievous wrongs that can befall an honored queen, and a devoted wife. Repudiated by her husband for senseless suspicions of her chastity, conceived without an excuse of foundation; thrown into prison, to give birth to a poor little princess; her first-born son dying of grief for his mother's disgrace; her infant condemned to death by its unnatural father; herself put to public shame—a second Grissel, Hermione endures all with scarce a murmur; not so much from patient love, however, as from an indomitable fortitude, a grand pride in her conscious innocence, which has all the exalting effect of martyrdom.

To Hermione, daughter of an emperor, wife to a king, and mother of a "hopeful prince," a serene, majestic composure belongs, as a birthright; and her soul is full of a repose as imperturbable as her bearing is royal. She has no passions: no violent demonstrations, no tears nor reproaches, resent her lord's injustice;

she is degraded, but in her ignominy she is still a queen. Absorbing as are her affections as wife and mother, the blow they suffer appears on the surface in no more accusing shape than a sublime, heroic patience; charged openly with adultery and treason, in the midst of the court where she has reigned a beloved and honored sovereign, her gracious lips can consent to frame no answer more ungentle than these touching words:

> How will this grieve you,
> When you shall come to clearer knowledge, that
> You thus have publish'd me? Gentle my lord,
> You scarce can right me throughly then, to say
> You did mistake.
> * * * * * * * * *
> * * * * * * * * *
> There's some ill planet reigns;
> I must be patient, till the heavens look
> With an aspéct more favorable.—Good my lords,
> I am not prone to weeping, as our sex
> Commonly are—the want of which vain dew,
> Perchance, shall dry your pities; but I have
> That honorable grief, lodg'd here, which burns
> Worse than tears drown.

Yet, though she can hide her bleeding heart away under the pall of a sorrow too grave for tears, though she can mourn her dearest loves as dead and make no sign, she may not thus proudly permit the filching of her good name—that inestimable dowry bestowed upon her by illustrious ancestors, a precious heritage to be transmitted to her children's children; and we feel that it is only in obedience to this lofty sense of duty that she condescends to justify herself—that she "stands to prate and talk before who please to come and hear."

By a woman of common temper this accusation of infidelity would have been silently spurned, in the face of its terrible consequences—the loss of her husband's love and the death of her children; but to the spotless majesty of Hermione's soul a charge of dishonor, which she is not able to disprove, is the very consummation of calamity; all the rest is but sorrow—this is shame.

The court scene, in the third act, of itself suffices to afford us a truthful conception of Hermione's character. At a time when, from merely physical causes, it would be natural to look for emotion even in her, this unhappy queen is as calm as if she were but a spectator, not the arraigned culprit, of the imposing concourse assembled to pronounce her sentence; her "nerves" are adamant; her whole bearing bespeaks the "queen o'er herself." Only when the oracle has been flouted which declared her chaste, and the death of her son is announced, does the heroic lady sink under her weight of woes.

Her appeal, not for pity nor for life, but for the re-establishment of her honor, is a model of dignified eloquence:

* * * * * * * * * *
* * * * * You, my lord, best know,
(Who least will seem to do so,) my past life
Hath been as continent, as chaste, as true,
As I am now unhappy—which is more
Than history can pattern, though devis'd,
And play'd, to take spectators; For behold me,—
A fellow of the royal bed, which owe
A moiety of the throne, a great king's daughter,
The mother to a hopeful prince,—here standing,
To prate and talk for life and honor 'fore
Who please to come and hear. For life, I prize it,
As I weigh grief, which I would spare; for honor—
'Tis a derivative from me to mine,
And only that I stand for.
* * * * * * * * *

Sir, spare your threats;
The bug, which you would fright me with, I seek.

To me can life be no commodity:
The crown and comfort of my life, your favor,
I do give lost—for I do feel it gone,
But know not how it went; my second joy,
And first-fruits of my body, from his presence
I am barr'd, like one infectious; my third comfort,
Star'd most unluckily, is from my breast,
The innocent milk in its most innocent mouth,
Haled out to murder; myself on every post
Proclaim'd a strumpet—with immodest hatred,
The child-bed privilege denied, which 'longs
To women of all fashion; lastly, hurried
Here to this place, i' the open air, before
I have got strength of limit. Now, my liege,
Tell me what blessings I have here, alive,
That I should fear to die? Therefore, proceed;
But yet hear this: mistake me not;——No! life,
I prize it not a straw;—but for mine honor,
(Which I would free,) if I shall be condemn'd
Upon surmises—all proofs sleeping else,
But what your jealousies awake—I tell you
'Tis rigor, and not law.

That Hermione was a beautiful woman, of the regal, Juno-like type, is surely established by many passages let fall at random through the text. When a gentleman of the court enthusiastically extols Perdita's beauty, Paulina, champion of her mistress's memory as she ever has been zealous in her service, exclaims:

O Hermione,
As every present time doth boast itself
Above a better gone, so must thy grave
Give way to what's seen now. Sir, you yourself
Have said, and writ so, (but your writing now
Is colder than that theme,) *She had not been,*
Nor was not to be, equal'd;—thus your verse
Flow'd with her beauty once; 'tis shrewdly ebb'd,
To say you have seen a better.
* * * * * * * * *

Leon. Good Paulina,—
Who hast the memory of Hermione,
I know, in honor,—O, that ever I
Had squar'd me to thy counsel!—then, even now,
I might have look'd upon my queen's full eyes,
Have taken treasure from her lips,——
Paul. And left them
More rich, for what they yielded.
* * * * * * * * *
Leon. Stars, very stars,
And all eyes else dead coals!—fear thou no wife;
I'll have no wife, Paulina.

And that Hermione was as excellent as she was beautiful is as well attested by the enduring respect and affection with which she is held in remembrance by her servants, and above all by her husband. One of his courtiers urges Leontes to marry—"to bless the bed of majesty again with a sweet fellow to 't;" but the wretched king can bear to think of no wife, save the one "done to death by sland'rous tongues:"

Whilst I remember
Her, and her virtues, I cannot forget
My blemishes in them, and so still think of
The wrong I did myself: which was so much,
That heirless it hath made my kingdom, and
Destroy'd the sweet'st companion that e'er man
Bred his hopes out of.
Paul. True, too true, my lord:
If, one by one, you wedded all the world—
Or, from the all that are took something good,
To make a perfect woman—she you kill'd
Would be unparallel'd.
Leon. I think so. Kill'd!
She I kill'd? I did so; but thou strik'st me
Sorely, to say I did; it is as bitter
Upon thy tongue as in my thought.
* * * * * * * * * *

Paul. There is none worthy,
Respecting her that's gone.
* * * * * * * * * *
Leon. Thou speak'st truth:
No more such wives; therefore, no wife.

The final, or "statue," scene—in which, after sixteen years of strict seclusion, she is restored to her husband, and the daughter who had been miraculously preserved to bless her patient heart—is one of the most effective in dramatic story.

If any thing could persuade us to forgive Leontes his unworthy doubts of such a woman as Hermione, it would be the sincere emotion he displays whilst gazing on what he believes to be the won drous statue of his wife:

Her natural posture!—
Chide me, dear stone, that I may say, indeed,
Thou art Hermione; or, rather, thou art she
In thy not chiding; for she was as tender
As infancy and grace.—But yet, Paulina,
Hermione was not so much wrinkled, nothing
So aged, as this seems.
Pol. O, not by much.
Paul. So much the more our carver's excellence,
Which lets go by some sixteen years, and makes her
As she liv'd now.
Leon. As now she might have done—
So much to my good comfort, as it is
Now piercing to my soul. O, thus she stood,
Even with such life of majesty, (warm life,
As now it coldly stands,) when first I woo'd her!
I am asham'd: Does not the stone rebuke me,
For being more stone than it?—O, royal piece,
There's magic in thy majesty, which has
My evils conjur'd to remembrance, and
From thy admiring daughter took the spirits,
Standing like stone with thee!
* * * * * * * * *

Leon. Do not draw the curtain.

Paul. No longer shall you gaze on 't, lest your fancy
May think anon it moves.

Leon. Let be, let be!
Would I were dead, but that, methinks, already—
What was he, that did make it?—See, my lord,
Would you not deem it breath'd? and that those veins
Did verily bear blood?

Pol. Masterly done!
The very life seems warm upon her lip.

Leon. The fixture of her eye has motion in 't,
As we are mock'd with art.

Paul. I'll draw the curtain;
My lord's almost so far transported that
He'll think anon it lives.

Leon. O sweet Paulina,
Make me to think so twenty years together;
No settled senses of the world can match
The pleasure of that madness. Let 't alone.

Paul. I am sorry, sir, I have thus far stir'd you; but
I could afflict you further.

Leon. Do, Paulina;
For this affliction has a taste as sweet
As any cordial comfort.—Still, methinks,
There is an air comes from her: What fine chisel
Could ever yet cut breath? Let no man mock me—
For I will kiss her.

Paul. Good my lord, forbear:
The ruddiness upon her lip is wet;
You'll mar it, if you kiss it—stain your own
With oily painting: Shall I draw the curtain?

Leon. No, not these twenty years.

MISTRESS FORD

Mistress Alice Ford is one of the two "Merry Wives of Windsor" whose mischievous pranks constitute the material for that very amusing, but somewhat too coarse, comedy. Sir John Falstaff, sojourning in Windsor, proposes to engage in certain amorous speculations with the wives of two well-to-do citizens, for his own pecuniary benefit. He accordingly indites love-letters to those jovial dames, who, being fast friends, at once inform each other of the audacious affront offered to their virtue, and together contrive a suitable revenge. By their excellent devices Falstaff is encouraged in both his suits, only to be betrayed into a series of humiliating situations, to the effect of which Master Ford, the jealous spouse of our quick-witted heroine, materially contributes by his counter-plotting, as well as by the punishment he receives for his groundless suspicions of his wife's virtue.

The underplot of the play is admirably sustained by the sentimental enterprises of three suitors for the hand of "Sweet Anne Page," daughter of Mistress Page, the famous coadjutor and fellow-sufferer of Mistress Ford; and Mistress Quickly, who, to her "respectable" calling of woman-of-all-work in a bachelor's establishment, adds the more questionable profession of go-between in all the amorous affairs—honorable or to the contrary—of her vil lage, plays no insignificant part in the laughable conspiracies of which the comedy consists.

The piquant original of these speaking "presentments" of Mistresses Ford and Page, existed, we have reason to believe, in the person of the beautiful Mrs. Davenant, hostess of the Crown Inn at Oxford, in whose sprightly company the Poet spent so many merry hours on his journeys from London to Stratford.

Without displaying any of those dainty refinements of character and manner which must always enter into one's ideas of a lady, Mistress Ford commands our good-natured sympathy by her many happy traits: her kindness of heart, her sound sense, her lively temper, and a certain jovial heartiness which pervades every thing she does or says.

To her conjugal honesty, so ill rewarded by her provoking husband, we pay a tribute of respect as genuine, if not so exalted, as that elicited by the more poetic chastity of the Princess Imogen; and it must be conceded that, notwithstanding the sacrifice of dramatic effect, her manner of punishing the "greasy knight" is far more practically sensible than provoking a duel to heal her wounded honor, or sacrificing her life to prove her husband a fool.

It is plain that Mistress Ford is a buxom beauty, in a state of remarkable preservation—"fat, fair," and very near "forty," but blest with the elastic spirits attendant on that robust health which makes English matrons the finest in the world. Allowing ample latitude for exaggeration, this matchless harangue of Gossip Quickly, on the importunities suffered by the handsome Merry Wife, quite glibly testifies to her exceeding comeliness, and suggests a very possible coquetry on her part, sufficient to avert from her poor, dear Ford a little of the contempt he appears to merit:

> *Fal.* Well! Mistress Ford:—what of her?
>
> * * * * * * * *
>
> *Quick.* Marry, this is the short and the long of it: you have brought her into such a canaries, as 'tis wonderful; the best courtier of them all, when the court lay at Windsor, could never have brought her to such a canary. Yet there has been knights, and lords, and gentlemen with their coaches—I warrant you, coach after coach, letter after letter, gift after gift—smelling so sweetly, (all musk,) and so rushling, I warrant you, in silk and gold; and in such alligant terms; and in such wine and sugar of the best, and the fairest, that would have won any woman's heart; and I warrant you, they could never get an eye-wink of her.—I had myself twenty angels given me this morning; but I defy all angels, (in any such sort, as they say,) but in the way of honesty:—and, I warrant you, they could never get her so much as sip on a cup with the proudest of them all; and yet there has been earls, nay, which is more, pensioners; but, I warrant you, all is one with her.

For a nicer personal description, though with even more liberal allowance for the flattery of the would-be gallant knight, we transcribe the first love-scene between him and the Merry Wife:

> *Fal. Have I caught* thee, *my heavenly jewel?* Why, now let me die, for I have lived long enough; this is the period of my ambition.—O this blessed hour!
>
> *Mrs. Ford.* O sweet Sir John!
>
> *Fal.* Mistress Ford, I cannot cog; I cannot prate, Mistress Ford. Now shall I sin in my wish: I would thy husband were dead; I'll speak it before the best lord—I would make thee my lady.
>
> *Mrs. Ford.* I your lady, Sir John! Alas, I should be a pitiful lady.

Fal. Let the court of France show me such another; I see how thine eye would emulate the diamond; thou hast the right arched bent of the brow, that becomes the ship-tire, the tire-valiant, or any tire of Venetian admittance.

Mrs. Ford. A plain kerchief, Sir John: my brows become nothing else; nor that well neither.

Fal. Thou art a traitor to say so: thou would'st make an absolute courtier; and the firm fixture of thy foot would give an excellent motion to thy gait, in a semicircled farthingale. I see what thou wert, if Fortune thy foe were not; Nature is thy friend:—Come, thou canst not hide it.

Mrs. Ford. Believe me, there's no such thing in me.

Fal. What made me love thee? Let that persuade thee there's something extraordinary in thee. * *
* * * * * * * * * *

MISTRESS PAGE.

By closely studying the characters of Mistress Page and Mistress Ford, one may detect a distinction, but it is a distinction almost without a difference. They are women of about the same age, the same position in life, of very similar temperaments and tastes—social, merry-hearted, fond of broad jests, but none the less chaste for that—and, moreover, friends, of long and confidential intimacy. It is certainly clear that Mistress Page is quite subordinate to Mistress Ford in the contrivance and execution of the novel self-avenging which has made them famous: it is Mistress Ford who grants Falstaff an interview at her own house during her husband's absence, and then sends him off, concealed in a basket of soiled linen, to be "dumped" into a foul ditch; it is Mistress Ford who, with excuses and cajolery, induces him to repeat his amorous visit, only to betray him to a sound drubbing from her enraged lord; and still Mistress Ford, who accords him an assignation in Windsor Park, and allows him one treacherous embrace before the dire consummation which occurs there.

We conclude, however, that this superior boldness on the part of Mistress Ford arises, not from a character dissimilar in that respect to that of Mistress Page, but rather from the constant temptation she finds in her husband's jealousy, to play upon his weakness; as she says to her friend:

> I know not which pleases me better—that my husband is deceiv'd, or Sir John.

And again:

> * * * * * * * * * *
> * * * O that my husband saw this letter! it would give eternal food to his jealousy.

Mistress Page, on the other hand, is evidently serious in her resentful reception of the insulting missive; her comments, as she reads it, are full of indignation, unalloyed by a trace of vanity:

> What! have I 'scaped love letters in the holiday time of my beauty, and am I now a subject for them? Let me see.
> * * * * * * * * * *
> * * * * * * * * * *
> What a Herod of Jewry is this?—O wicked, wicked world!—one that is well-nigh worn to pieces with age, to show himself a young gallant! What an unweighed behavior hath this Flemish drunkard picked (with the devil's name) out of my conversation, that he dares in this manner assay me? Why, he hath not been thrice in my company!—What should I say to him?—I was then frugal of my mirth:—Heaven forgive me!—Why, I'll exhibit a bill in the parliament for the putting down of men. How shall I be revenged on him? for revenged I will be.

Contrast this with Mistress Ford's jolly *double-entendres*—though she becomes serious enough when she discovers that Falstaff is not even honest in his infamous overtures:

> *Mrs. Ford.* O woman, if it were not for one trifling respect, I could come to such honor!

Mrs. Page. Hang the trifle, woman; take the honor. What is it!—dispense with trifles;—what is it?

Mrs. Ford. If I would but go to hell for an eternal moment or so, I could be knighted.

* * * * * * * * * *

Here, read, read!—perceive how I might be knighted.—I shall think the worse of fat men as long as I have an eye to make difference of men's liking. And yet he would not swear, praised women's modesty, and gave such orderly and well-behaved reproof to all uncomeliness, that I would have sworn his disposition would have gone to the truth of his words.

* * * * * * * *

How shall I be revenged on him? I think the best way were to entertain him with hope. * * * * *

Mrs. Page. Letter for letter—but that the name of Page and Ford differs!—To thy great comfort in this mystery of ill opinions, here's the twin-brother of thy letter: but let thine inherit first; for I protest mine never shall. I warrant he hath a thousand of these letters, writ with blank space for different names, (sure more;) and these are of the second edition.

* * * * * * * * * *

Mrs. Ford. Why this is the very same—the very hand, the very words! What doth he think of us?

Mrs. Page. Nay, I know not; it makes me almost ready to wrangle with mine own honesty. I'll entertain myself like one that I am not acquainted withal.

* * * * * * * * * *

Let's be revenged on him; let's appoint him a meeting, give him a show of comfort in his suit, and lead him on with a fine baited delay, till he hath pawn'd his horses to mine host of The Garter.

Mrs. Ford. Nay, I will consent to act any villainy against him, that may not sully the chariness of our honesty.

ANNE PAGE.

"Sweet Anne Page" is one of those rare bits of poetic sketching which, with scarcely a defined outline, and not a touch of vivid coloring, leave on the fancy an indelible impression of refined beauty.

In her graceful quiet, her lady-like reserve, her pretty, modest ways, she is so far removed from those among whom we find her, and whose coarse good-humor, and cordial, homely virtues, are utterly devoid of taste or delicate sentiment, that we may almost regard her as a second Perdita—a gem of the first water, shining all the more brightly for the roughness of its setting.

The subtile, indescribable charm which accompanies this "pretty virginity" is evidently felt by her coarse companions, without being perceived or understood by them. Of her three lovers, two of them—the half-witted booby, Slender, (with whom, nevertheless, originated her inseparable surname, "Sweet,") and the old French doctor, Caius—cannot be supposed to have the faintest appreciation of her character, however profoundly they may be impressed by her first-rate gentility and her father's money-bags. We do not wonder, then, that her maiden preference is bestowed on "young Master Fenton, who dances, has eyes of youth, writes verses, speaks holiday, smells April and May, has kept company with the wild prince, and is of too high a region" for her; in the one glimpse allowed us of their love-making, there is, in her two brief replies to Fenton's appeals, a delightful touch of unconscious coquetry. In the "why then," at the end, how much of vague hope, fear, delicious uncertainty, for the nice distinctions of a lover's heart:

Fent. I see I cannot get thy father's love;
Therefore no more turn me to him, sweet Nan.
Anne. Alas! how then?
Fent. Why, thou must be thyself.
He doth object I am too great of birth;
And that, my state being gall'd with my expense,
I seek to heal it only by his wealth.
Besides these, other bars he lays before me—
My riots past, my wild societies—
And tells me 'tis a thing impossible
I should love thee, but as a property.
Anne. May be, he tells you true.
Fent. No, Heaven so speed me in my time to come!
Albeit, I will confess, thy father's wealth
Was the first motive that I woo'd thee, Anne;
Yet, wooing thee, I found thee of more value
Than stamps in gold, or sums in sealed bags;
And 'tis the very riches of thyself
That now I aim at.
Anne. Gentle Master Fenton,
Yet seek my father's love; still seek it, sir:
If opportunity and humblest suit
Cannot attain it—*why then.*

But alas for the boasted guilelessness of this most innocent of maids! Love teaches even her shyness to be bold, and insinuates deceitful invention into that heart where loyal obedience and submission to parental will would seem to have built their throne: pretending to acquiesce in the contending views of both her father and her mother, she plays them false, to consummate her own fond designs. Her stratagem, in which she shows herself not inferior in ready wit to the Merry Wives, is thus described by Fenton to mine host of the Garter Inn:

From time to time I have acquainted you
With the dear love I bear to fair Anne Page,
Who, mutually, hath answer'd my affection
(So far forth as herself might be her chooser,)
Even to my wish. I have a letter from her,
Of such contents as you will wonder at—
The mirth whereof so larded with my matter,
That neither, singly, can be manifested
Without the show of both—wherein fat Falstaff
Hath a great scene; the image of the jest
[*Showing the letter.*
I'll show you here at large. Hark, good mine host!
To-night at Herne's oak, just 'twixt twelve and one,
Must my sweet Nan present the fairy queen—
The purpose why is here; in which disguise,
While other jests are something rank on foot,
Her father hath commanded her to slip
Away with Slender, and with him at Eton
Immediately to marry: she hath consented.
Now, sir,
Her mother, even strong against that match,
And firm for Dr. Caius, hath appointed
That he shall likewise shuffle her away,
While other sports are tasking of their minds,
And at the deanery, where a priest attends,
Straight marry her; to this her mother's plot
She, seemingly obedient, likewise hath
Made promise to the doctor.—Now thus it rests:
Her father means she shall be all in white;
And in that habit, when Slender sees his time
To take her by the hand, and bid her go,
She shall go with him. Her mother hath intended,
The better to denote her to the doctor,
(For they must all be masked and vizarded,)

That, quaint in green, she shall be loose enrob'd,
With ribands pendant, flaring 'bout her head;
And when the doctor spies his vantage ripe,
To pinch her by the hand—and, on that token,
The maid hath given consent to go with him.
Host. Which means she to deceive? father or mother?
Fent. Both, my good host, to go along with me;
And here it rests—that you'll procure the vicar
To stay for me at church, 'twixt twelve and one,
And, in the lawful name of marrying,
To give our hearts united ceremony.

And as lovers' excuses for their own misdemeanors are always the best, we cannot do better for our sweet Anne Page than to quote the plea of that plausible young Fenton:

The offence is holy that she hath committed,
And this deceit loses the name of craft,
Of disobedience, or unduteous title;
Since therein she doth evitate and shun
A thousand irreligious cursed hours,
Which forced marriage would have brought upon her.

ISABELLA.

ISABELLA of Vienna, a novice of the Sisterhood of St. Clare, was the sister of Claudio, a young man under sentence of death for having seduced a lady betrothed to him in marriage.

Vicentio, the reigning Duke of Vienna, becoming conscious of an injudicious clemency in his administration of the laws, appointed Lord Angelo his deputy, and, pretending to set out, incognito, on a long journey, remained in his dukedom, disguised as a friar, to take personal note of the effect produced on his people by the severe discipline of an austere ruler.

Claudio chanced to be the first detected in the violation of a law which, from long neglect to enforce it, had become a dead letter; and to establish an example for the salutary contemplation of its many outragers, Angelo, without hesitation, condemned him to die.

Isabella, who was on the point of taking the veil in the convent where she had served her novitiate, being sent for by her brother, abandoned her strict seclusion, to implore his pardon at the feet of Angelo, who at first was inexorable; but, seeming-virtuous as he was, he finally became enamoured of the beautiful vestal, and offered her Claudio's life in exchange for her honor. His vile proposal was indignantly rejected; and in recounting to her brother, in prison, the details of the insult, Isabella was overheard by the duke, who, as a friar, had visited Claudio to administer the consolations of religion, and to acquaint himself with the facts of the case. On parting from her brother, Isabella was accosted by the friar, who bade her seem to acquiesce in Angelo's proposition, and appoint him an assignation at night, taking every precaution, however, to insure strict secrecy; and he promised that he would procure a substitute for her, in the person of Mariana, a young lady to whom Angelo had been betrothed, who still loved him, whom he had deserted on some dishonorable pretext, but whom he would be compelled to marry after this visit—such being the friar's motive for interference.

Isabella consented to this subterfuge, the more readily that it was advised by a holy father; and it was accordingly executed as the duke had proposed. Angelo, however, with a treachery to be expected from his hypocritical sanctity, although he confidently believed that he had won the immaculate Isabella, resolved not to fulfil the terms of his own infamous bargain—he feared the vengeance of Claudio, the order for whose immediate execution was now set aside only through the intervention of the friar, who produced the duke's signet as evidence of his superior authority.

The return of Vicentio was then proclaimed throughout the city of Vienna; and all persons having grievances to complain of against the State were commanded to make public declaration of them before the duke.

Isabella, who believed that her brother had been executed, notwithstanding Angelo's promise to her, was the first to enter complaint against that corrupt judge; whereupon, after some intricate preliminaries, the lord deputy's wickedness was exposed, and he was forced to make restitution to the wronged but faithful

Mariana, by marrying her. Claudio, pardoned by the duke, was united to the victim of his selfish passion; and, finally, the spotless Isabella was created Duchess of Vienna by Vicentio, whose gracious preference she had won by her uncompromising virtue.

The character of Isabella presents a notable example of the inefficacy of a purely intellectual virtue to command our sympathy or admiration, or in any way to advance the cause of Religion.

In critical, as well as popular, appreciation, Isabella occupies a position of cool toleration—although in some opinions she has risen from that questionable status, to be denominated "an angel of light," and by another order of minds has been assailed with vituperative violence, as a coarse, vixenish prude. The prudent preservation of a temperate course, between these two exaggerations, will perhaps be the shortest and the surest road to strict justice toward one who would, herself, desire no more.

Cold, faultless, severe in moral rectitude, not liable to the weaknesses which "make the whole world kin," and utterly incapable of sympathy for them, this *réligieuse* stands, in a manner, arrayed against her fellows: existing, not only physically, but morally, apart from them, permitting herself no tie of reciprocal feeling to keep her united with the human family—the type of a class of mistaken but sincere religionists of all sects, who, by their repulsive self-sufficiency, fatally subvert the very interests to which they have consecrated their lives.

Isabella is no hypocrite—that is, consciously; her flawless excellence commands our exalted respect, our honorable recognition, however it may repel any more enthusiastic admiration; to the impregnability of her chastity, the prominent feature of her strongly marked individuality, full honor must be awarded; yet self-sacrifice, without a reservation, has become so inseparably associated with all that is most lovable in woman, that it would have been far easier to forgive the actual offence, than conscientiously to applaud her moral grandeur, remembering the beautiless details of her victory.

We do not "doubt the angelic purity of Isabella;" and, but for the instance of eccentric depravity furnished by her lover Angelo, we should believe only one event to be less possible than her "lapse from virtue"—that, notwithstanding her beauty, it should ever have sustained a temptation.

Isabella's complaints of the too lax discipline of her order are construed by her panegyrist, Mrs. Jameson, to signify that she desires a "more strict restraint," "from the consciousness of strong intellectual and imaginative power, and of *overflowing sensibility*," in herself, which require it. With all respect, we would suggest that this "very virtuous maid" is supplied with the latter qualities only from the abundant stores of the accomplished authoress herself. Isabella's strong intellectual power no one questions—it is conclusively established in her logical tilt of wits with the lord deputy; but of imagination, or sensibility, she is as destitute as an Audrey. Her appetite for severer penances and sharper mortifications is natural to the morbid devotee—and by no means peculiar to her, or of any special significance.

The austerity of Isabella's heart and soul, as well as of her outward life—her freedom from emotion, almost incredible in one so young—cannot be better illustrated than by the dialogue between her and Angelo, wherein she proves her dreadful insensibility to the peril of her brother's situation by the cool, self-possessed, equipoised arguments with which she pleads for him. It is plain that her words are doing violence to her convictions, that in suing for his pardon she is conscious of wronging her rigid conscientiousness; and she is quite willing to retire, on the slightest pretext, and leave justice triumphant over the mercy for which she argues —even over the life of her wretched brother·

Isab. I am a woeful suitor to your honor,
Please but your honor hear me.
Ang. Well; what's your suit?
Isab. There is a vice that most I do abhor,
And most desire should meet the blow of justice—
For which I would not plead, but that I must—
For which I must not plead, but that I am
At war 'twixt will, and will not.
Ang. Well; the matter?
Isab. I have a brother is condemn'd to die:
I do beseech you, let it be his fault,
And not my brother.
Ang. Condemn the fault, and not the actor of it!
Why, every fault's condemn'd ere it be done:
Mine were the very cipher of a function,
To find the faults whose fine stands in record,
And let go by the actor.
Isab. O just, but severe law!
I had a brother then.—Heaven keep your honor!
[*Retiring.*
Lucio. [*To* Isab.] Give't not o'er so; to him again, entreat him;
Kneel down before him, hang upon his gown;
You are too cold: if you should need a pin,
You could not with more tame a tongue desire it.
To him, I say!
Isab. Must he needs die?
Ang. Maiden, no remedy.
Isab. Yes; I do think that you might pardon him,
And neither heaven nor man grieve at the mercy.
* * * * * * * * *
Ang. He's sentenc'd; 'tis too late.
Isab. Too late? why, no; I that do speak a word
May call it back again: Well, believe this:

No ceremony that to great ones 'longs,
Not the king's crown, nor the deputed sword,
The marshal's truncheon, nor the judge's robe,
Become them with one half so good a grace
As mercy does.
* * * * * * *
* * * O, it is excellent
To have a giant's strength; but it is tyrannous
To use it like a giant.

Her interview with her brother in prison is even more characteristic: her first speech to him, when, agonized with suspense, he awaits the issue of her prayers to the lord deputy, is almost inconceivably harsh and unwomanly; Isabella tricks out the fatal intelligence in a sustained figure, substitutes rhetoric for the consoling tenderness of a sister, and a sister of charity:

Claud. Now, sister, what's the comfort?
Isab. Why, as all comforts are—most good indeed.
Lord Angelo, having affairs to heaven,
Intends you for his swift embassador,
Where you shall be an everlasting lieger:
Therefore your best appointment make with speed—
To-morrow you set on.
Claud. Is there no remedy?
Isab. None, but such remedy as, to save a head,
To cleave a heart in twain.
Claud. But is there any?
Isab. Yes, brother, you may live;
There is a devilish mercy in the judge,
If you'll implore it, that will free your life,
But fetter you till death.
* * * * * * * *
Claud. Thou shalt not do 't.
Isab. O, were it but my life,
I'd throw it down for your deliverance
As frankly as a pin.
Claud. Thanks, dear Isabel.
Isab. Be ready, Claudio, for your death to-morrow.

Claud. Yes.—Has he affections in him,
That thus can make him bite the law by the nose,
When he would force it? Sure it is no sin;
Or of the deadly seven it is the least.
Isab. Which is the least?
Claud. If it were damnable, he being so wise,
Why would he for the momentary trick
Be perdurably fin'd?—O Isabel!
Isab. What says my brother?
Claud. Death is a fearful thing—
Isab. And shamed life a hateful.
* * * * * * * *
Claud. Sweet sister, let me live:
What sin you do to save a brother's life,
Nature dispenses with the deed so far
That it becomes a virtue.
Isab. O you beast!
O faithless coward! O dishonest wretch!
Wilt thou be made a man out of my vice?
* * * * * * * *
* * * * Take my defiance.
Die, perish! might but my bending down
Reprieve thee from thy fate, it should proceed:
I'll pray a thousand prayers for thy death,
No word to save thee.

CLEOPATRA.

This world-renowned princess was the daughter of Ptolemy Auletes, king of Egypt, at whose death, she, with her brother, ascended the throne. The *motif* of Shakspeare's play, of which she is the heroine, consists of the episode, with its final catastrophe, of her intrigue with Mark Antony, the Roman hero—commencing with his first visit to Alexandria, whither he had followed Cleopatra after that triumphant excursion to Tarsus, so glowingly described in the text:

The barge she sat in, like a burnish'd throne,
Burn'd on the water: the poop was beaten gold;
Purple the sails, and so perfumed that
The winds were love-sick with them; the oars were silver,
Which to the tune of flutes kept stroke, and made
The water, which they beat, to follow faster,
As amorous of their strokes. For her own person,
It beggar'd all description: she did lie
In her pavilion, (cloth of gold, of tissue,)
O'er-picturing that Venus, where we see
The fancy outwork nature; on each side her
Stood pretty dimpled boys, like smiling Cupids,
With divers-color'd fans, whose wind did seem
To glow the delicate cheeks which they did cool,
And what they undid, did.

* * * * * * * *

Her gentlewomen, like the Nereides,
So many mermaids, tended her i' the eyes,
And made their bends adornings; at the helm
A seeming mermaid steers; the silken tackle
Swell with the touches of those flower-soft hands,
That yarely frame the office. From the barge
A strange invisible perfume hits the sense
Of the adjacent wharfs.

Here, in the palace of the Ptolemies, abandoning himself to the fascinations of his imperial mistress, and the bewildering revels with which she besotted and enchained him, the "triple pillar of the world" forgot his glory, his wife, and his country. One day, however, in the midst of his ignoble ease, messengers from Rome arrived at the Egyptian court, with tidings for Antony of internal wars at home, and of the death of his wife, Fulvia. This intelligence awakening his patriotism and his remorse, he shook off his sensual sloth and returned at once to Rome, to find Octavius Cæsar, one of his associate triumvirs, highly incensed by the rumors which had reached them of his dishonorable self-indulgence, while his wife, Fulvia, "to have him out of Egypt" at any cost, had been waging war against Cæsar. In a spirit of true penitence, Antony acknowledged his criminal remissness; and, to renew their friendly relations the more securely, he married the virtuous Octavia, Cæsar's sister.

But internal jealousies soon again divided their interests; and Octavia having left her husband to visit her brother in Rome, for the purpose of reconciling them once more, Antony rejoined Cleopatra in Alexandria, with imposing ceremonials bestowed upon her a large addition to her dominions, and proclaimed his sons by her "the kings of kings."

War between Antony and Cæsar was now hotly waged, to be

finally decided by a naval contest at Actium; where, by a mere accident, Antony lost the day, and fled to Egypt. He offered various terms of capitulation to Cæsar; but that victorious hero would content himself with nothing less than the death of the man who had outraged his sister's honor, and scoffed at his avenging power; he, however, sent secret messages to Cleopatra, assuring her of his protection if she would give up her lover. The artful queen pretended to receive these advances with humble gratitude, and Antony, apprised of her conduct, suspected and accused her of treachery toward himself.

To dissipate his doubts of her constancy, Cleopatra betook herself, with her women, to a tower, which she had erected as her monument, and, as a final stroke of coquetry, caused it to be reported that she had killed herself. Antony, in despair at the news of her death, threw himself upon his sword, just as Cleopatra, fearful of the effect of her artifice, had sent to contradict the dangerous tidings; he ordered his attendants to bear him into her presence, and died in her arms.

Cæsar, thus robbed of half his triumph, resolved to secure Cleopatra as a captive and a trophy, to glorify his return to Rome. Through her maternal pride and affection he prevented her from starving herself; but when she found that he was proof against her charms, and learned beyond doubt for what ignominious purpose she was spared, she procured an asp, and died of its venomous bite—her faithful attendants sharing her fate.

Eternal and unfading as the glory of her Egyptian skies, this "serpent of old Nile" shall unwind her coils from about the hearts of men, only when Time shall cease to be. Her spells, as potent to-day as when she reigned, a score of centuries since, survive the subtle enchantress from whom they emanated, to mock us with something of her own imperial coquetry, when we fain would shut our eyes against their dazzling charms, and bring our steady reason to bear upon her intrinsic claims to admiration and respect.

The very faults of Cleopatra, emblazoned with all the mystic extravagance of Eastern story, constitute her most fatal fascination; they bewilder one's moral sense, overwhelm it with kaleidoscopic brilliancies, tinge its grave conclusions with the spirit of their maddest intoxication, till, like Mark Antony, we find ourselves wondering, applauding, paying participating tribute, where we had thought to sit in austere judgment.

Complexity, contradiction, "infinite variety," instantaneous transmutations, are the exponents of Cleopatra's character; she is consistent only in being inconsistent—each particular idiosyncrasy, keen, flashing, meteoric, is "like the lightning, which doth cease to be, ere we can say It lightens." With towering, audacious consciousness of power, she one moment challenges our contempt, by the coarse wrangling of a vixenish temper, only the more absolutely to compel our recognition of her royal elegance and classic grace, the next; she unites in herself all that is luxurious in voluptuousness, unscrupulous in the gratification of passion, reckless in the procurement of debasing pleasure, and insolent in self-assertion, with rare intellect, superior attainments, and elegant accomplishments, a lively and intense imagination, magnificent tastes, a grand, self-reliant spirit, a warm, generous heart, and a perfection in the art of coquetry never attained by woman before or since—this last being the more remarkable, in that she was not possessed of extraordinary beauty.

The Cleopatra of Shakspeare—among a multitude of abortive creations which have taken her name in vain—is, alone, the faith ful reflection of that Oriental Circe who holds our imaginations captive in "her strong toil of grace;" only she realizes to one's senses the glowing ideal suggested by her very name. In delineating her, Shakspeare employed to the utmost his wonderful faculty of perfectly identifying himself for the time with the character he was in the act of portraying; his sublime insight alone, unaided by fancy or invention, was concerned in bringing out this living portrait; for even the minutest dramatic effect he adhered strictly to historical facts, "spreading over the whole a richness like the overflowing of the Nile."

The most characteristic display of Cleopatra's antithetical peculiarities is afforded by the scenes immediately following her lover's departure: First, where, "feeding herself with most delicious poison," she lolls in restless, longing, luxurious languor, calling for drugged draughts, that she may "sleep out this great gap of time her Antony is away"—teasing her attendants with her lovesick petulance, beguiling the heavy hours with passionate fancies:

Cleo. O Charmian,
Where think'st thou he is now? Stands he, or sits he?
Or does he walk? or is he on his horse?
O happy horse, to bear the weight of Antony!
Do bravely, horse! for wot'st thou whom thou mov'st?
The demi-Atlas of this earth, the arm
And burgonet of men.—He's speaking now,
Or murmuring, *Where's my serpent of old Nile?*
For so he calls me;

* * * * * * * *

Met'st thou my posts?
Alex. Ay, madam, twenty several messengers:
Why do you send so thick?
Cleo. Who's born that day
When I forget to send to Antony,
Shall die a beggar.—Ink and paper, Charmian.—

Welcome, my good Alexas.—Did I, Charmian,
Ever love Cæsar so?
Char. O that brave Cæsar!
Cleo. Be chok'd with such another emphasis!
Say the brave Antony.
Char. The valiant Cæsar!
Cleo. By Isis! I will give thee bloody teeth,
If thou with Cæsar paragon again
My man of men.
Char. By your most gracious pardon,
I sing but after you.
Cleo. My salad days,
When I was green in judgment:—Cold in blood,
To say as I said then!—But, come, away:
Get me ink and paper; he shall have every day
A several greeting, or I'll unpeople Egypt.

In strong contrast to this tremendous trifling, is the scene where she receives the messenger from Italy: with what half-prescient emotion she anticipates the evil tidings that cling to his tongue! With what shocking transitions Hope and Fear toss alternately, from her lips, promises full of gracious elegance, and coarse threats of personal violence, till they have lashed up a tempest in her torrid soul, to vent its impotent fury on the innocent cause of her anguish:

Mess. Madam, madam,—
Cleo. Antony's dead?—
If thou say so, villain, thou kill'st thy mistress;
But well and free,
If thou so yield him, there is gold, and here
My bluest veins to kiss—a hand that kings
Have lipp'd, and trembled kissing.
Mess. First, madam, he's well.
Cleo. Why, there's more gold. But, sirrah, mark! we use
To say the dead are well: bring it to that,
The gold I give thee will I melt, and pour
Down thy ill-uttering throat.

Mess. Good madam, hear me.
Cleo. Well, go to, I will;
But there's no goodness in thy face. If Antony
Be free, and healthful,—why so tart a favor
To trumpet such good tidings? If not well,
Thou should'st come like a fury crown'd with snakes
Not like a formal man.
Mess. Will 't please you hear me?
Cleo. I have a mind to strike thee, ere thou speak'st;
Yet, if thou say Antony lives, is well,
Or friends with Cæsar, or not captive to him,
I'll set thee in a shower of gold, and hail
Rich pearls upon thee.
Mess. Madam, he's well.
Cleo. Well said.

* * * * * * * * * *

In state of health, thou say'st; and, thou say'st, free.
Mess. Free, madam! no; I made no such report:
He's bound unto Octavia.
Cleo. For what good turn.

* * * * * * * *

Mess. Madam, he's married to Octavia.
Cleo. The most infectious pestilence upon thee!
[*Strikes him down.*
—Hence,
Horrible villain! or I'll spurn thine eyes
Like balls before me; I'll unhair thy head;
Thou shalt be whipp'd with wire, and stew'd in brine,
Smarting in ling'ring pickle.
Mess. Gracious madam,
I, that do bring the news, made not the match.
Cleo. Say 'tis not so, a province I will give thee,
And make thy fortunes proud; the blow thou had'st
Shall make thy peace, for moving me to rage;
And I will boot thee with what gift beside
Thy modesty can beg.
Mess. He's married, madam.
Cleo. Rogue, thou hast liv'd too long.
[*Draws a dagger.*

But the rude storm spent, this wrathful queen is as love-lorn and pitiful, in her tears and swooning sorrow, as any heart-wrung wretch of to-day:

> *Cleo.* In praising Antony, I have disprais'd Cæsar.
> *Char.* Many times, madam.
> *Cleo.* I am paid for 't now.
> Lead me from hence—
> I faint! O Iras, Charmian!—'Tis no matter:—
> Go to the fellow, good Alexas; bid him
> Report the feature of Octavia, her years,
> Her inclination; let him not leave out
> The color of her hair:—bring me word quickly.—
> Let him forever go—Let him not—Charmian,
> Though he be painted one way like a Gorgon,
> T' other way he's a Mars.—Bid you Alexas
> Bring me word how tall she is.—Pity me, Charmian;
> But do not speak to me.—Lead me to my chamber.

Hazlitt says of Cleopatra that "she had great and unpardonable faults, but the beauty of her death almost redeems them." It would, indeed, quite redeem them, if we did not find the motive that prompted her death, "after the high Roman fashion," more plainly evinced in her haughty horror of being paraded through Rome, than in her anguish at surviving the lover whom she had, in a manner, murdered; for a woman of equally intense passions, and less egotism, the last would have sufficed; but with Cleopatra, Self was paramount to Love, and all the gods.

Antony, brought to the foot of the monument, mortally wounded, implores her to come down to him; yet even at that moment of shocked surprise and overwhelming agony, she answers him thus—a selfish consideration uppermost even then:

> I dare not, dear;
> (Dear my lord, pardon,) I dare not,

Lest I be taken. Not the imperious show
Of the full-fortun'd Cæsar ever shall
Be brooch'd with me; if knife, drugs, serpents, have
Edge, sting, or operation, I am safe.
Your wife, Octavia, with her modest eyes
And still conclusion, shall acquire no honor
Demuring upon me.

Then, with the assistance of her women, "Cleopatra, stooping down her head, putting to all her strength to her uttermost power, did lift him up with much ado, and never let go her hold."

And thus, again, to Cæsar's messenger:

Know, sir, that I
Will not wait pinion'd at your master's court;
Nor once be chastis'd with the sober eye
Of dull Octavia. Shall they hoist me up,
And show me to the shouting varletry
Of censuring Rome? Rather a ditch in Egypt
Be gentle grave to me! rather on Nilus' mud
Lay me stark naked, and let the water-flies
Blow me into abhorring! rather make
My country's high pyramides my gibbet,
And hang me up in chains!

But in the following burst, addressed to one of her women, and repeated in detailed offensiveness, the better to strengthen her own timid purpose, speaks all the woman—the sumptuous Sybarite to whom coarseness of association or diet was immeasurably worse than the profoundest moral degradation of "purple and fine linen:"

* * * * * * * *

* * Now, Iras, what think'st thou?
Thou, an Egyptian puppet, shalt be shown
In Rome, as well as I: mechanic slaves
With greasy aprons, rules, and hammers, shall

Uplift us to the view; in their thick breaths,
Rank of gross diet, shall we be enclouded,
And forc'd to drink their vapor.
* * * * * * * *
Saucy lictors
Will catch at us, like strumpets; and scald rhymers
Ballad us out o' tune; the quick comedians
Extemporally will stage us, and present
Our Alexandrian revels; Antony
Shall be brought drunken forth, and I shall see
Some squeaking Cleopatra boy my greatness.

The death scene imparts additional and gorgeous vividness to our vision of Cleopatra; it proves indisputably that coquetry is not with her a merely convenient art, acquired and cultivated for a purpose, but part of her very being. *Effect*, even in the "article of death," is her ruling passion. It is not enough that she should give up grandly her illustrious ghost; she must die picturesquely, berobed and jewelled; and her success is, as ever, perfect: the glorious legend of the "Venus of the Nile," robed in imperial vestures, crowned, and dead—looking like sleep, "as she would catch another Antony in her strong toil of grace," is spendidly emblazoned on the panes of fancy, in imperishable dyes.

Two delicate touches of the "pure womanly" throw a mournful tenderness over the last moments of the unhappy queen. One is her allusion to the grand triumph of her life, the adventure of the Cydnus, in which she likens this dreadful setting-forth to that first journey to her lover:

Show me, my women, like a queen:—Go fetch
My best attires;—I am again for Cydnus,
To meet Mark Antony:
* * * * * * * *
Give me my robe; put on my crown.
* * * Quick!—Methinks I hear
Antony call.

And again:

> *Char.* O eastern star!
> *Cleo.* Peace, peace!
> Dost thou not see my baby at my breast,
> That sucks the nurse asleep?

Here it is not only "the contrast between the beauty of the image and the horror of the situation" which produces so touching an effect, but the reproduction, with startling reality, of the very sensations experienced by Cleopatra in the act of *suffering* this quick and "easy way to die." Had not Shakspeare written thus, we should be sure that none but a mother could with such reality conceive of the luxurious, dreamy, half-unconscious languor, peculiar to her most beautiful office, and which, through an image as tender as it is subtile, conveys to our minds the only idea we can associate with the death of Cleopatra—a voluptuous, intoxicated sleep, rather than death.

We are tempted to transcribe a few condensed expressions of character, scattered throughout the play, as affording the truest index to Cleopatra's distinguished peculiarities. For examples of her coquetry:

> *Cleo.* Where is he?
> *Char.* I did not see him since.
> *Cleo.* See where he is, who's with him, what he does—
> I did not send you.—If you find him sad,
> Say I am dancing; if in mirth, report
> That I am sudden sick: Quick, and return. [*Exit* ALEX.
> *Char.* Madam, methinks if you did love him dearly,
> You do not hold the method to enforce
> The like from him.
> *Cleo.* What should I do I do not?
> *Char.* In each thing give him way, cross him in nothing.
> *Cleo.* Thou teachest like a fool—the way to lose him.

Char. Tempt him not so too far; I wish, forbear.
In time we hate that which we often fear.

Ant. I must be gone.

Eno. * * * * * * * * * * Cleopatra, catching but the least noise of this, dies instantly; I have seen her die twenty times upon far poorer moment. I do think there is mettle in death, which commits some loving act upon her, she hath such a celerity in dying.

Ant. She is cunning past man's thought.

Eno. Alack, sir, no; her passions are made of nothing but the finest part of pure love. We cannot call her winds and waters sighs and tears; they are greater storms and tempests than almanacs can report: this cannot be cunning in her; if it be, she makes a shower of rain as well as Jove.

Cleo. Cut my lace, Charmian, come!—
But let it be;—I am quickly ill, and well.
So Antony loves.

To the monument!—
Mardian, go tell him I have slain myself;
Say that the last I spoke was Antony,
And word it, pr'ythee, piteously. Hence,
Mardian; and bring me how he takes my death.

I know, by that same eye, there's some good news.
What says the married woman?—You may go;
'Would she had never given you leave to come!
Let her not say 'tis I that keep you here—
I have no power upon you; hers you are.
* * * * * * * *

Ant. Cleopatra,—

Cleo. Why should I think you can be mine and true,
Though you in swearing shake the throned gods,
Who have been false to Fulvia? Riotous madness,
To be entangled with those mouth-made vows,
Which break themselves in swearing!

Ant. Most sweet queen,—
Cleo. Nay, pray you, seek no color for your going,
But bid farewell, and go. When you sued staying,
Then was the time for words—no going then;
Eternity was in our lips and eyes,
Bliss in our brows' bent.

And finally these speaking portraits:

Ant. Fye, wrangling queen!
Whom every thing becomes—to chide, to laugh,
To weep; whose every passion fully strives
To make itself in thee fair and admired!

O this false soul of Egypt! this grave charm,
Whose eye beck'd forth my wars, and call'd them home.

Age cannot wither her, nor custom stale
Her infinite variety: Other women
Cloy th' appetites they feed; but she makes hungry
Where most she satisfies; for vilest things
Become themselves in her.

CRESSIDA.

This fair but frail beauty was the daughter of Calchas, a Trojan priest, who, in the great war between his countrymen and the Greeks—provoked by the abduction of Helen, Menelaus' queen, by Paris, one of the king of Troy's sons—took part with the Greeks, and fled to their camp outside the walls of the "many-gated city," leaving Cressida with her uncle Pandarus.

Prince Troilus, Priam's youngest son, became blindly infatuated with the beautiful Cressida, who secretly returned his passion, but with coquettish dissimulation held herself aloof, despite the well-laid plans of her intriguing uncle to consummate the tender hopes of Troilus. At last, however, beset on every side, Cressida yielded to the importunate suit of her lover, and confessed herself won; but the very next day, the Greeks, moved by the prayers of Calchas, sent a herald to the Trojans, to proffer Antenor, one of the Trojan commanders whom they had taken prisoner, in exchange for Cressida, the priest's daughter; and the offer was joyfully accepted.

Cressida, accordingly, departed for the camp, escorted by Diomed, a Grecian general, on whom, notwithstanding her vows of fidelity to Troilus—himself the most constant of lovers—she at once bestowed her perfidious favors; the Greek, for all his valor, was not proof against her charms.

Shortly afterward, during a truce, and a friendly interview of Hector and Troilus with the Greek heroes, on the latter's own ground, Troilus was made aware of Cressida's perfidy, and from a concealed position witnessed certain love passages between her and Diomed, in which she presented her new lover with the very same *gage d'amour* that she had accepted from him when she left Troy. On the morrow, during the engagements by single combat between the most puissant of the Greeks and Trojans, Troilus fought valiantly with [illegible]al, Diomed, who tauntingly displayed Cressida's gift on his helmet; but the rash, unpractised stripling could not cope with the tried skill of the Greek; Diomed succeeded in dismounting the "amorous Trojan," and sent his charger as a trophy to the lady Cressid.

On that same day the valiant Hector—who had gone forth to battle despite the tears and prayers of his wife Andromache, despite the entreaties of his royal father, and the foreboding utterances of the forlorn Cassandra, whose ravings might well have been accepted as inspirations—was treacherously murdered by Achilles, the champion of the Greeks.

In puny contrast with Egypt's queen of voluptuousness—the same in kind, but immeasurably below her in degree—stands Cressida, the type of coquettes of little ambitions and less brains, flirting, jilting, silly wantons, whose insignificant amours lack every quality of sentiment or taste which might appeal to one's toleration—most of all, that intellectual element which may impart even to her sin a certain dignity.

Cressida is but another name for an inconstancy tenfold more hopeless than downright treachery, in that it implies an inherent incapability of being true; the involuntary breaking of her solemn oaths to her lover, uttered in all sincerity perhaps, betrays a nature far more hopelessly depraved than if she had, from the first, meant to deceive him. Selfish love of admiration possesses her completely; her life is devoted to the gratification of a petty vanity, and the study of a very low order of seductions to procure it; not once do her faults rise to the dignity of bad passions, nor are they ever honored with more indignation than a contemptuous disgust. Her penchant for the handsome young Troilus is utterly without taste, "tenderness, passion, or poetry;" it is only the diluted romance of a giddy-pated girl. Her confession of *love* for him, in which she judges him by her own fickleness and wanton exercise of power, is characteristic:

> *Cres.* Boldness comes to me now, and brings me heart:—
> Prince Troilus, I have lov'd you night and day,
> For many weary months.
> *Tro.* Why was my Cressid then so hard to win?
> *Cres.* Hard to seem won; but I was won, my lord,
> With the first glance that ever—Pardon me;—
> If I confess much, you will play the tyrant.
> I love you now; but not, till now, so much
> But I might master it.—In faith, I lie;
> My thoughts were like unbridled children, grown
> Too headstrong for their mother.—See, we fools!
> Why have I blabb'd? Who shall be true to us,
> When we are so unsecret to ourselves?
> But, though I lov'd you well, I woo'd you not;
> And yet, good faith, I wish'd myself a man;
> Or that we women had men's privilege
> Of speaking first. Sweet, bid me hold my tongue;
> For, in this rapture, I shall surely speak
> The thing I shall repent. See, see! your silence,
> Cunning in dumbness, from my weakness draws

My very soul of counsel: Stop my mouth.
Tro. And shall, albeit sweet music issues thence.
* * * * * * * * *
Cres. My lord, I do beseech you, pardon me—
'Twas not my purpose, thus to beg a kiss;
I am asham'd;—O heavens! what have I done?
* * * * * * * * *
Cres. Pr'ythee, tarry;
You men will never tarry.—
O foolish Cressid!—I might have still held off,
And then you would have tarried.

And even more Cressid-like is her explanation of the mean philosophy that prompted [illegible]ming "stubborn-chastity against all suit," which so captivated her hero-lover:

But more in Troilus thousand fold I see
Than in the glass of Pandar's praise may be;
Yet hold I off. Women are angels, wooing;
Things won are done—joy's soul lies in the doing
That she belov'd knows nought, that knows not this—
Men prize the thing ungain'd more than it is;
That she was never yet that ever knew
Love got so sweet, as when Desire did sue:
Therefore this maxim out of love I teach,—
Achievement is command; ungain'd, beseech.
Then though my heart's content firm love doth bear,
Nothing of that shall from mine eyes appear.

In the parting scene she makes much of her pretty poutings and her spoilt-child petulance; the threatened destruction of her beauty is an exquisite touch of nature, while her high-sounding oaths are ludicrous only to those who have anticipated the sequel:

Cres. O you immortal gods!—I will not go.
Pan. Thou must.
Cres. I will not, uncle: I have forgot my father;
I know no touch of consanguinity;

No kin, no love, no blood, no soul so near me
As the sweet Troilus.—O you gods divine!
Make Cressid's name the very crown of falsehood,
If ever she leave Troilus! Time, Force, and Death,
Do to this body what extremes you can;
But the strong base and building of my love
Is as the very centre of the earth,
Drawing all things to it.—I'll go in, and weep,—
* * * * * * * * * *
Tear my bright hair, and scratch my praised cheeks,
Crack my clear voice with sobs, and [illegible] my heart
With sounding Troilus. I will not [illegible] Troy.
* * * * * * * * * *
* * * * * * * * * *
If I be false, or sw[illegible] fr[illegible]
When Time is old [illegible] forgot [illegible]
When waterdrops have [illegible]rn the sto[illegible],
And blind Oblivion swa[illegible]w'd cities u[illegible]
And mighty states, characterless, are grated
To dusty nothing—yet let memory,
From false to false, among false maids in love,
Upbraid my falsehood! * * * *
* * * * * * * * *
Yea, let them say, to stick the heart of falsehood,
As false as Cressid

We cannot more appropriately conclude our remarks on a subject that certainly tempts us but little, than by quoting the trenchant description of the sage Ulysses:

Fye, fye upon her!
There's language in her eye, her cheek, her lip—
Nay, her foot speaks; her wanton spirits lo[illegible]
At every joint and motive of her body.
O, these encounterers, so glib of tongue,
That give a coasting welcome ere it comes,
And wide unclasp the tables of their thoughts
To every ticklish reader! set them down
For sluttish spoils of opportunity,
And daughters of the game.

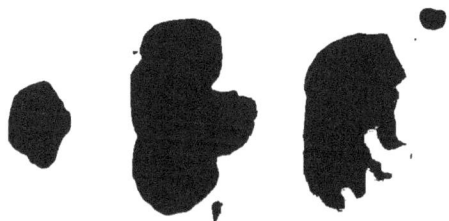

HELEN.

THIS "beautiful trouble" of the Trojan War, the most admired woman of her time, was the "begotten of Jupiter," by Leda, wife of King Tyndarus. From her birth she was a marvel of beauty; and when she had arrived at marriageable age, many of the Greek princes became suitors for her hand. Finally she made choice of Menelaus, and the others joined in a chivalrous compact to protect his marital rights against the world. Paris, son of Priam, king of Troy, smitten by the mere report of her charms, visited Lacedæmon on the pretext of sacrificing to Apollo; and in the absence of Menelaus, he prevailed on the beautiful Helen to fly with him to Troy.

True to their vow, the Grecian princes held a solemn council, and resolved to make war against the Trojans; but first they sent an embassy to Priam's court, demanding the restoration of Helen. This refused, war was declared at once, and the Grecian forces surrounded the walled city of Troy. The tedious siege lasted ten years; Paris having been killed in the ninth year, Helen married another of Priam's sons; and when Troy fell, she betrayed her husband into the hands of the conquerors, to procure the favor of Menelaus.

A few years later, Menelaus, who had received again his unworthy wife, died; and Helen, driven from his court by his illegitimate sons, took refuge in Rhodes, where she was put to death by order of the queen, Polyxo, in revenge for the loss of her husband, who had been killed in the Trojan war.

The sketch of Helen, in the play of *Troilus and Cressida*, is not less incomplete than that of "the mad Cassandra;" still, from that mere outline of her history the inference is safe, that she was as fickle and false as she was incomparably fair—a faithless wife, and a treacherous mistress—a woman who could abandon herself to the most frivolous pleasures while the best blood of two nations was being wasted for the glory of possessing her person. Diomed, the Grecian general, who fell so easy a victim to Cressida of infamous memory, is scarcely one from whom to expect impressive lessons in morality; but his appreciation of Helen is nevertheless just:

Par. And tell me, noble Diomed—faith, tell me true,
Even in the soul of sound good-fellowship—
Who, in your thoughts, merits fair Helen best—
Myself or Menelaus?
Dio. Both alike:
He merits well to have her, that doth seek her
(Not making any scruple of her soilure,)
With such a hell of pain, and world of charge;
And you as well to keep her, that defend her
(Not palating the taste of her dishonor,)
With such a costly loss of wealth and friends:
* * * * * * * * * *
Par. You are too bitter to your countrywoman.
Dio. She's bitter to her country: Hear me, Paris.—
For every false drop in her bawdy veins
A Grecian's life hath sunk; for every scruple

Of her contaminated carrion weight,
A Trojan hath been slain; since she could speak,
She hath not given so many good words breath
As for her Greeks and Trojans suffer'd death.

But this

Mortal Venus, the heart-blood of beauty, love's invisible soul,

seems to have cast the spell of her abominable charms over her Trojan defenders; Paris, indeed, "speaks like one besotted on his sweet delights:"

Sir, I propose not merely to myself
The pleasures such a beauty brings with it;
But I would have the soil of her fair rape
Wip'd off, in honorable keeping her.
What treason were it to the ransack'd queen,
Disgrace to your great worths, and shame to me,
Now to deliver her possession up,
On terms of base compulsion? Can it be,
That so degenerate a strain as this
Should once set footing in your generous bosoms?
There's not the meanest spirit on our party,
Without a heart to dare, or sword to draw,
When Helen is defended; nor none so noble,
Whose life were ill-bestow'd, or death unfam'd,
Where Helen is the subject: then, I say,
Well may we fight for her whom, we know well,
The world's large spaces cannot parallel.

But the simple-minded, brave, honorable Troilus is scarcely less enthusiastic when there is question among the assembled sages of Troy whether or not to restore Helen to her husband:

* * * * * * * * * *
He brought a Grecian queen, whose youth and freshness
Wrinkles Apollo's, and makes pale the morning.

* * * * * * * * *

Is she worth keeping? why, she is a pearl,
Whose price hath launch'd above a thousand ships,
And turn'd crown'd kings to merchants.
If you'll avouch 'twas wisdom Paris went,
(As you must needs, for you all cry'd—*Go, go!*)
If you'll confess he brought home noble prize,
(As you must needs, for you all clapp'd your hands,
And cry'd—*Inestimable!*) why do you now
The issue of your proper wisdoms rate,
And do a deed that fortune never did—
Beggar the estimation which you priz'd
Richer than sea and land? * * *

* * * * * * * *

She is a theme of honor and renown,
A spur to valiant and magnanimous deeds,
Whose present courage may beat down our foes,
And fame, in time to come, canonize us.

CASSANDRA.

Cassandra was the daughter of Priam, and twin-sister of Helenus. In her early youth she was beloved by Apollo, who endowed her with the gift of prophecy, and demanded her love in return. This was indignantly refused by the virgin princess; wherefore, enraged by her refusal, Apollo left her in possession of her supernatural faculty, but set a cruel curse on her predictions—that they should never be believed.

Thus she suffered all the anguish of foreseeing the fate of her beloved Troy, without being able to persuade the people to give up Helen—the unworthy cause of that disastrous war. They deemed her warnings mere "brain-sick raptures:"

> *Cas.* Cry, Trojans, cry! lend me ten thousand eyes,
> And I will fill them with prophetic tears.
> *Hect.* Peace, sister, peace!
> *Cas.* Virgins and boys, mid age and wrinkled elders,
> Soft infancy, that nothing canst but cry,
> Add to my clamors! let us pay betimes
> A moiety of that mass of moan to come.
> Cry, Trojans, cry! practise your eyes with tears!
> Troy must not be, nor goodly Ilion stand;
> Our fire-brand brother, Paris, burns us all.

Cry, Trojans, cry! a Helen, and a woe!
Cry, cry! Troy burns, or else let Helen go. [*Exit.*
Hect. Now, youthful Troilus, do not these high strains
Of divination in our sister work
Some touches of remorse? or is your blood
So madly hot that no discourse of reason,
Nor fear of bad success in a bad cause,
Can qualify the same?
Tro. Why, brother Hector,
We may not think the justness of each act
Such and no other than event doth form it;
Nor once deject the courage of our minds,
Because Cassandra's mad; her brain-sick raptures
Cannot distaste the goodness of a quarrel
Which hath our several honors all engag'd
To make it gracious.

The scene where, foreseeing the death of her hero-brother, Hector, the strong arm of Troy, she beseeches him not to go forth to battle on that unlucky day, is full of highly-wrought tragic effects; her frantic pre-vision of his death, which she interprets with all the despairing grief of a sister and the fervid conviction of a prophetess—and her hopeless, resigned "farewell," when it fails to move him, and she remembers her curse, abound in touching eloquence:

Cas. Where is my brother Hector?
And. Here, sister—arm'd and bloody in intent.
Consort with me in loud and dear petition—
Pursue we him on knees; for I have dream'd
Of bloody turbulence, and this whole night
Hath nothing been but shapes and forms of slaughter.
Cas. O, it is true.
Hect. Ho! bid my trumpet sound!
Cas. No notes of sally, for the heavens, sweet brother.
Hect. Begone, I say! the gods have heard me swear.
Cas. The gods are deaf to hot and peevish vows;

They are polluted offerings, more abhorr'd
Than spotted livers in the sacrifice.
And. O! be persuaded. Do not count it holy
To hurt by being just; it is as lawful,
For we would give much, to use violent thefts,
And rob in the behalf of charity.
Cas. It is the purpose that makes strong the vow;
But vows to every purpose must not hold.
Unarm, sweet Hector.

* * * * * * * *

Lay hold upon him, Priam—hold him fast:
He is thy crutch; now, if thou lose thy stay,
Thou on him leaning, and all Troy on thee,
Fall all together.
Pri. Come, Hector, come! go back:
Thy wife hath dream'd; thy mother hath had visions;
Cassandra doth foresee; and I myself
Am like a prophet suddenly enrapt,
To tell thee—that this day is ominous;
Therefore, come back.

* * * * * * * * *

Tro. This foolish, dreaming, superstitious girl
Makes all these bodements.
Cas. O farewell, dear Hector.
Look, how thou diest! look, how thy eye turns pale!
Look, how thy wounds do bleed at many vents!
Hark, how Troy roars! how Hecuba cries out!
How poor Andromache shrills her dolors forth!
Behold, destruction, frenzy, and amazement,
Like witless antics, one another meet,
And all cry—Hector! Hector's dead! O Hector!
Tro. Away!—Away!
Cas. Farewell.—Yet, soft.—Hector, I take my leave:
Thou dost thyself, and all our Troy, deceive.

The Cassandra of Shakspeare is but a sketch—one of those half-mad sibyls of the East who generally exercised so potent an influence over the popular mind, and whose counsels were so highly esteemed in the world's romantic age. Her subsequent fate was as wretched as the Shakspearian episode of her life is melancholy: according to classical authority, Cassandra was violated by Ajax, one of the Greek heroes, in a sacred temple, whither she had fled with her maidens for protection when Troy was taken. Falling to the share of Agamemnon, he bore her to Mycene, where they were both murdered by his wife, Clytemnestra.

THE SHREW.

Katharina was the elder daughter of Baptista Minola, a wealthy citizen of Padua. So notorious was she for her violent temper and unruly tongue, that, although she was handsomely dowered, and very beautiful, not a gallant in the city was bold enough to take her to wife. But it happened that Petruchio, a gentleman from Verona, having fallen into possession of his property by the death of his father, had come to "wive it wealthily in Padua," where certain lovers of Bianca, Katharina's sister, who were interested in the marrying of the Shrew—inasmuch as Baptista would not think of wedding his younger daughter first—informed Petruchio of this most excellent chance for him to get a rich wife, as he had declared to them that only riches were indispensable to his choice.

So he straightway went to Baptista and made proposals for Katharina, which were accepted, on condition that the young signior should find favor with the Shrew. Katharina did not fail to treat her suitor promptly to a spice of her unlovely temper; but Petruchio, well prepared, took no notice of her saucy rejoinders, except to construe them as amiable manifestations; and when her father rejoined them, he informed him that Kate had promised to become his wife on the following Sunday.

Old Baptista, delighted at the prospect of marrying "Katharina the curst," made handsome preparations for the wedding, to which Petruchio came in such strange attire, and with such odd behavior, that he was regarded by the bride and the guests as half crazed. At the church he conducted himself even more wildly, and immediately after the wedding, insisted upon starting for his own home, in spite of the entreaties of his father-in-law that he would stay to the feast he had prepared, and the downright, but unavailing, refusal of his bride to accompany him.

Arrived at their own house, Petruchio, madder than before, began beating the servants and storming at every thing; clearing the table before his wife had eaten a morsel, on pretence that the viands were not cooked fit for his dainty Kate; tearing her bed to pieces, because it was not properly made; keeping her awake night after night with railing, after her own fashion—till, with hunger and fatigue, Katharina's "mad and headstrong humor" was tamed down sufficiently to receive with edification the course of lessons her husband had projected for her benefit.

Soon after their marriage he proposed a journey to her father's house; and while on the road thither, because his wife presumed to correct him for saying "how goodly shines the moon," in bright mid-day, he immediately ordered their horses to be taken back; nor would he consent to proceed, until Katharina swore it should be sun, moon, rush-candle, or what he pleased. And still more oddly to test her submission, he caused her to greet an old man on the highway as a "young and budding virgin"—and in the next breath, as he really was, a wrinkled graybeard. But the final triumph of his discipline was reserved to be displayed in her father's house, where, at his command, she read a lecture on conjugal obedience to her sister Bianca and a pert widow, who had just been made brides, and who had been exhibiting signs of waywardness towards "their lords, their kings, their governors."

It is scarcely possible to consider the character of Katharina with gravity; her shrewishness is so wildly extravagant, so inconceivable in any maiden, "young, beauteous, and brought up as best becomes a gentlewoman," that she may serve but as the heroine of the extravaganza wherein she figures—and as a burlesque "moral and example" to those "not impossible shes" who are curst, within the bounds of probability, with her unamiable proclivities.

The predicaments of this brawling Kate are extremely ludicrous; but we cannot be so charitable towards her peculiar sin against womanhood as to pity them, even when she is most hardly pressed—she deserves even more than she suffers, at the hands of her mad Petruchio; and the outward fruits of her trials and tribulations are highly satisfactory. Nevertheless, we own we have but little faith in the enduring quality of a "taming" which is procured by almost the same means as are employed in the subduing of a wild animal, and by a husband who neither loves nor is loved by her; we much fear that—the keeper and his lash out of sight—this human wild-cat, "convinced against her will," would be "of the same opinion still."

One is amused at Hazlitt's absurdities about Petruchio's metamorphosing his wife's senses at his will—as if he believed that Katharina actually sees what her husband pretends to see; so far from affording satisfaction to a man of less blunted sensibilities than her husband, Kate's ready acquiescence in his palpable nonsense would be full of sarcasm, ten times more insulting, more spiteful, than her honest railing.

For two of the "eleven and twenty" tricks of Petruchio, we give the incidents of the journey to Padua:

Pet. Come on, o' God's name; once more toward our father's.
Good Lord, how bright and goodly shines the moon!
Kath. The moon!—the sun; it is not moonlight now.
Pet. I say it is the moon that shines so bright.
Kath. I know it is the sun that shines so bright.
Pet. Now, by my mother's son, and that's myself,
It shall be moon, or star, or what I list,
Or ere I journey to your father's house:—
Go on, and fetch our horses back again.—
Evermore cross'd, and cross'd; nothing but cross'd!
Hor. Say as he says, or we shall never go.
Kath. Forward, I pray, since we have come so far;
And be it moon, or sun, or what you please;
And if you please to call it a rush candle,
Henceforth I vow it shall be so for me.
Pet. I say it is the moon.
Kath. I know it is.
Pet. Nay, then you lie; it is the blessed sun.
Kath. Then, God be blessed, it is the blessed sun;
But sun it is not, when you say it is not;
And the moon changes, even as your mind.
What you will have it nam'd, even that it is;
And so it shall be so, for Katharina.

Pet. Tell me, sweet Kate—and tell me truly too—
Hast thou beheld a fresher gentlewoman?
Such war of white and red within her cheeks!
What stars do spangle heaven with such beauty
As those two eyes become that heavenly face?—
Fair lovely maid, once more good day to thee:—
Sweet Kate, embrace her for her beauty's sake.
Kath. Young budding virgin, fair, and fresh, and sweet,
Whither away? or where is thy abode?
Happy the parents of so fair a child;

Happier the man whom favorable stars
Allot thee for his lovely bed-fellow!
Pet. Why, how now, Kate! I hope thou art not mad:
This is a man, old, wrinkled, faded, wither'd—
And not a maiden, as thou say'st he is.
Kath. Pardon, old father, my mistaking eyes,
That have been so bedazzled with the sun
That every thing I look on seemeth green;
Now I perceive thou art a reverend father:
Pardon, I pray thee, for my mad mistaking.

The final trotting out of his trained wife before his friends, for a wager, is worthy of the man who "came to Padua to wive it wealthily"—

Be she as foul as was Florentius' love,
As old as Sibyl, and as curst and shrewd
As Socrates' Xantippe, or a worse.

But she gets off her little speech, with which, by the by, no one out of the dangerous circle of Woman's Rights can possibly find fault; and she receives her reward—a kiss from the husband, whom we are sure, for all her fine talk, she hates cordially:

Pet. Nay, I will win my wager better yet,
And show more sign of her obedience—
Her new-built virtue and obedience.
See! where she comes, and brings your froward wives
As prisoners to her womanly persuasion.—
Katharine, that cap of yours becomes you not;
Off with that bauble, throw it under foot.
[KATHARINA *pulls off her cap, and throws it down.*
* * * * * * * * * *
Pet. Katharine, I charge thee, tell these headstrong women
What duty they do owe their lords and husbands.
* * * * * * * * * *
Kath. Fye, fye! unknit that threat'ning, unkind brow,
And dart not scornful glances from those eyes,

To wound thy lord, thy king, thy governor;
It blots thy beauty, as frosts bite the meads—
Confounds thy fame, as whirlwinds shake fair buds;
And in no sense is meet or amiable.
A woman mov'd is like a fountain troubled,
Muddy, ill-seeming, thick, bereft of beauty;
And, while it is so, none so dry or thirsty
Will deign to sip, or touch one drop of it.
Thy husband is thy lord, thy life, thy keeper,
Thy head, thy sovereign; one that cares for thee,
And for thy maintenance—commits his body
To painful labor, both by sea and land,
To watch the night in storms, the day in cold,
While thou liest warm at home, secure and safe;
And craves no other tribute at thy hands
But love, fair looks, and true obedience—
Too little payment for so great a debt.
Such duty as the subject owes the prince,
Even such a woman oweth to her husband;
And when she's froward, peevish, sullen, sour,
And not obedient to his honest will,
What is she but a foul contending rebel,
And graceless traitor to her loving lord?—
I am asham'd that women are so simple,
To offer war where they should kneel for peace;
Or seek for rule, supremacy, and sway,
When they are bound to serve, love, and obey.
Why are our bodies soft, and weak, and smooth,
Unapt to toil, and trouble, in the world,
But that our soft conditions, and our hearts,
Should well agree with our external parts?
Come, come, you froward and unable worms!
My mind hath been as big as one of yours,
My heart as great—my reason, haply, more,
To bandy word for word, and frown for frown;
But now I see our lances are but straws,
Our strength as weak, our weakness past compare—
That seeming to be most which we least are.

HELENA.

Helena was the daughter of Gerard de Narbon, a poor but famous physician, who, at his death, left her to the motherly care of the noble and wealthy Countess of Rousillon. This lady having lately lost her husband, who was in high favor with the king of France, his Majesty despatched one of his courtiers to the countess's palace, with commands for her son Bertram, that he should forthwith accompany the messenger to court; the young count obeyed with alacrity.

The good king was at this time suffering acutely, with a disease that baffled all the skill of his physicians. Helena—who was hopelessly in love with Bertram, and to whom any suggestion was welcome that afforded her an excuse for following him to Paris—was moved by the melancholy case of the king to try the virtues of a precious prescription left by her father, and which he had declared infallible in the very disease of which the French monarch languished.

So she besought permission of her generous mistress to go to Paris and tender her services to the king, which was readily granted. At the same time the shrewd countess took advantage of the occasion to extort from her gentlewoman a confession of her love for the count; nor did the discovery displease her, for she loved Helena as a daughter, and was well pleased at the prospect of being her mother in reality.

At court Helena encountered no little difficulty in inducing the king to believe in the efficacy of her father's prescription; but won over by her beauty and her eloquence, as much as by her absolute conviction of the infallibility of her remedy, he consented to give it a trial, on her own condition: that if he should be cured, he would bestow upon her the husband of her choice—but if not, that she should die for her presumption.

Happily for Helena, the medicine wrought a miracle: the king was restored to health in a few days; and eager to discharge his debt of gratitude, he summoned the young nobles into his presence, that Helena might choose a husband from among them. Of course, she laid claim to Bertram, who—his ancestral pride outraged at the idea of marrying a "poor physician's daughter," his mother's humble dependant—protested against so arbitrary a disposal of his person and honorable name; but the king's word was given, and he commanded that the marriage should proceed.

Thus Helena was made Countess of Rousillon; but that same day her husband sent her home with a letter for his mother, informing her of his intention to leave the country unceremoniously, and protesting that until he had no wife he had nothing in France. He added a few cruel lines for Helena, in which he gave her the right to call him husband only when she could get possession of a certain ring that should never leave his finger, and show him a son of hers of which he should be the father. This unkindness so afflicted Helena—especially the thought that she had driven him from his home—that she stole away from her good mother-in-law, and set forth on a pilgrimage to St. Jaques.

At Florence she sought shelter and rest beneath the roof of a poor widow, who was accustomed to entertain pilgrims on their way to the shrine. Here she learned that the widow's fair young daughter, Diana, was wooed by one Count Rousillon, a countryman of hers; but the fact of his extraordinary marriage being known, Diana, a discreet maiden, had virtuously repulsed his dishonorable advances. Helena, inspired by love, confided her story to the two women, and procured their co-operation in her plot, by money as well as by the persuasive eloquence of her sorrows.

Following her instructions, Diana made an appointment for Count Bertram to visit her bed-chamber by night, on which occasion Helena, personating Diana, gave him the ring the king had bestowed on her, and obtained from him in exchange his ring, "bequeathed down from many ancestors." With this trophy she returned to France, accompanied by Diana and her mother, who were necessary to the accomplishment of her design.

Helena had caused it to be reported that she was dead; whereupon Bertram hastened back to Paris, in the hope of procuring the king's pardon, and obtaining the hand of a lady at court; but his majesty discovered on the count's finger the ring that Helena had promised should never leave hers, except for some grave necessity; and suspecting that some foul wrong had been done her by her husband, he instituted inquiries which, somewhat circuitously, but not the less certainly, resulted in the happiness of this heroic lady and devoted wife, by securing to her the favor of her husband, Count Bertram of Rousillon.

In Helena we have the remarkable case of a very interesting female character, which is, nevertheless, deficient in one of the chief charms of womanhood; her virtue is above suspicion; her mind well balanced, and marked by sterling good sense, rather than brilliancy; she has ardent affections, deep devotion, indomitable energy, and genuine modesty—but with scarcely a trace of that higher order of delicacy which should be first in such a combination.

This formidable accusation is sustained by the simple fact that Helena permits herself to be married to a proud man against his will, even in spite of his expressed abhorrence of the union and dislike of herself; yet it must be confessed that she maintains this graceless position with marvellous tact.

In mitigation of so coarse a shock to the finest instincts of the sex which must "be wooed, and not unsought be won," it may be argued for Helena that in her self-abandonment to a controlling passion, on which her every emotion, every thought, are concentrated, all her other feelings, instincts even, are for the time repudiated, except as they tend towards the one great aim of her life—the happy consummation of her love.

Yet however intense and absorbing her passion may be, she is as guiltless of senseless sentimentality as that very Hebe in love, Rosalind; she has staked her life on its successful issue, and to that end she is ready to sacrifice every consideration, short of honor.

She never, for an instant, permits herself to entertain a doubt of her ultimate triumph—because she knows that her only hope lies in her own unwavering conviction that she is capable, in herself, of achieving it. This proud self-reliance is a marked feature of Helena's character, and is finely portrayed in her soliloquy after Bertram's departure:

> Our remedies oft in ourselves do lie,
> Which we ascribe to heaven; the fated sky
> Gives us free scope—only doth backward pull
> Our slow designs when we ourselves are dull.

What power is it which mounts my love so high—
That makes me see, and cannot feed mine eye?
The mightiest space in fortune nature brings
To join like likes, and kiss like native things.
Impossible be strange attempts to those
That weigh their pains in sense, and do suppose
What hath been cannot be. Who ever strove
To show her merit that did miss her love?
The king's disease—my project may deceive me;
But my intents are fix'd, and will not leave me.

No heroine could desire a more flattering passport to general favor than that afforded by the friendship for Helena of the noble old countess, who is never more staunchly devoted to her foster-child than when she is returned to her—a daughter-in-law, and a bride, but worse than widowed. The closeted interview between Helena and the countess is very characteristic of both women: Helena's conduct throughout is distinguished by candor and simplicity; she exhibits, at first, a natural reluctance to declare plainly that she loves the young Count of Rousillon, but she prepares his mother by unmistakable innuendoes for a confession which, when it comes, is full of chaste dignity:

Count. I say I am your mother.
* * * * * * * * * *
Hel. You are my mother, madam; 'Would you were
(So that my lord, your son, were not my brother,)
Indeed my mother!—or were you both our mothers
I care no more for than I do for heaven,
So I were not his sister: Can 't no other,
But, I your daughter, he must be my brother?
Count. Yes, Helen, you might be my daughter-in-law;
God shield you mean it not! daughter, and mother,
So strive upon your pulse. What, pale again?
My fear hath catch'd your fondness; now I see
The mystery of your loneliness, and find
Your salt tears' head. Now to all sense 'tis gross:

26

You love my son; invention is asham'd,
Against the proclamation of thy passion,
To say thou dost not; therefore tell me true;
* * * * * * * * * *

Hel. Your pardon, noble mistress!
Count. Love you my son?
Hel. Do not you love him, madam?
Count. Go not about; my love hath in 't a bond
Whereof the world takes note. Come, come! disclose
The state of your affection; for your passions
Have to the full appeach'd.
Hel. Then I confess,
Here on my knee, before high heaven and you,
That before you, and next unto high heaven,
I love your son.
My friends were poor, but honest; so 's my love.
Be not offended; for it hurts not him
That he is lov'd of me: I follow him not
By any token of presumptuous suit;
Nor would I have him till I do deserve him—
Yet never know how that desert should be.
I know I love in vain, strive against hope;
Yet, in this captious and intenible sieve,
I still pour in the waters of my love,
And lack not to lose still; thus, Indian-like,
Religious in mine error, I adore
The sun, that looks upon his worshipper,
But knows of him no more.

Side by side with this passionate picture we place another, even more intensely painted; its beauty is vouched for by its universal popularity:

I am undone; there is no living, none,
If Bertram be away. It were all one
That I should love a bright particular star,
And think to wed it—he is so above me:
In his bright radiance and collateral light
Must I be comforted, not in his sphere.

The ambition in my love thus plagues itself;
The hind that would be mated by the lion
Must die for love. 'Twas pretty, though a plague,
To see him every hour—to sit and draw
His arched brows, his hawking eye, his curls,
In our heart's table—heart too capable
Of every line and trick of his sweet favor;
But now he's gone, and my idolatrous fancy
Must sanctify his relics.

Not less characteristic than her deportment with the countess, is Helena's bearing during the very trying ordeal of the husband-choosing; nothing can be more modest than her manner of forcibly taking possession of her beloved Bertram—for it amounts to that, as she well knows:

I dare not say I take you; but I give
Me and my service, ever whilst I live,
Into your guiding power.—This is the man!

Yet she is none the less persistent in her purpose, for all his scorn of her low origin, and his assertion that he neither loves her "nor will strive to do't"—his "recantation" to the king's anger being a mere satire, even more insulting than his plain-spoken rejection.

Once married, however, Helena is all discretion, modesty, sweetness; there is a world of plaintive tenderness in her reception of Bertram's letter—her self-reproach the more bitter because in the realization of her dearest hopes she finds only the source of endless sorrow:

Hel. Till I have no wife, I have nothing in France.
Nothing in France, until he has no wife!
Thou shalt have none, Rousillon, none in France;
Then hast thou all again. Poor lord! is 't I
That chase thee from thy country, and expose

Those tender limbs of thine to the event
Of the none-sparing war? and is it I
That drive thee from the sportive court, where thou
Wast shot at with fair eyes, to be the mark
Of smoky muskets? O you leaden messengers,
That ride upon the violent speed of fire,
Fly with false aim; move the still-piercing air,
That sings with piercing—do not touch my lord!
Whoever shoots at him, I set him there;
Whoever charges on his forward breast,
I am the caitiff that do hold him to it;
And, though I kill him not, I am the cause
His death was so effected. Better 'twere
I met the ravin lion when he roar'd
With sharp constraint of hunger; better 'twere
That all the miseries which nature owes
Were mine at once: No, come thou home, Rousillon,
Whence honor but of danger wins a scar
As oft it loses all. I will be gone;
My being here it is that holds thee hence:
Shall I stay here to do 't? no, no, although
The air of Paradise did fan the house,
And angels offic'd all. I will be gone—
That pitiful rumor may report my flight,
To consolate thine ca

We should repose more faith in the disinterestedness of Helena's flight from her husband's home, if she did not steer straight for Florence, where she knows he is quartered, and if she were less munificently provided with money and jewels, inappropriate to the estate of pilgrims. But—

All's well that ends well.

TITANIA.

Titania, wife of Oberon, was queen of a band of fairies, who held nightly revel in the beautiful wood "a league from the town" of Athens.

An ancient law of that city invested a father with the power of dooming his daughter to death or celibacy, if she refused the husband of his choosing; accordingly, Egeus, a citizen of Athens, came before Duke Theseus and demanded that this law be enforced against his daughter Hermia, because she refused to marry Demetrius, whom he had selected for a son-in-law. In defence, Hermia urged that she loved, and was betrothed to, Lysander; moreover, that Demetrius was beloved by her dearest friend, Helena, for whom until lately he had professed ardent affection.

Notwithstanding the justice of her pleas, Theseus had no right to put aside the law, and Hermia was allowed four days only—to choose between death and a life of "single blessedness," in preference to marriage with a man whose fickle, faithless passion she despised.

Lysander came promptly to the rescue of his lady fair. He proposed that she should fly from her father's house to the fairy-haunted wood; there he would meet her, and conduct her thence to another city, where they could be married. Hermia joyfully accepted this timely suggestion, and confided her secret to Helena, who, for the poor pleasure of having the company of her recreant lover to the wood and back again, told Demetrius—knowing that he would follow Hermia, but knowing also that it would be in vain.

Now, between Oberon and Titania, king and queen of the fairies, there was at this time pending a conjugal quarrel, the cause being a beautiful little Indian boy belonging to the queen, whom Oberon ardently desired for a page, but whom Titania firmly refused to give up. On the very night when the Athenian lovers agreed to meet in the wood, Oberon had made a last appeal to his wife, with no better result than before; and he determined to punish her for what he considered her undutiful and contumacious behavior, and to acquire by stratagem what he had failed to gain by fair means or foul words. So he summoned into his presence a fairy by the name of Puck, renowned for his expertness in all mischievous tricks, and commanded him to find a little flower called "Love in Idleness," at the same time confiding to him the use to which he intended to put it:

> Fetch me that flower—the herb I show'd thee once;
> The juice of it, on sleeping eyelids laid,
> Will make or man or woman madly dote
> Upon the next live creature that it sees.
>
> * * * * * * *
>
> * * * Having once this juice,
> I'll watch Titania when she is asleep,
> And drop the liquor of it in her eyes.
> The next thing then she waking looks upon,
> (Be it on lion, bear, or wolf, or bull,
> On meddling monkey, or on busy ape,)
> She shall pursue it with the soul of love;
> And ere I take this charm off from her sight,

> (As I can take it, with another herb,)
> I'll make her render up her page to me.

Before Puck returned with the flower, Demetrius passed by, followed by Helena, whose love he repulsed so cruelly that Oberon, touched with compassion, resolved to redress her wrongs by laying the same spell on Demetrius that he intended for Titania. Accordingly, he commanded Puck, when he returned, to follow this Athenian, whom he would know by his dress, and to take care to touch his eyes with the magic juice just when the object they must next rest upon would be Helena.

Forthwith Puck started on his errand; but it chanced that the first Athenian he saw was Lysander, who, at a respectful distance from Hermia, was stretched on the turf fast asleep, as likewise was the lady. So Puck anointed Lysander's eyes; but when he awoke, the first thing he perceived was Helena, who, deserted by Demetrius, was trying to find her way out of the wood. Immediately his love was transferred from Hermia to Helena, and leaving his true love still sleeping, he followed his new love with compliments and courtship.

About this time, Theseus, Duke of Athens, was on the eve of marriage with Hippolyta, queen of the Amazons, and a company of actors who were preparing "a sweet comedy" to be performed in their august presence, in honor of the nuptials, assembled in this wood to rehearse the play. It happened that the spot selected for this purpose was near the "close and consecrated bower" of Queen Titania, wherein she now lay sleeping. Oberon, hastening to play his magic trick upon his wife, noted these "hempen homespuns," and selected Bottom, a coarse, ignorant weaver, from among them, to be the first object that Titania should behold on awaking.

Of course the exquisite Titania straightway doted on this

"monster," whom Oberon had made even more ridiculous, by placing an ass's head on his brawny shoulders; she lured him away from his companions, heaped upon him her sweet favors, and put her sprites at his command.

Meantime Hermia awoke, to find her lover gone; and in looking for him she came upon Demetrius, who at once resumed his unwelcome suit. Oberon, passing that way, overheard their conversation, and discovered the mischief Puck had done by mistaking Lysander for Demetrius; but the blunder was easily rectified by the fairy king, who anointed the lovers' eyes with his love-juice, and then had their respective ladies brought before them at the proper moment.

Oberon found little difficulty in securing his page, now that his queen's whole soul was occupied only with Bottom, the weaver; and having accomplished his purpose, he took pity upon her ridiculous delusion, and released her from the spell. Then, all being harmony again, Oberon caused the events of the night to appear, to the "human mortals" concerned, but as a Midsummer Night's Dream.

Of course the lovers were married according to their hearts' desire, and the beneficent purposes of the "wee folk:"

"Farewell rewards and fairies!
  Good housewives now may say,
For now foule sluts in dairies
  Doe fare as well as they;
And though they sweepe their hearths no less
  Than mayds were wont to doe,
Yet who of late for cleanlinesse
  Finds sixepence in her shoe?"

Had we lived in the days of a more beautiful and less sophisticated superstition than that of this table-tipping generation, we had scarcely ventured to arraign a *bona fide* fairy queen before our vulgar tribunal; indeed, as it is, we have "screwed our courage to the sticking-point" of this task, only by remembering that we have nothing to say that could offend faërial majesty, or tempt its prompt revenge.

Since those Swedenborgs of the elfin faith—Hans Christian Andersen and the Brothers Grimm—have spoken, no one can deny to the tricksy sprites strongly marked individualities, physical and mental; among no people are the pure affections more tenderly cultivated, the unworthy more severely rooted up—the lives of most of them being devoted to the rewarding of virtue and the punishing of vice.

Titania, however, is not to be classed with these moral economists: she is a sort of queen-bee in the fairy hive; her sole business is to be beautiful, and to enjoy the beautiful. She is the perfect fairy queen—exquisite, dainty, luxurious, self-willed, capricious, coquettish; and thoroughly royal in one and all. In her feud with her husband, King Oberon, she compels our sympathy throughout; she is in the right, and she maintains her position with commendable firmness and dignity. As to the shameful trick played upon her delicate fancy, we overlook the ridicule in which it involves her "style," to admire her tender solicitude for her new love, her graceful dalliance, and her lavish hospitality.

Though Titania is introduced to us in the heat of her temporary hostility to her liege lord, it must be confessed that their misunderstanding, especially on her part, is widely removed from the vulgar squabbles of "human mortals." The queen's argument for peace—not on her own account. but because their dissension is fraught with consequences disastrous to the inhabitants of Earth—is in the highest degree lofty:

Obe. Ill met by moon-light, proud Titania.
Tita. What! jealous Oberon? Fairy, skip hence;
I have forsworn his bed and company.
Obe. Tarry, rash wanton! Am not I thy lord?
Tita. Then I must be thy lady. But I know
When thou hast stol'n away from fairy land,
And in the shape of Corin sat all day,
Playing on pipes of corn, and versing love
To amorous Phillida. Why art thou here,
Come from the farthest steep of India?
But that, forsooth, the bouncing Amazon,
Your buskin'd mistress, and your warrior love,
To Theseus must be wedded; and you come
To give their bed joy and prosperity.
Obe. How canst thou thus, for shame, Titania,
Glance at my credit with Hippolyta,
Knowing I know thy love to Theseus?
Didst thou not lead him through the glimmering night
From Perigenia, whom he ravished?
And make him with fair Ægle break his faith,
With Ariadne, and Antiopa?
Tita. These are the forgeries of jealousy;
And never, since the middle summer's spring,
Met we on hill, in dale, forest, or mead,
By paved fountain, or by rushy brook,
Or on the beachy margent of the sea,
To dance our ringlets to the whistling wind,
But with thy brawls thou hast disturb'd our sport.
Therefore the winds, piping to us in vain,
As in revenge, have suck'd up from the sea
Contagious fogs; which, falling in the land,
Have every pelting river made so proud,
That they have overborne their continents:
* * * * * * * *
And this same progeny of evils comes
From our debate, from our dissension;
We are their parents and original.

Obe. Do you amend it then; it lies in you.
Why should Titania cross her Oberon?
I do but beg a little changeling boy
To be my henchman.
Tita. Set your heart at rest—
The fairy land buys not the child of me.
His mother was a vot'ress of my order;
And, in the spiced Indian air, by night,
Full often hath she gossip'd by my side,
And sat with me on Neptune's yellow sands,
Marking the embarked traders on the flood.
But she, being mortal, of that boy did die;
And, for her sake, I do rear up her boy;
And, for her sake, I will not part with him.

It is as unnecessary to comment on the mean selfishness of Oberon's answer to her appeal in behalf of the distressed earth, as on the generosity and faithful friendship that distinguish Titania's concluding remarks. Let us peep at the fairy queen in love:

Tita. I pray thee, gentle mortal, sing again;
Mine ear is much enamour'd of thy note—
So is mine eye enthralled to thy shape;
And thy fair virtue's force perforce doth move me,
On the first view, to say, to swear, I love thee.
Bot. Methinks, mistress, you should have little reason for that; and yet, to say the truth, Reason and Love keep little company together now-a-days.

* * * * * * * * *

Tita. Out of this wood do not desire to go;
Thou shalt remain here, whether thou wilt or no.
I am a spirit, of no common rate;
The summer still doth tend upon my state,
And I do love thee: therefore, go with me;
I'll give thee fairies to attend on thee;
And they shall fetch thee jewels from the deep,
And sing while thou on pressed flowers dost sleep;
And I will purge thy mortal grossness so,

That thou shalt like an airy spirit go.—
Peas-blossom! Cobweb! Moth! and Mustard-seed!

* * * * * * * *

Be kind and courteous to this gentleman;
Hop in his walks, and gambol in his eyes;
Feed him with apricocks and dewberries,
With purple grapes, green figs, and mulberries;
The honey bags steal from the humble bees;
And, for night-tapers, crop their waxen thighs,
And light them at the fiery glow-worm's eyes,
To have my love to bed, and to arise;
And pluck the wings from painted butterflies,
To fan the moon-beams from his sleeping eyes:
Nod to him, elves, and do him courtesies.

Come, sit thee down upon this flowery bed,
  While I thy amiable cheeks do coy,
And stick musk-roses in thy sleek smooth head,
  And kiss thy fair large ears, my gentle joy.

* * * * * * * * *

Or say, sweet love, what thou desir'st to eat.

Bot. Truly, a peck of provender; I could munch your good dry oats. Methinks I have a great desire to a bottle of hay: good hay, sweet hay, hath no fellow.

Tita. I have a venturous fairy that shall seek
The squirrel's hoard, and fetch thee new nuts.

Bot. I had rather have a handful or two of dried peas. But, I pray you, let none of your people stir me; I have an exposition of sleep come upon me.

Tita. Sleep thou, and I will wind thee in my arms.
Fairies, begone—and be all ways away.
So doth the woodbine, the sweet honeysuckle,
Gently entwist—the female ivy so
Enrings the barky fingers of the elm.
O, how I love thee! how I dote on thee!

One glance at the household habits of a fairy court, and then we shall have awakened from this Midsummer Night's Dream, which is "like wandering through a grove by moonlight," and "breathes a sweetness, like odors thrown from beds of flowers."

Obe. I know a bank whereon the wild thyme blows,
Where ox-lips and the nodding violet grows—
Quite over-canopied with lush woodbine,
With sweet musk-roses, and with eglantine;
There sleeps Titania, some time of the night
Lull'd in these flowers with dances and delight;
And there the snake throws her enamell'd skin,
Weed wide enough to wrap a fairy in.

Tita. Come, now a roundel, and a fairy song;
Then, for the third part of a minute, hence:
Some to kill cankers in the musk-rose buds;
Some war with rear-mice for their leathern wings,
To make my small elves coats; and some keep back
The clamorous owl, that nightly hoots, and wonders
At our quaint spirits. Sing me now asleep;
Then to your offices, and let me rest.

SONG.

I.

You spotted snakes with double tongue,
Thorny hedgehogs, be not seen;
Newts, and blind-worms, do no wrong;
Come not near our fairy queen!

CHORUS.

Philomel, with melody,
Sing in our sweet lullaby:
Lulla, lulla, lullaby! lulla, lulla, lullaby!
Never harm, nor spell, nor charm,
Come our lovely lady nigh;
So, good night, with lullaby!

II.

Weaving spiders, come not here;
Hence, you long-legg'd spinners, hence;
Beetles black, approach not near;
Worm, nor snail, do no offence!

CHORUS.

Philomel, with melody,
Sing in our sweet lullaby:
Lulla, lulla, lullaby! lulla, lulla, lullaby!
Never harm, nor spell, nor charm,
Come our lovely lady nigh;
So, good night, with lullaby!

CONSTANCE.

Constance, daughter and heiress of Conan IV., Duke of Bretagne, was the widow of Geffrey, son of Henry II. of England, and mother of Arthur, his heir. John, the younger brother of Geffrey, having usurped the English throne, Philip of France demanded its restoration to the rightful king—the young Duke of Bretagne; and held himself in readiness to maintain the boy's claim with force of arms.

To chastise this insolent interference with his self-constituted authority, King John invaded France with a large army. At first he was valiantly repulsed by the French and Austrian troops; but, after several indecisive battles, Philip forgot his royal promise to Constance, to defend the rights of her son, and yielded to the strong temptation of selfish interests. He concluded a peace with King John, by receiving in marriage for his son Louis, the Dauphin, Blanche of Castile, a princess of rare perfections, and niece of King John, who dowered her with the very territories that Philip had demanded for Arthur.

But in the midst of the wedding feasts came a "holy legate of the Pope," commanding Philip, on pain of excommunication, to break his alliance with a king who had flouted the authority of the

Church, and set her dignitaries at defiance, and again to take up arms against him—this time, in her name. Philip dared not disobey; but in obeying he lost every thing. Arthur was taken prisoner and carried to England, leaving his wretched mother so distraught with grief and disappointment that she "died in a frenzy" shortly after; the royal child himself, having, through the humanity of his jailer, escaped an assassination planned by his cruel uncle, met his death, accidentally, in attempting to escape from prison.

Louis, the Dauphin, invaded England, and set up a claim to the throne in the name of his wife; but his expedition was unsuccessful. King John dying, poisoned, his son ascended the throne as Henry III.

Constance of Bretagne exists to our sympathy only in her maternal relation; in her affection for her son, Arthur, all other emotions are swallowed up; in him are concentred all her ambitions, hopes, desires; so it is not surprising that we forget the heiress of a sovereign duchy, and her strictly personal misfortunes—which, alone, should suffice to invest her with peculiar interest—to bestow our pity upon the mother of a fair young prince, despoiled of his birthright, and betrayed by those who had promised to befriend him.

Her dramatic situation—"the mother-eagle wounded, and bleeding to death, yet stretched over her young in the attitude of defiance"—may be, critically considered, unsurpassed in sublimity, but its painfulness is too unmitigated to constitute it a source of pleasure to even the most stoical reader.

The spectacle of an utterly helpless being—weak and defenceless only by reason of her sex; with no weapon but words, "full of sound and fury," availing nothing; perfectly conscious of her impotency, yet resisting desperately to the last—oppresses the mind with something of its own overwhelming weight of forlornness. The only forms of sorrow to be pleasurably contemplated in woman are pious resignation and heroic fortitude; the violent passion of grief, as "torn to tatters" in the person of Constance, defeats itself; the mental exhaustion consequent upon the effort to follow it, is exactly similar to the physical prostration it produces in its victim.

The maternal love of Constance, as a dramatic effect, is very beautiful; but it partakes too much of sentiment, too little of pure instinct, to command our undivided admiration; we feel, as she did, that it depends for its devotion, in great measure, on her son's poetic attributes, of beauty, high birth, and princely presence—not, as it should, on the simple, all-sufficing *because*—because he is the fruit of her womb. The following speech to the boy-prince illustrates our meaning, and has left its impress of unloveliness on our high ideal of Constance; a mother after our own heart could never have found it in hers to give utterance to such a libel on the only love which is indifferent to physical, moral, or mental perfections in its object:

> *Arth.* I do beseech you, madam, be content.
> *Const.* If thou, that bid'st me be content, were grim,
> Ugly, and sland'rous to thy mother's womb,
> Full of unpleasing blots and sightless stains,
> Lame, foolish, crooked, swart, prodigious,
> Patch'd with foul moles and eye-offending marks—
> I would not care, I then would be content;
> For then I should not love thee; no, nor thou
> Become thy great birth, nor deserve a crown.
> But thou art fair; and at thy birth, dear boy,
> Nature and fortune joined to make thee great:
> Of nature's gifts thou may'st with lilies boast,

And with the half-blown rose. But fortune, O!
She is corrupted, chang'd, and won from thee;
She adulterates hourly with thine uncle John;
And with her golden hand hath pluck'd on France
To tread down fair respect of sovereignty.

Constance is distinguished by her imagination, the natural vivacity of which is intensified by suffering till it assumes an almost morbid predominance over every other faculty; this exaggerates even her desperate sorrows, and colors every event with its extravagance—hyperbole is its natural language, and frenzy its legitimate realm. Her eloquence is the declamation of exalted passion, which can scarce find images grand enough to express its concentrated vehemence; of this we have a fine example in her refusal to obey the summons of the kings, after their ignoble treaty has betrayed her rights:

Sal. Pardon me, madam—
I may not go without you to the kings.
Const. Thou may'st, thou shalt, I will not go with thee.
I will instruct my sorrows to be proud;
For grief is proud, and makes his owner stout.
To me, and to the state of my great grief,
Let kings assemble; for my grief's so great
That no supporter but the huge firm earth
Can hold it up: here I and Sorrow sit;
Here is my throne—bid kings come bow to it.

And again, in her interview with their perjured majesties, when they do, indeed, come to her:

K. Phi. By heaven, lady! you shall have no cause
To curse the fair proceedings of this day;
Have I not pawn'd to you my majesty?
Const. You have beguil'd me with a counterfeit,
Resembling majesty—which, being touch'd, and tried,

Proves valueless. You are forsworn, forsworn:
You came in arms to spill mine enemies' blood,
But now, in arms, you strengthen it with yours;
The grappling vigor and rough frown of war
Is cold in amity and painted peace;
And our oppression hath made up this league:—
Arm, arm, you heavens, against these perjured kings!
A widow cries; be husband to me, heavens!
Let not the hours of this ungodly day
Wear out the day in peace; but, ere sunset,
Set armed discord 'twixt these perjur'd kings!
Hear me, O, hear me!
Aust. Lady Constance, peace!
Const. War! war! no peace! peace is to me a war.
O Lymoges! O Austria! thou dost shame
That bloody spoil! Thou slave, thou wretch, thou coward!
Thou little valiant, great in villainy!
Thou ever strong upon the stronger side!
Thou fortune's champion, that dost never fight
But when her humorous ladyship is by
To teach thee safety! thou art perjur'd too,
And sooth'st up greatness. What a fool art thou,
A ramping fool—to brag, and stamp, and swear,
Upon my party! Thou cold-blooded slave,
Hast thou not spoke like thunder on my side?
Been sworn my soldier—bidding me depend
Upon thy stars, thy fortune, and thy strength?
And dost thou now fall over to my foes?
Thou wear a lion's hide! doff it for shame,
And hang a calf's skin on those recreant limbs.

This last speech, to Austria, is a glory of rage, contempt, and sarcasm; we can almost see the archduke of fair promises "hiding his diminished head" from the swelling storm.

There is something in the bewildered, helpless despair of Constance that reminds us of Lear; yet her frenzy is that of a mind distraught, not overthrown—she, herself, draws a fine distinction between the two mental conditions:

Thou art not holy to belie me so;
I am not mad: this hair I tear is mine;
My name is Constance; I was Geffrey's wife;
Young Arthur is my son, and he is lost:
I am not mad;—I would to heaven I were!
For then 'tis like I should forget myself;
O, if I could, what grief should I forget!—
Preach some philosophy to make me mad,
And thou shalt be canoniz'd, cardinal;
For, being not mad, but sensible of grief,
My reasonable part produces reason
How I may be deliver'd of these woes,
And teaches me to kill or hang myself;
If I were mad, I should forget my son,
Or madly think a babe of clouts were he:
I am not mad; too well, too well I feel
The different plague of each calamity.

But it is not in wild ravings, bitter taunts, lofty invocations, or logical arguments, that the eloquence of this unhappy duchess lives in our memory; let us rather turn to those simple, natural strains of pathos in which she bewails her lost child—that universal language which goes straight to the heart of the bereaved mother, whether in hut or palace, and is understood alike by both, by both alike repeated.

The "holy legate" admonishes her for so immoderately indulging her sorrow:

Const. He talks to me, that never had a son.
K. Phi. You are as fond of grief as of your child.
Const. Grief fills the room up of my absent child,
Lies in his bed, walks up and down with me,
Puts on his pretty looks, repeats his words,
Remembers me of all his gracious parts,
Stuffs out his vacant garments with his form;
Then have I reason to be fond of Grief.
Fare you well: had you such a loss as I,
I could give better comfort than you do.—

* * * * * * * *

And father cardinal, I have heard you say
That we shall see and know our friends in heaven:
If that be true, I shall see my boy again;
For, since the birth of Cain, the first male child,
To him that did but yesterday suspire,
There was not such a gracious creature born.
But now will canker sorrow eat my bud,
And chase the native beauty from his cheek,
And he will look as hollow as a ghost,
As dim and meagre as an ague's fit;
And so he'll die; and, rising so again,
When I shall meet him in the court of heaven
I shall not know him: therefore never, never
Must I behold my pretty Arthur more.

* * * * * * * *

O lord! my boy, my Arthur, my fair son!
My life, my joy, my food, my all the world!
My widow-comfort, and my sorrows' cure!

CORDELIA.

CORDELIA, the youngest of three sisters, was a daughter of Lear, king of Britain. That venerable monarch, weary of the cares of state, having almost fulfilled his allotted time on earth, determined to divide his kingdom between his children—two of whom had husbands—that he might pass his last days in honored repose. The fond, foolish old father called his daughters together; and making known to them his inclination to share his domain among them according to the affection they respectively entertained for him, he questioned the two married princesses as to the fervor of their filial love. Goneril and Regan replied with all the fulsome flattery of mercenary tongues, and so put to the blush the true-minded Cordelia, that when it was her turn to speak she refused to acknowledge any more affection for her father than her duty compelled. This answer so incensed the choleric king that he cast her off utterly, and divided her portion between her two sisters.

There were then at the court of Britain two suitors for Cordelia's hand—the Duke of Burgundy and the King of France: when the duke learned that she would be dowerless, he withdrew his suit; but the King of France was so touched by her lofty spirit, and her forlorn condition, that he married her, and made her queen over his fair kingdom.

The condition on which King Lear had abdicated his sovereign rights, in favor of his daughters and their husbands, was: that he, attended by a hundred chosen knights, should be entertained at their palaces alternately, while he should retain the name and all "the additions to a king."

It was not long before Goneril found it irksome to accommodate her father's attendants, and regarded them as an unnecessary expense; her own servants were therefore instructed to annoy his majesty with petty indignities; and when he remonstrated, she rebuffed him with a cool contempt that astounded him. Appealing from Goneril to Regan, the unhappy father fared even worse; for the latter co-operated with her sister to divest him of all the outward shows of state; and at last she drove him forth in a howling storm at night, when the exposure, added to the sharp sense of his children's ingratitude, drove the poor old man mad.

He was blessed, however, in one faithful follower—the Earl of Kent, whom he had banished for interceding in behalf of Cordelia, but who, in disguise, had returned to the service of his beloved master. This loyal nobleman housed the king in his own castle, and sent letters to the court of France for Cordelia, who was ignorant of her father's wretchedness. Hastening, with an army contributed by her husband, to the rescue of her outraged parent, she found him almost hopelessly crazed; but by kind nursing he was restored sufficiently to recognize and bless her. Unfortunately for the brave and devoted lady, her army was defeated by the superior force with which Goneril and Regan opposed it; Lear and Cordelia were consigned to a prison, where she was hung, by order of Goneril and her paramour; and her father, paralyzed by this last blow, breathed his last on her beloved corse.

In Cordelia we have an exalted example of pure filial devotion, unalloyed by any less heroic passion—a character every attribute of which is subordinate to the highest conception of duty. The admiration she commands is entirely independent of the lighter graces, or those pretty tricks of unconscious coquetry which have attained a legitimate position in the "affairs of woman;" she is a silent, shy, undemonstrative girl, quite outshone in her father's court by the "scornful beauty" and the ready tongues of her sisters.

Compared with any less perfect, but not less charming, lady of this sisterhood, Cordelia will appear transcendently superior, by as much as she who follows the dictates of true religious principle must ever take moral precedence of the creature of mere impulses, whether of passion or caprice; but side by side with Goneril and Regan—those diabolical creations, who are women only physically—she shines an angel of light. It is only by careful study of the few master-strokes with which Cordelia is delineated that we can make out a faithful portrait of this matchless daughter; in fact, throughout the moving record of madness and crime, of which she is the heroine, her "heavenly beauty of soul" is felt rather than seen; although she is almost excluded from the action, her purity is ever present to the mind's eye, in dazzling contrast to the outer darkness of her surroundings.

In the first scene, where Cordelia incurs her royal father's displeasure, she might, by a superficial observer, be accused of sullen obstinacy, in persisting to seem less fond than we know she is, at heart; but it must be remembered that she is not only disgusted with her sisters' deceit, and mortified at the doting credulity of her father, but that she has been virtually bribed to exceed even their bombastic protestations:

* * * * What can you say, to draw
A third more opulent than your sisters? Speak.

Her loyal soul revolts from such mockery of its dearest duty, she answers with simple truthfulness, not devoid of a trace of sarcasm for her sisters' palpable lies; and even imposes restraint upon those expressions of fondness which under other circumstances would be natural to her:

Unhappy that I am, I cannot heave
My heart into my mouth: I love your majesty
According to my bond; nor more, nor less.
* * * * * * * *
* * * * * Good my lord,
You have begot me, bred me, loved me; I
Return those duties back as are right fit—
Obey you, love you, and most honor you.
Why have my sisters husbands, if they say
They love you all? Haply, when I shall wed,
That lord, whose hand must take my plight, shall carry
Half my love with him, half my care, and duty;
Sure, I shall never marry like my sisters,
To love my father all.
Lear. But goes this with thy heart?
Cor. Ay, good my lord.
Lear. So young, and so untender?
Cor. So young, my lord, and true.
Lear. Let it be so—thy truth then be thy dower:
For, by the sacred radiance of the sun,
The mysteries of Hecate, and the night—
By all the operations of the orbs,
From whom we do exist, and cease to be—
Here I disclaim all my paternal care,
Propinquity and property of blood,
And as a stranger to my heart and me
Hold thee, from this, forever.

In the next scene, in which Lear summons Cordelia's suitors to inform them of her fall from his favor, and to receive their final decision, her conduct is eminently characteristic; nothing can exceed in serene dignity and inherent honor her appeal to her father, in answer to her royal lover's amazed reception of this intelligence—for which the effect upon her future husband is voucher enough:

France. This is most strange!
That she, that even but now was your best object,
The argument of your praise, balm of your age,
Most best, most dearest, should in this trice of time
Commit a thing so monstrous, to dismantle
So many folds of favor! Sure, her offence
Must be of such unnatural degree
That monsters it, or your fore-vouch'd affection
Fall into taint: which to believe of her,
Must be a faith that reason without miracle
Could never plant in me.
Cor. I yet beseech your majesty,
(If for I want that glib and oily art,
To speak, and purpose not; since what I well intend,
I'll do't before I speak,) that you make known
It is no vicious blot, murder, or foulness,
No unchaste action, or dishonor'd step,
That hath deprived me of your grace and favor;
But even for want of that for which I am richer—
A still soliciting eye, and such a tongue
That I am glad I have not, though not to have it
Hath lost me in your liking.
* * * * * * * *
France. Is it but this? a tardiness in nature,
Which often leaves the history unspoke
That it intends to do? * * * *
* * * * * * * * *
Fairest Cordelia, thou art most rich, being poor;
Most choice, forsaken; and most lov'd, despis'd!
Thee and thy virtues here I seize upon:
Be it lawful, I take up what's cast away.
Gods, gods! 'tis strange, that from their cold'st neglect
My love should kindle to inflam'd respect.—

Thy dowerless daughter, king, thrown to my chance,
Is queen of us, of ours, and our fair France;
Not all the dukes of wat'rish Burgundy
Shall buy this unpriz'd precious maid of me.

In her charge to her unnatural sisters, at parting, she still maintains the calm majesty of demeanor that befits her grave misfortune:

The jewels of our father, with wash'd eyes
Cordelia leaves you. I know you what you are;
And, like a sister, am most loath to call
Your faults as they are nam'd. Use well our father:
To your professed bosoms I commit him;
But yet, alas! stood I within his grace,
I would prefer him to a better place.
So farewell to you both.

With this, the Cordelia of an incorruptible and somewhat rigid virtue disappears, and in her place we have the tenderest child that ever blessed a doting father. The following extracts are beautifully illustrative of that steadfast self-command, born of a most shrinking modesty, which has become habitual with her, even on occasions of extraordinary trial, and which, in later examples, is too often mistaken for insensibility, pride, or heartlessness:

Kent. Did your letters pierce the queen to any demonstration of grief?
Gent. Ay, sir; she took them, read them in my presence;
And now and then an ample tear trill'd down
Her delicate cheek: it seem'd she was a queen
Over her passion, who, most rebel-like,
Sought to be king o'er her.
Kent. O, then it moved her.
Gent. Not to a rage; patience and sorrow strove
Who should express her goodliest. You have seen
Sunshine and rain at once: her smiles and tears
Were like a better day. Those happy smiles,
That play'd on her ripe lip, seem'd not to know

What guests were in her eyes; which parted thence,
As pearls from diamonds dropp'd.—In brief, sorrow
Would be a rarity most belov'd, if all
Could so become it.
Kent. Made she no verbal question?
Gent. 'Faith, once or twice she heav'd the name of *father*
Pantingly forth, as if it press'd her heart;
Cried, *Sisters! sisters!—Shame of ladies! sisters!*
Kent! father! sisters! What! i' the storm i' the night?
Let pity not be believ'd!—There she shook
The holy water from her heavenly eyes,
And clamor moisten'd:—then away she started,
To deal with grief alone.

But the crowning beauty of Cordelia's character, as well as one of the master-pieces of this "best tragedy," is achieved in the scene where, having returned home to find her father hopelessly crazed by his children's cruelty, she bends, a pitying angel, over that sad wreck of manhood and of majesty:

O my dear father! Restoration hang
Thy medicine on my lips; and let this kiss
Repair those violent harms, that my two sisters
Have in thy reverence made!
Kent. Kind and dear princess.
Cor. Had you not been their father, these white flakes
Had challeng'd pity of them. Was this a face
To be expos'd against the warring winds?
To stand against the deep dread-bolted thunder?
In the most terrible and nimble stroke
Of quick, cross-lightning? to watch (poor perdu!)
With this thin helm? Mine enemy's dog,
Though he had bit me, should have stood that night
Against my fire. And wast thou fain, poor father,
To hovel thee with swine, and rogues forlorn,
In short and musty straw? Alack, alack!
'Tis wonder that thy life and wits at once
Had not concluded all.—He wakes; speak to him.
Phys. Madam, do you; 'tis fittest.

Cor. How does my royal lord? How fares your majesty?
* * * * * * * * * *
* * * * * * * * * *
* * * * * O, look upon me, sir;
And hold your hands in benediction o'er me:—
No, sir, you must not kneel.
Lear. Pray, do not mock me:
I am a very foolish, fond old man—
Fourscore and upward; and, to deal plainly,
I fear I am not in my perfect mind.
Methinks I should know you, and know this man—
Yet I am doubtful; for I am mainly ignorant
What place this is; and all the skill I have
Remembers not these garments; nor I know not
Where I did lodge last night. Do not laugh at me;
For, as I am a man, I think this lady
To be my child Cordelia.
Cor. And so I am, I am.

The great Master has not weakened his imposing work by a single allusion to her mere personality; let us not then vulgarly descend to guess at what he has left veiled, assured that such inner glory as Cordelia's would diffuse its radiance over any but a monstrous exterior. If, in conclusion, we confess that Cordelia presents to us few points of congeniality on which we may freely hang a familiar preference, the acknowledgment can be prejudicial only to ourself; for we feel that to be capable of worthily understanding and loving her, one must possess virtue as heroic, a heart as pure, and a conscience as void of offence, as her own.

THE ABBESS.

Æmilia, lady-abbess of a convent at Ephesus, had been, during her secular life, the wife of Ægeon, a wealthy Syracusan merchant. While on a visit to Epidamnum with her husband, she became the mother of twin sons, who were marvellously alike in person, and to whom they gave the same name, Antipholus. A poor woman, in the inn where Æmilia lodged, gave birth at the same time to twin sons, who also precisely resembled each other, and were both named Dromio; so Ægeon, for the pretty sentiment of the thing, purchased them, with the intention of bringing them up with his own boys, to be their companions and servants.

On their way home with the four little ones, a terrific storm threatened to destroy the ship in which they had taken passage; the sailors abandoned her, in the boats, and left Ægeon and his helpless family to their fate. In this extremity the poor gentleman bound his wife, and one Antipholus with his accompanying Dromio, to a mast, and secured himself with the other two children in the same manner—so that when the vessel sank the spars still kept them afloat.

Æmilia was separated from her husband by the violence of the sea, but was rescued by some fishermen. Ægeon was picked up by a ship which conveyed him to Syracuse; but for many a day the fate of his wife and son remained for him a painful mystery.

The fishermen who had saved Æmilia landed her in safety at Ephesus, but took the two boys, and sold them to a wealthy nobleman; so the unhappy mother—widowed and childless, as it seemed—entered a convent, of which she eventually became the abbess.

When the Antipholus who was saved with his father had grown to manhood, he set out on a journey with his faithful Dromio, to seek his long-lost mother and brother. Two years had he been absent from Syracuse on this almost hopeless errand, when his old father, fearing he would lose him also, set forth to find him and urge him to return.

Ægeon had journeyed year after year through distant countries, without discovering a trace of his son, when finally he came to Ephesus, and found that by so doing he had forfeited his life—according to an Ephesian law which forbade a Syracusan to enter the city, on pain of death.

The Antipholus sold by the fisherman had been adopted by the duke of Ephesus, and was living in that city, married to a wealthy lady named Adriana. The other Antipholus, by a happy chance, came to Ephesus in search of his brother, while Ægeon was there under sentence of death; and through a bewildering concatenation of fortuitous circumstances, the whole family were once more united. It is almost unnecessary to add that the duke gladly pardoned the father of his foster-son, and rejoiced with them that rejoiced.

The *Comedy of Errors* turns chiefly on the ludicrous mistakes arising out of the personal resemblance between the two Antipholuses, and the two Dromios.

The Abbess is a woman of sound sense, reliable judgment, and ready knowledge of human nature. As her position—attained through personal merit alone—indicates, she is of grave presence, and held in high esteem for her piety and good works; her character is marked by dignified simplicity, but at the same time evinces capacity for firm, decisive action.

The scene where, having given refuge to the Syracusan Antipholus, whom Adriana pursues with her servants, believing him to be her husband, and mad, the Abbess "betrays" that perplexed lady "to her own reproof," finely displays the *finesse* so requisite in her calling, and which she possesses in an eminent degree:

> *Abb.* Be quiet, people! Wherefore throng you hither?
> *Adr.* To fetch my poor distracted husband hence:
> Let us come in, that we may bind him fast,
> And bear him home for his recovery.
> * * * * * * * * * *
> *Abb.* How long hath this possession held the man?
> *Adr.* This week he hath been heavy, sour, sad,
> And much, much different from the man he was;
> But, till this afternoon, his passion
> Ne'er brake into extremity of rage.
> *Abb.* Hath he not lost much wealth by wreck at sea—
> Buried some dear friend? Hath not else his eye
> Stray'd his affection in unlawful love?—
> A sin prevailing much in youthful men,
> Who give their eyes the liberty of gazing.
> Which of these sorrows is he subject to?
> *Adr.* To none of these, except it be the last—
> Namely some love, that drew him oft from home.
> *Abb.* You should for that have reprehended him.
> *Adr.* Why, so I did.
> *Abb.* Ay, but not rough enough.
> *Adr.* As roughly as my modesty would let me.
> *Abb.* Haply, in private.
> *Adr.* And in assemblies too.
> *Abb.* Ay, but not enough.

Adr. It was the copy of our conference:
In bed, he slept not for my urging it;
At board, he fed not for my urging it;
Alone, it was the subject of my theme;
In company, I often glanced it;
Still did I tell him it was vile and bad.
Abb. And thereof came it that the man was mad;
The venom clamors of a jealous woman
Poison more deadly than a mad dog's tooth.
It seems his sleeps were hinder'd by thy railing;
And therefore comes it that his head is light.
Thou say'st his meat was sauc'd with thy upbraidings:
Unquiet meals make ill digestions—
Thereof the raging fire of fever bred;
And what's a fever but a fit of madness?
Thou say'st his sports were hinder'd by thy brawls:
Sweet recreation barr'd, what doth ensue
But moody and dull Melancholy,
(Kinsman to grim and comfortless Despair,)
And, at her heels, a huge infectious troop
Of pale distemperatures, and foes to life?
In food, in sport, and life-preserving rest
To be disturb'd, would mad or man or beast:
The consequence is then, thy jealous fits
Have scar'd thy husband from the use of wits.

An episode of the same adventure shows our lady-abbess invested with her canonical authority:

Adr. * * * * * * * * *
Good people, enter, and lay hold on him!
Abb. No, not a creature enters in my house.
Adr. Then let your servants bring my husband forth.
Abb. Neither; he took this place for sanctuary,
And it shall privilege him from your hands
Till I have brought him to his wits again,
Or lose my labor in assaying it.
Adr. I will attend my husband, be his nurse,
Diet his sickness; for it is my office,

And will have no attorney but myself;
And therefore let me have him home with me.
Abb. Be patient; for I will not let him stir,
Till I have used the approved means I have,
With wholesome syrups, drugs, and holy prayers,
To make of him a formal man again:
It is a branch and parcel of mine oath,
A charitable duty of my order;
Therefore depart, and leave him here with me.
Adr. I will not hence, and leave my husband here;
And ill it doth beseem your holiness,
To separate the husband and the wife.
Abb. Be quiet, and depart; thou shalt not have him.

Yet, at the last, we see that twenty-five years of self-mortification, and contempt of earthly ties, have failed to eradicate the strong affections of Æmilia, the wife and the mother. Our sympathy with this Rachel, who mourned for her children because she believed they were not, is as cordial as our congratulations on their restoration are sincere; and to her gracious invitation we reply in the words of the duke—"With all our heart, we'll gossip at this feast:"

Abb. * * * Vouchsafe to take the pains
To go with us into the abbey here,
And hear at large discoursed all our fortunes;
And all that are assembled in this place,
That by this sympathized one day's error
Have suffer'd wrong, go, keep us company,
And we shall make full satisfaction.—
Twenty-five years have I but gone in travail
Of you, my sons; nor, till this present hour,
My heavy burdens are delivered:—
The duke, my husband, and my children both,
And you, the calendars of their nativity,
Go to a gossip's feast, and go with me;
After so long grief, such nativity!

KATHARINE OF ARRAGON.

Queen Katharine, of sorrowful memory, was the daughter of Ferdinand, king of Arragon, and first wife of the infamous Henry VIII. of England. In her seventeenth year she was married to Arthur, prince of Wales, the eldest son of Henry VII.; but he died a few months after; and her royal father-in-law, anxious to secure the alliance, as well as the magnificent dowry, of the Infanta, procured a dispensation from the Pope to betroth her to his second son, Henry, then a child of twelve years.

This marriage was consummated five years later, when Henry had ascended the throne. Katharine was six years older than her boy-husband, and they possessed not a point of character in common; yet he was devotedly attached to her, and they had lived in undisturbed harmony for nearly twenty years, when the beautiful Anne Bullen came to court, as maid of honor to the queen.

Henry was fascinated by this lady's charms, and as she was proof against a dishonorable suit, he proceeded to rid himself of Katharine by divorce—pretending that his conscience would no longer permit him to cohabit with his brother's widow, and that his marriage with her was illegal.

The wretched queen opposed this contemplated degrading of

herself and daughter with all the spirit and pertinacity of her Spanish blood; but the divorce, which to the last she refused to acknowledge, was granted by Archbishop Cranmer, in open contempt of the Pope's authority; and Anne Bullen, whom Henry had secretly married previous to that decision, was crowned at Westminster with magnificent ceremony.

The play of *King Henry VIII.*, of which Katharine is the heroine, extends through about twelve years of his abominable reign, commencing with the disgrace of the Duke of Buckingham, and ending with the christening of Elizabeth, infant daughter of Anne Bullen, previous to which, by an allowable anachronism, the death of the heart-broken queen occurs.

The Katharine of *King Henry VIII.* is, almost without doubt, a faithful portrait of the unhappy lady whose virtues and wrongs command a tribute of pity from all true and tender hearts.

Apart from her overweening pride of birth, and jealous exaction of the homage due to her exalted rank, which was engendered in her Castilian blood—aside from her austere and narrow-minded bigotry, the result of a rigorous education—Katharine was remarkable for her quiet, domestic virtues, conjugal devotion, simple tastes, and genuine piety. She was not endowed with the brilliant mental gifts of her mother, the famous Isabella; but that her intellect was by no means of low order is proved by the decided influence she exerted over her violent husband, and by the confidence with which, in his absence, he intrusted to her judgment affairs of national importance.

In his portrait of Katharine, Shakspeare has followed historical records for all personal details, with the most conscientious exactness, depending for effect simply on the unembellished story of her misfortunes; in many of her speeches the words are the very same imputed to her by the old chroniclers.

The queen first appears on the scene of action in all the enjoyment of acknowledged dignities, and her royal husband's respect and favor; her appeal to Henry in behalf of his people, mercilessly taxed by Wolsey, which is granted even before it is concluded, is a natural emanation from her strict integrity, her kindness of heart, and her sound judgment. But our sympathies for her are not fairly aroused until, stripped of all the insignia of her state, all the honors of her chaste matronhood, she stands arraigned for trial, one of the most pitiful objects in history—the devoted wife of twenty years' fidelity, the mother of many children, repudiated by her husband for no more honorable reason than the gratification of a new and illicit passion.

The perfectly natural pathos of her address to the king, on this occasion, is exquisite, even as a merely dramatic effect, but doubly touching in that it is a faithful paraphrase of the very words uttered by the queen in her own defence:

Sir, I desire you do me right and justice,
And to bestow your pity on me; for
I am a most poor woman, and a stranger,
Born out of your dominions—having here
No judge indifferent, nor no more assurance
Of equal friendship and proceeding. Alas, sir,
In what have I offended you? what cause
Hath my behavior given to your displeasure,
That thus you should proceed to put me off,
And take your good grace from me? Heaven witness,
I have been to you a true and humble wife,
At all times to your will conformable—
Ever in fear to kindle your dislike—
Yea, subject to your countenance, glad, or sorry,
As I saw it inclin'd. When was the hour

I ever contradicted your desire,
Or made it not mine too? Or which of your friends
Have I not strove to love, although I knew
He were mine enemy? What friend of mine
That had to him deriv'd your anger, did I
Continue in my liking? nay, gave notice
He was from thence discharg'd? Sir, call to mind
That I have been your wife, in this obedience,
Upward of twenty years, and have been blest
With many children by you; if, in the course
And process of this time, you can report,
And prove it too, against mine honor aught,
My bond to wedlock, or my love and duty,
Against your sacred person—in God's name,
Turn me away, and let the foul'st contempt
Shut door upon me; and so give me up
To the sharpest kind of justice.

In characteristic contrast to this is her conference with Cardinal Wolsey, wherein, in spite of the severe discipline of her daily life, her hot temper gets the better of her self-control, and relieves its virtuous indignation in rebukes as scathing as they are shrewd:

Lord cardinal,
To you I speak.
* * * * * I do believe,
Induc'd by potent circumstances, that
You are mine enemy; and make my challenge—
You shall not be my judge; for it is you
Have blown this coal betwixt my lord and me,—
Which God's dew quench!—Therefore, I say again,
I utterly abhor, yea, from my soul
Refuse you for my judge, whom, yet once more,
I hold my most malicious foe, and think not
At all a friend to truth.
Wol. I do profess
You speak not like yourself, who ever yet
Have stood to charity, and display'd the effects

Of disposition gentle, and of wisdom
O'ertopping woman's power. Madam, you do me wrong:
I have no spleen against you. * * * *
Q. Kath. My lord, my lord,
I am a simple woman, much too weak
To oppose your cunning. You are meek, and humble-
mouth'd;
You sign your place and calling in full seeming
With meekness and humility; but your heart
Is cramm'd with arrogancy, spleen, and pride.
You have, by fortune, and his highness' favors,
Gone slightly o'er low steps; and now are mounted
Where powers are your retainers; and your words,
Domestics to you, serve your will, as 't please
Yourself pronounce their office. I must tell you,
You tender more your person's honor than
Your high profession spiritual; that again
I do refuse you for my judge; and here,
Before you all, appeal unto the Pope,
To bring my whole cause 'fore his holiness,
And to be judg'd by him.

In the scene where she gives audience to the Cardinals, Wolsey and Campeius (Campeggio), her individuality, with all its strong points of contrast, is admirably delineated—her simple, housewifely habits opposed to her jealous exaction of the honors which are her birthright:

Q. Kath * * * * * *
* * * * * I was set at work
Among my maids; full little, God knows, looking
Either for such men, or such business.
For her sake that I have been, (for I feel
The last fit of my greatness,) good your graces,
Let me have time and counsel for my cause;
Alas! I am a woman, friendless, hopeless.
* * * * * * * *
* * * * * * * *
Cam. I would your grace
Would leave your griefs, and take my counsel.

Q. Kath. How, sir?
Cam. Put your main cause into the king's protection;
He's loving, and most gracious; 'twill be much
Both for your honor better, and your cause;
For if the trial of the law o'ertake you,
You'll part away disgrac'd.
Wol. He tells you rightly.
Q. Kath. Ye tell me what ye wish for both, my ruin.
Is this your Christian counsel? Out upon ye!
Heaven is above all yet; there sits a judge
That no king can corrupt.
Cam. Your rage mistakes us.
Q. Kath. The more shame for ye; holy men I thought ye—
Upon my soul, two reverend cardinal virtues;
But cardinal sins, and hollow hearts, I fear ye:
Mend them, for shame, my lords. Is this your comfort—
The cordial that ye bring a wretched lady,
A woman lost among ye, laugh'd at, scorn'd?
* * * * * * * * *
Woe upon ye,
And all such false professors! Would ye have me
(If you have any justice, any pity—
If ye be any thing but churchmen's habits)
Put my sick cause into his hands that hates me?

And this fearless denunciation of the hypocrisy of her saintly visitors, who would persuade her to relinquish her pretensions as queen-consort, is again contrasted with the most pitiful self-contemplation:

Alas! he has banish'd me his bed already—
His love, too long ago: * * *
* * * Have I liv'd thus long—(let me speak myself,
Since virtue finds no friends,)—a wife, a true one—
A woman (I dare say, without vain-glory,)
Never yet branded with suspicion?
Have I with all my full affections
Still met the king, lov'd him next heaven, obey'd him,
Been, out of fondness, superstitious to him,
Almost forgot my prayers to content him?

And am I thus rewarded? 'Tis not well, lords.
Bring me a constant woman to her husband,
One that ne'er dream'd a joy beyond his pleasure,
And to that woman, when she has done most,
Yet will I add an honor,—a great patience.

'Would I had never trod this English earth,
Or felt the flatteries that grow upon it!
Ye have angels' faces, but Heaven knows your hearts.
What will become of me now, wretched lady?
I am the most unhappy woman living,—
Shipwreck'd upon a kingdom where no pity,
No friends, no hope; no kindred weep for me,
Almost no grave allow'd me:—Like the lily,
That once was mistress of the field, and flourish'd,
I'll hang my head, and perish.

Katharine's estimate of the popular feeling with regard to herself was not altogether just to English hearts; her cause elicited much sympathy, much tender pity—especially among the women, who in her wrongs saw their own rights threatened—but it was timid and unavailing. Her virtues were universally acknowledged; and of two beautiful tributes to her worth, the first, which Shakspeare has ascribed to her husband, is historically attested:

* * * * * *

That man i' the world who shall report he has
A better wife, let him in nought be trusted
For speaking false in that. Thou art, alone,
(If thy rare qualities, sweet gentleness,
Thy meekness saint-like, wife-like government,
Obeying in commanding,—and thy parts,
Sovereign and pious else, could speak thee out,)
The queen of earthly queens:—She is noble born;
And like her true nobility she has
Carried herself towards me.

He counsels a divorce—a loss of her
That, like a jewel, has hung twenty years

About his neck, yet never lost her lustre—
Of her that loves him with that excellence
That angels love good men with—even of her
That, when the greatest stroke of fortune falls,
Will bless the king.

The death of Queen Katharine—who lives to see her beautiful supplanter elevated to the throne she humbly waited on, and her own daughter, Mary, illegitimized to make way for new heirs—is full of majestic pathos. Her long probation of trial, which in a less heroic woman would have subdued every vestige of pride, had served but to intensify her ruling passion, fulfilling her own words: "nothing but death shall e'er divorce my dignities."

Still constant in her duty and grave affection to Henry, she dictates a farewell letter to him, over which even he, monster as he is, sheds tears; and having carefully instructed her women as to their last sad offices, she gives up her troubled ghost:

I thank you, honest lord. Remember me
In all humility unto his highness:
Say his long trouble now is passing
Out of this world; tell him in death I bless'd him,
For so I will.—Mine eyes grow dim.—Farewell,
My lord!—Griffith, farewell!—Nay, Patience,
You must not leave me yet. I must to bed;
Call in more women.—When I am dead, good wench,
Let me be used with honor; strew me over
With maiden flowers, that all the world may know
I was a chaste wife to my grave; embalm me,
Then lay me forth; although unqueen'd, yet like
A queen, and daughter to a king, inter me.
I can no more.— * * * *
* * * * * * * *

Pat. Do you note
How much her grace is alter'd on a sudden—
How long her face is drawn? How pale she looks,
And of an earthly cold! Mark you her eyes?
Grif. She is going, wench; pray, pray!

ANNE BULLEN.

Anne Bullen was the daughter of Sir Thomas Bullen, and second wife to Henry VIII. of England. While still very young, she, as maid of honor, accompanied Henry's sister, the Princess Mary, to France, when the latter was united to Louis XII.; and afterwards she served in the same capacity in the households of several royal ladies of that country. On returning home she was appointed to attend on Queen Katharine of Arragon, and at once entered upon her elegant duties.

In the story of Henry's first wife, Katharine, we have told how Anne supplanted her mistress in the affections of her husband; and how, for her sake, the Spanish woman was put away, and the famous court-beauty crowned queen. Of this marriage was born Elizabeth, with whose christening the play of *King Henry VIII.* concludes.

Anne Bullen's supremacy over the fickle mind of her royal husband was of but short duration; for she, in her turn, was supplanted by one of her maids of honor, Jane Seymour. Anne was accused of infidelity, tried, and condemned to die; she suffered on the scaffold, only a few months after the death of Katharine.

Anne Bullen reminds us of one of those rarer hot-house plants, which, perfected in an artificial atmosphere, exposed only to influences quite foreign to their nature, still retain much of their original freshness and perfume. Her whole life, from childhood, was passed amid the dissolute surroundings, the unwholesome pleasures, the empty etiquette of a court; she was surpassingly beautiful, gay, fascinating, witty. While yet a young woman—of twenty-five or thereabouts—she came to be maid of honor to Katharine, fresh from the careless coquetries and the lax principles of the French court, where she had been a favorite belle; to Henry, therefore, her sparkling vivacity presented a welcome contrast to the distasteful austerity of his wife.

Yet with all her vanity, her love of display, her giddy enjoyment of the homage her charms commanded, this our Anne Bullen is gentle, compassionate, affectionate. Shakspeare has, with exceeding skill, introduced her plaintively commenting on the much agitated question of the queen's divorce, of which she already suspects herself the cause, though she dare not, for an instant, ponder the certain consequences, so much does she desire, yet fear them. It is noticeable that Anne does not sympathize with her mistress in her conjugal distress—as would be most natural to a young and love-inspiring woman—but only in her loss of position:

> *Anne.* Not for that neither;—here's the pang that pinches:
> His highness having liv'd so long with her; and she
> So good a lady, that no tongue could ever
> Pronounce dishonor of her,—by my life,
> She never knew harm-doing!—O now, after
> So many courses of the sun enthron'd,
> Still growing in a majesty and pomp—the which
> To leave is a thousand-fold more bitter than
> 'Tis sweet at first to acquire—after this process
> To give her the avaunt! it is a pity
> Would move a monster.

Old L. Hearts of most hard temper
Melt and lament for her.
Anne. O, God's will! much better
She had never known pomp: though it be temporal,
Yet, if that quarrel fortune do divorce
It from the bearer, 'tis a sufferance, panging
As soul and body's severing.
Old L. Alas, poor lady!
She's a stranger now again.
Anne. So much the more
Must pity drop upon her. Verily,
I swear, 'tis better to be lowly born,
And range with humble livers in content,
Than to be perk'd up in a glistering grief,
And wear a golden sorrow.

* * * * * * * * *

By my troth,
I would not be a queen!
Old L. Beshrew me, I would—
And so would you,
For all this spice of your hypocrisy:
You, that have so fair parts of woman on you,
Have too a woman's heart, which ever yet
Affected eminence, wealth, sovereignty—
Which, to say sooth, are blessings, and which gifts
(Saving your mincing) the capacity
Of your soft cheveril conscience would receive,
If you might please to stretch it.
Anne. Nay, good troth,—
Old L. Yes, troth, and troth!—You would not be a queen?
Anne. No, not for all the riches under heaven.
Old L. 'Tis strange: a three-pence bowed would hire me,
Old as I am, to queen it.

And this is not hypocrisy, but a manifestation of weakness—when we consider "what follows"—far more culpable in its results. Even as Anne is conversing with the *Old Lady*, the lord chamberlain waits on her, to bestow a title upon her:

Cham. Good morrow, ladies. What were 't worth to know
The secret of your conference?
Anne. My good lord,
Not your demand; it values not your asking:
Our mistress' sorrows we were pitying.
Cham. It was a gentle business, and becoming
The action of good women. There is hope
All will be well.
Anne. Now I pray God, amen!
Cham. You bear a gentle mind, and heavenly blessings
Follow such creatures. That you may, fair lady,
Perceive I speak sincerely, and high note's
Ta'en of your many virtues, the king's majesty
Commends his good opinion to you, and
Does purpose honor to you, no less flowing
Than marchioness of Pembroke; to which title
A thousand pound a-year, annual support,
Out of his grace he adds.
Anne. I do not know
What kind of my obedience I should tender;
More than my all is nothing; nor my prayers
Are not words duly hallow'd, nor my wishes
More worth than empty vanities; yet prayers, and wishes,
Are all I can return. 'Beseech your lordship,
Vouchsafe to speak my thanks, and my obedience,
As from a blushing handmaid to his highness—
Whose health and royalty I pray for.
Cham. Lady,
I shall not fail to approve the fair conceit
The king hath of you.—I have perus'd her well!
[*Aside.*
Beauty and honor in her are so mingled
That they have caught the king. * * *
* * * * * * * * * *
* * * * * * * * * *
Old L. * * * * * * * *
The marchioness of Pembroke!
A thousand pounds a-year, for pure respect!
No other obligation: By my life,
That promises more thousands! Honor's train
Is longer than his foreskirt. By this time,

I know, your back will bear a duchess;—Say,
Are you not stronger than you were?
Anne. Good lady,
Make yourself mirth with your particular fancy,
And leave me out on 't. 'Would I had no being,
If this salute my blood a jot; it faints me,
To think what follows.
The queen is comfortless, and we forgetful,
In our long absence. Pray, do not deliver
What here you have heard, to her.
Old L. What do you think me?

Anne Bullen's errors spring from innate weakness of character, deplorably aggravated by a pernicious education. Her vanity lays successful snares for her good impulses—impulses only, they never rise to the dignity of principle. She can pity her royal rival from her very soul; but when she is brought face to face with the dazzling temptation, she is not sufficiently heroic to refuse for her fair brows the diadem of a betrayed wife, or the wooing of a guilty husband for her dainty hand. It may indeed "faint her to think what follows"—as well it might, poor lady!—but the power to resist is not in her.

To the scene of her coronation, at Westminster Abbey, we must look for the most striking mention of her personal beauty:

The rich stream
Of lords and ladies, having brought the queen
To a prepar'd place in the choir, fell off
A distance from her, while her grace sat down
To rest a while, some half an hour or so,
In a rich chair of state, opposing freely
The beauty of her person to the people;
* * * * * * *
* * * * which when the people
Had the full view of, such a noise arose
As the shrouds make at sea in a stiff tempest,

As loud, and to as many tunes: hats, cloaks,
(Doublets, I think,) flew up; and had their faces
Been loose, this day they had been lost. Such joy
I never saw before. * * * * * *
* * * * * * * * * *
At length her grace rose, and with modest paces
Came to the altar, where she kneel'd, and, saint-like,
Cast her fair eyes to heaven, and prayed devoutly.
Then rose again, and bow'd her to the people;
When by the archbishop of Canterbury
She had all the royal makings of a queen:
As holy oil, Edward Confessor's crown,
The rod, and bird of peace—and all such emblems
Laid nobly on her; which perform'd, the choir,
With all the choicest music of the kingdom,
Together sung *Te Deum*. So she parted,
And with the same full state pac'd back again
To York-place, where the feast is held.

THE PRINCESS OF FRANCE.

This royal lady, while yet a maiden, was despatched by her bed-ridden father, the King of France, on an important mission to the court of Ferdinand, King of Navarre, to confer with that prince concerning the surrender of Aquitaine—a fair domain then in his possession, but to which France laid claim.

As the august party approached Navarre, the princess learned that his majesty, with sundry of his gentlemen, had recently made a solemn vow to devote the coming three years to painful study—to mortify the flesh by fasting, to speak to no woman, and to forbid the approach of any woman within a mile of the royal palace.

So the lady halted, even where she was, and sent a messenger within the gates, to King Ferdinand, craving an interview "on serious business." But the king, already informed of her approach, had taken counsel with his fellow-devotees, and, concluding that this must constitute an exception to the rigor of their abstinence, was already on the road, gallantly attended, to bid her highness welcome to Navarre. Much to his mortification he was compelled, for his oath's sake, to deny the princess, and her suite, access to his court; but he caused tents to be erected at some distance from the palace, and entertained them with great splendor—he and his favorite gentlemen paying their respects daily to the fair embassy.

The result of these visits to the lively French maids was, as might be anticipated, fatal to the peace of the "matchless Navarre" and his lords; his majesty fell in love with the princess at sight, and his followers were severally fascinated by her highness's ladies. The merry demoiselles amused themselves to their hearts' content with the love-making of the amateur ascetics—passing the days in sports, invented for their entertainment by their lovers, and all the graceful coquetries in which the ladies of that nation are expert.

But in the midst of the merry-making came a messenger from France, with the sad intelligence of the king's death; and at once preparations were made for the princess's return home. And now Navarre and his lords urged their suits more seriously; but the ladies showed themselves, by their answers, as wise as they were fair and witty: the princess set the example by condemning her royal suitor to a twelvemonth of severe seclusion, to expiate his broken oaths; and her ladies imitated their mistress in the disposition of their lovers, imposing upon each some penance adapted to his peculiar case.

This "French king's daughter" is drawn after the established model for princesses—"a maid of grace and complete majesty," beautiful, of imposing presence, and much given to a sententious sort of wit. But under all her ostentation and moral formalities, which seem assumed as necessary addenda to her rank, she is a natural woman in her love of admiration, coquetry, and frolic.

At first, somewhat piqued at being compelled "to attend like humbly-visag'd suitors," on the king's high will—herself, a monarch's daughter, "lodged in a field, like one that came to besiege his court," rather than to demand a right—the princess receives the royal courtesy with sharp retorts:

> *King.* Fair princess, welcome to the court of Navarre.
> *Prin.* Fair I give you back again; and welcome I have not yet: the roof of this court is too high to be yours; and welcome to the wild fields too base to be mine.
> *King.* You shall be welcome, madam, to my court.
> *Prin.* I will be welcome then; conduct me thither.
> *King.* Hear me, dear lady; I have sworn an oath.
> *Prin.* Our lady help my lord! he'll be forsworn.
> *King.* Not for the world, fair madam, by my will.
> *Prin.* Why, will shall break it—will, and nothing else.
> *King.* Your ladyship is ignorant what it is.
> *Prin.* Were my lord so, his ignorance were wise,
> Where now his knowledge must prove ignorance.
> I hear your grace hath sworn out house-keeping:
> 'Tis deadly sin to keep that oath, my lord—
> And sin to break it.
> But pardon me—I am too sudden bold;
> To teach a teacher ill beseemeth me.
> Vouchsafe to read the purpose of my coming,
> And suddenly resolve me in my suit.

But all more dignified emotions soon yield to her mischievous enjoyment of the ludicrous plight of these gentlemen-hermits, who fall in love with the first women they meet, after their loud denunciations of the sex. Notwithstanding their hearty response to the protestations of the gallant Navarrese, the princess and her ladies spare no opportunity to heap humiliations upon them: mocking their amorous verses as "huge translations of hypocrisy, vilely compil'd" and "too long by half a mile;" turning their elaborate entertainments to ridicule; and yet, withal, making themselves more and more fascinating to the infatuated knights. But when the announcement of the death of the King of France puts an end to their mad "revels, dances, masks, and merry hours," the princess, recalled to her stateliness, apologizes for their perhaps indecorous folly, with a dignity truly royal:

> I thank you, gracious lords,
> For all your fair endeavors, and entreat,
> Out of a new-sad soul, that you vouchsafe,
> In your rich wisdom, to excuse, or hide,
> The liberal opposition of our spirits;
> If over boldly we have borne ourselves
> In the converse of breath, your gentleness
> Was guilty of it.—Farewell, worthy lord!
> A heavy heart bears not an humble tongue:
> Excuse me so, coming so short of thanks
> For my great suit so easily obtain'd.

And her reply to Navarre, that "sole inheritor of all perfections that a man may owe," when in good earnest he proffers his heart, is marked by sound sense, and jealous regard for her honor, as well as by the chivalric spirit of the time, when a lady's love was not to be had for the asking, however her own heart might "own the soft impeachment:"

> We have receiv'd your letters, full of love—
> Your favors, the ambassadors of love;
> And in our maiden council rated them
> At courtship, pleasant jest, and courtesy,
> As bombast, and as lining to the time:
> But more devout than this, in our respects,
> Have we not been; and therefore met your loves
> In their own fashion, like a merriment.
> *Dum.* Our letters, madam, show'd much more than jest.
> *Long.* So did our looks.

* * * * * * * *

King. Now, at the latest minute of the hour,
Grant us your loves.
Prin. A time, methinks, too short
To make a world-without-end bargain in.
No, no, my lord; your grace is perjur'd much—
Full of dear guiltiness; and therefore this—
If for my love (as there is no such cause)
You will do aught, this shall you do for me:
Your oath I will not trust; but go with speed
To some forlorn and naked hermitage,
Remote from all the pleasures of the world;
There stay, until the twelve celestial signs
Have brought about their annual reckoning;
If this austere insociable life
Change not your offer made in heat of blood—
If frosts, and fasts, hard lodging, and thin weeds,
Nip not the gaudy blossoms of your love,
But that it bear this trial, and last love—
Then, at the expiration of the year,
Come challenge, challenge me by these deserts,
And, by this virgin palm, now kissing thine,
I will be thine; and, till that instant, shut
My woeful self up in a mourning house,
Raining the tears of lamentation
For the remembrance of my father's death.
If this thou do deny, let our hands part—
Neither intitled in the other's heart.

The opening address of the princess is, of course, only a coquettish ruse, not to be thought "too quickly won"—no one is better assured than she of the sincerity of the passion conveyed in those fantastic letters, and the rich gifts which bid fair to "wall about with diamonds" the "girls of France;" and none more happily confident that these "moon-like men" will steadfastly devote their twelvemonth of probation to the consummation of their loves.

MARGARET OF ANJOU.

THE eventful history of this celebrated princess, who "excelled all other in beauty and favor, as in wit and policy," constitutes the leading interest of the tedious, three-parted tragedy of *King Henry VI.*, wherein she appears, first as the daughter of Reignier, Duke of Anjou and Count of Provence, and afterwards as Queen Margaret of England, wife of Henry VI.

The action of this play, the legitimacy of which has been disputed and maintained, with equal astuteness, by Shakspearian scholars, is laid amid the turbulent scenes of the York and Lancaster struggle. Part First opens with the death of Henry V., whereupon his youthful son, Henry, ascends the throne under the protectorate of his uncle, the Duke of Gloster; it treats more particularly of the war with France, memorable for the heroism of Joan of Arc. In Part Second, the young king is married to the Princess Margaret of Anjou, who prevails upon her weak-minded husband to assume the reins of government—soon after which the kingdom is embroiled in the Civil War of the Roses; while Part Third is occupied with Henry's deposition from the throne, and Margaret's intriguing efforts to reinstate him—concluding with his murder by the Duke of Gloster.

Were the Margaret of Shakspeare—for it is not the Margaret of History of whom we have to speak—invested with any personal claims to our pathetic interest, a more pitiful picture than that afforded by the simple circumstances of her story could scarcely be offered to our sympathetic contemplation. A woman of excelling beauty and accomplishments, of indomitable spirit and unquailing courage, who, having been elevated to the exalted station of England's queen, lives to see her husband treacherously deposed from his throne, and finally murdered—her son having suffered the same fate before her eyes; her enemies in the full enjoyment of their guilty triumph; herself an outcast, so wretched that her life is not thought worth the taking: such a woman would seem to constitute an object of commiseration for the sternest beholder, aside from all individual attributes whatsoever; but Shakspeare has converted pity into detestation, by depicting Margaret as a faithless wife to a husband, noted for his gentle virtues, who idolized her—a ferocious, unrelenting enemy, a woman of petty spites and coarse cruelty.

This Margaret has all the ambition of Lady Macbeth; but, unlike hers, it is essentially vulgar in quality: she prefers to gain her ends by trivial, transparent subtleties, such as the dashing boldness of the thane's wife would have grandly disdained. She has the true Frenchwoman's love of political intrigue, without her proverbial tact; whatever she may achieve by her scheming, she as surely spoils by her maladroit rashness. The only situations in which we are permitted to regard Margaret with even tolerable kindness are these two: where she parts with her lover, Suffolk, who is banished by Henry after the murder of the "good duke Humphrey:"

> *Q. Mar.* Enough, sweet Suffolk: thou torment'st thyself;
> And these dread curses—like the sun 'gainst glass,
> Or like an overcharged gun—recoil,

And turn the force of them upon thyself.
Suf. You bade me ban, and will you bid me leave?
Now, by the ground that I am banish'd from,
Well could I curse away a winter's night,
Though standing naked on a mountain top,
Where biting cold would never let grass grow,
And think it but a minute spent in sport!
Q. Mar. O, let me entreat thee, cease! Give me thy hand,
That I may dew it with my mournful tears;
Nor let the rain of heaven wet this place,
To wash away my woeful monuments.
O could this kiss be printed in thy hand—
That thou might'st think upon these by the seal,
Through whom a thousand sighs are breathed for thee!

* * * * * * * * *

I will repeal thee—or, be well assured,
Adventure to be banished myself;
And banished I am, if but from thee.
Go! speak not to me; even now begone.—
O, go not yet!—Even thus two friends condemn'd
Embrace, and kiss, and take ten thousand leaves,
Loather a hundred times to part than die.
Yet now farewell; and farewell life with thee!
Suf. Thus is poor Suffolk ten times banished:
Once by the king, and three times thrice by thee.
'Tis not the land I care for, wert thou hence—
A wilderness is populous enough,
So Suffolk had thy heavenly company;
For where thou art, there is the world itself,
With every several pleasure in the world;
And where thou art not, desolation.
I can no more:—Live thou to joy thy life—
Myself no joy in nought, but that thou liv'st.

* * * * * * * *

Q. Mar. Away! Though parting be a fretful corrosive,
It is applied to a deathful wound.
To France, sweet Suffolk: Let me hear from thee;
For wheresoe'er thou art in this world's globe,
I'll have an Iris that shall find thee out.

—and where she upbraids her husband for having ignobly ceded his son's right of succession for the assurance of a peaceful reign to himself:

> Ah, wretched man! 'would I had died a maid,
> And never seen thee, never borne thee son,
> Seeing thou hast proved so unnatural a father!
> Hath he deserved to lose his birthright thus?
> Had'st thou but loved him half so well as I—
> Or felt that pain which I did for him once—
> Or nourish'd him, as I did with my blood—
> Thou wouldst have left thy dearest heart-blood there,
> Rather than made that savage duke thine heir,
> And disinherited thine only son.
> * * * * * * * * *
> *K. Hen.* Pardon me, Margaret;—pardon me, sweet son;—
> The earl of Warwick, and the duke, enforced me.
> *Q. Mar.* Enforced thee! Art thou king, and wilt be forc'd?
> I shame to hear thee speak. Ah, timorous wretch!
> Thou hast undone thyself, thy son, and me;
> And given unto the house of York such head
> As thou shalt reign but by their sufferance.
> To entail him and his heirs unto the crown,
> What is it but to make thy sepulchre,
> And creep into it far before thy time?
> * * * * * * *
> Had I been there, which am a silly woman,
> The soldiers should have toss'd me on their pikes,
> Before I would have granted to that act.
> But thou preferr'st thy life before thine honor;
> And, seeing thou dost, I here divorce myself,
> Both from thy table, Henry, and thy bed,
> Until that act of parliament be repealed,
> Whereby my son is disinherited.

Here her indignation is most just, its lofty spirit equally becoming to the mother and the queen.

Henry lives to see her words made good: the Duke of York is to all intents and purposes king, under the title of lord-protector;

while his final overthrow by Margaret, whose vigilance and energy in her husband's forlorn cause are untiring, displays with fine dramatic effect all the inhuman attributes of her character. The gibing malignity of her address to him, after he has been taken prisoner, is worthy of this "she-wolf of France," and inseparable from her characteristic spitefulness:

* * * * * * * * *
* * * * * * * * *

What! was it you that would be England's king?
Was 't you that revel'd in our parliament,
And made a preachment of your high descent?
Where are your mess of sons to back you now—
The wanton Edward, and the lusty George?
And where's that valiant crook-back prodigy,
Dicky your boy, that with his grumbling voice,
Was wont to cheer his dad in mutinies?
Or, with the rest, where is your darling Rutland?
Look, York! I stain'd this napkin with the blood
That valiant Clifford, with his rapier's point,
Made issue from the bosom of the boy;
And, if thine eyes can water for his death,
I give thee this to dry thy cheeks withal.
Alas, poor York! but that I hate thee deadly,
I should lament thy miserable state.
I pr'ythee grieve, to make me merry, York;
Stamp, rave, and fret, that I may sing and dance.
What! hath thy fiery heart so parch'd thine entrails,
That not a tear can fall for Rutland's death?
Why art thou patient, man? thou should'st be mad;
And I, to make thee mad, do mock thee thus.
Thou would'st be fee'd, I see, to make me sport;
York cannot speak, unless he wear a crown.—
A crown for York;—and, lords, bow low to him.—
Hold you his hands, whilst I do set it on.—
[*Putting a paper crown on his head.*
Ay, marry, sir, now looks he like a king!
Ay, this is he that took King Henry's chair;
And this is he was his adopted heir.—

But how is it that great Plantagenet
Is crown'd so soon, and broke his solemn oath?
As I bethink me, you should not be king,
Till our King Henry had shook hands with death.

After that murder of an innocent child, to avenge herself on the father, we can scarcely sympathize with her clamorous grief when her own son is pitilessly hacked to death at her feet; her denunciation of his "butchers" is no better than mockery, from the lips of a woman guilty of the same crime, committed in the wantonest spirit of malignity:

Q. Mar. O Ned, sweet Ned! speak to thy mother, boy!
Canst thou not speak? O traitors! murderers!—
They that stabb'd Cæsar shed no blood at all,
Did not offend, nor were not worthy blame,
If this foul deed were by, to equal it:
He was a man—this, in respect, a child;
And men ne'er spend their fury on a child.
What's worse than murderer, that I may name it?
No, no; my heart will burst, an if I speak;—
And I will speak, that so my heart may burst:—
Butchers and villains, bloody cannibals!
How sweet a plant have you untimely cropp'd!
You have no children, butchers! if you had,
The thought of them would have stir'd up remorse;
But if you ever chance to have a child,
Look in his youth to have him so cut off,
As, deathsmen, you have rid this sweet young prince!

We have the apparition of Queen Margaret in the play of *King Richard III.* also, where she presents the melancholy spectacle of defeated hopes, and a desolate old age spent in bitter imprecations, which seem to recoil with tenfold power upon her own head. Here she "stalks around the seat of her former greatness, like a terrible phantom of departed majesty," or like a "grim prophetess of evil," "filling the world with words" whose intensity of cursing seems, as she says, to "ease the heart." And it would appear that her curses were true inspirations, not simply vindictive volubility, for she survives to see them fulfilled with appalling exactness:

Q. Eliz. O, thou didst prophesy the time would come
That I should wish for thee to help me curse
That bottled spider, that foul bunch-back'd toad.
Q. Mar. I call'd thee, then, vain flourish of my fortune;
I call'd thee, then, poor shadow, painted queen—
The presentation of but what I was,
The flattering index of a direful pageant—
One heaved a-high, to be hurl'd down below:
A mother only mock'd with two fair babes;
A dream of what thou wast; a garish flag,
To be the aim of every dangerous shot;
A sign of dignity, a breath, a bubble;
A queen in jest, only to fill the scene.
Where is thy husband now? where be thy brothers?
Where be thy two sons? wherein dost thou joy?
Who sues, and kneels, and says,—God save the queen?
Where be the bending peers that flatter'd thee?
Where be the thronging troops that follow'd thee?
Decline all this, and see what now thou art:
For happy wife, a most distressed widow;
For joyful mother, one that wails the name;
For one being sued to, one that humbly sues;
For queen, a very caitiff crown'd with care.

The scene where, after the murder of the young princes in the Tower, the three women—Margaret, Queen Elizabeth, and the old Duchess of York—sworn foes till then, meet at the foot of the scaffold of their appalling wrongs and sorrows, is wrought with terrible effect:

Q. Mar. If ancient sorrow be most reverent,
Give mine the benefit of seniory,
And let my griefs frown on the upper hand.

If sorrow can admit society, [*Sitting down with them.*
Tell o'er your woes again by viewing mine:
I had an Edward, till a Richard kill'd him;
I had a husband, till a Richard kill'd him:
Thou hadst an Edward, till a Richard kill'd him;
Thou hadst a Richard, till a Richard kill'd him.
Duch. I had a Richard too, and thou didst kill him;
I had a Rutland too—thou holp'st to kill him.
Q. Mar. Thou hadst a Clarence too, and Richard kill'd him.
From forth the kennel of thy womb hath crept
A hell-hound, that doth hunt us all to death—
That dog, that had his teeth before his eyes,
To worry lambs, and lap their gentle blood—
That foul defacer of God's handy-work—
That excellent grand tyrant of the earth,
That reigns in galled eyes of weeping souls!
* * * * * * * *
Duch. O, Harry's wife, triumph not in my woes;
God witness with me, I have wept for thine.
Q. Mar. Bear with me; I am hungry for revenge,
And now I cloy me with beholding it.
Thy Edward he is dead, that kill'd my Edward;
Thy other Edward dead, to quit my Edward;
Young York he is but boot, because both they
Match not the high perfection of my loss.
Thy Clarence he is dead, that stabb'd my Edward,
And the beholders of this tragic play,
The adulterate Hastings, Rivers, Vaughan, Grey,
Untimely smother'd in their dusky graves.
Richard yet lives, hell's black intelligencer—
Only reserv'd their factor, to buy souls,
And send them thither. But at hand, at hand,
Ensues his piteous and unpitied end:
Earth gapes, hell burns, fiends roar, saints pray,
To have him suddenly convey'd from hence;—
Cancel his bond of life, dear God, I pray,
That I may live to say the dog is dead!

JOAN OF ARC.

It is a cruel trial for one's cherished romance to be compelled to turn from the spotless enthusiast, the gentle martyr of history, who has made this name famous, to the poor counterfeit and impostor who appears as the heroine of the first part of *King Henry VI.* The "La Pucelle" of Shakspeare is painted with the bitterest English prejudice, as half witch, half charlatan—a coarse, fighting, blood-thirsty Amazon, who, when made prisoner, condescends to an ignominious subterfuge to escape the death-sentence.

She is introduced to the prince-dauphin, during the desperate straits of the siege of Orleans, by the Bastard of Orleans, who addresses his royal master in these words:

> Methinks your looks are sad, your cheer appall'd;
> Hath the late overthrow wrought this offence?
> Be not dismay'd, for succor is at hand:
> A holy maid hither with me I bring,
> Which, by a vision sent to her from heaven,
> Ordained is to raise this tedious siege,
> And drive the English forth the bounds of France.
> The spirit of deep prophecy she hath,
> Exceeding the nine sibyls of old Rome;
> What's past, and what's to come, she can descry.

And to Charles, himself, she thus relates her story, and declares the mission she is charged with:

Dauphin, I am by birth a shepherd's daughter—
My wit untrain'd in any kind of art.
Heaven, and our Lady gracious, hath it pleas'd
To shine on my contemptible estate:
Lo, whilst I waited on my tender lambs,
And to sun's parching heat display'd my cheeks,
God's mother deigned to appear to me,
And, in a vision full of majesty,
Will'd me to leave my base vocation,
And free my country from calamity;
Her aid she promis'd, and assur'd success;
In complete glory she reveal'd herself;
And, whereas I was black and swart before,
With those clear rays which she infus'd on me
That beauty am I bless'd with which you see.
Ask me what question thou canst possible,
And I will answer unpremeditated;
My courage try by combat, if thou dar'st,
And thou shalt find that I exceed my sex.
Resolve on this: Thou shalt be fortunate,
If thou receive me for thy warlike mate.

La Pucelle is as good as her word; she forces an entrance to the town of Orleans, in the very teeth of the redoubtable John Talbot, "the scourge of France;" and at once the shepherd's daughter is deified by her grateful sovereign and her enthusiastic countrymen:

Puc. Advance our waving colors on the walls;
Rescu'd is Orleans from the English wolves:—
Thus Joan la Pucelle hath perform'd her word.
Char. Divinest creature, bright Astræa's daughter,
How shall I honor thee for this success?
Thy promises are like Adonis' gardens,
That one day bloom'd, and fruitful were the next.—

France, triumph in thy glorious prophetess!—
Recover'd is the town of Orleans;
More blessed hap did ne'er befall our state.
Reig. Why ring not out the bells throughout the town?
Dauphin, command the citizens make bonfires,
And feast and banquet in the open streets,
To celebrate the joy that God hath given us.

* * * * * * * *

Char. 'Tis Joan, not we, by whom the day is won;
For which I will divide my crown with her,
And all the priests and friars in my realm
Shall, in procession, sing her endless praise.
A statelier pyramis to her I'll rear
Than Rhodope's, or Memphis', ever was;
In memory of her, when she is dead,
Her ashes, in an urn more precious
Than the rich jewell'd coffer of Darius,
Transported shall be at high festivals
Before the kings and queens of France.
No longer on Saint Denis will we cry,
But Joan la Pucelle shall be France's saint.

One passage from the lips of our Joan of Arc is worthy of her great namesake—her exhortation to the Duke of Burgundy, who has joined the English forces against France:

Look on thy country, look on fertile France,
And see the cities and the towns defac'd
By wasting ruin of the cruel foe!
As looks the mother on her lowly babe,
When death doth close his tender dying eyes,
See, see, the pining malady of France;
Behold the wounds, the most unnatural wounds,
Which thou thyself hast given her woful breast!
O, turn thy edged sword another way—
Strike those that hurt, and hurt not those that help!
One drop of blood, drawn from thy country's bosom,
Should grieve thee more than streams of foreign gore;
Return thee, therefore, with a flood of tears,
And wash away thy country's stained spots!

Bur. Either she hath bewitch'd me with her words,
Or nature makes me suddenly relent.

In the Fifth Act we are treated to an episode of genuine witchcraft, over which the "holy maid" presides; by the desertion of her "familiars" we are prepared for her speedy downfall:

Puc. Now help, ye charming spells, and periapts;
And ye choice spirits that admonish me,
And give me signs of future accidents! [*Thunder.*
You speedy helpers, that are substitutes
Under the lordly monarch of the north,
Appear, and aid me in this enterprise!

Enter Fiends.

This speedy quick appearance argues proof
Of your accustom'd diligence to me.
Now, ye familiar spirits, that are cull'd
Out of the powerful regions under earth,
Help me this once, that France may get the field.
[*They walk about, and speak not.*
O, hold me not with silence over-long!
Where I was wont to feed you with my blood,
I'll lop a member off, and give it you,
In earnest of a further benefit;
So you do condescend to help me now.—
[*They hang their heads.*
No hope to have redress?—My body shall
Pay recompense, if you will grant my suit.
[*They shake their heads.*
Cannot my body, nor blood-sacrifice,
Entreat you to your wonted furtherance?
Then take my soul—my body, soul, and all—
Before that England give the French the foil.
[*They depart.*
See! they forsake me. Now the time is come,
That France must vail her lofty-plumed crest,
And let her head fall into England's lap.
My ancient incantations are too weak.

In the next martial encounter, therefore, we are not surprised to find her captured by the Duke of York, and at once condemned to die:

> *York.* Take her away; for she hath liv'd too long,
> To fill the world with vicious qualities.
> *Puc.* First, let me tell you whom you have condemn'd:
> *Not me begotten of a shepherd swain,*
> *But issu'd from the progeny of kings;*
> Virtuous, and holy; chosen from above,
> By inspiration of celestial grace,
> To work exceeding miracles on earth.
> I never had to do with wicked spirits;
> But you,—that are polluted with your lusts,
> Stain'd with the guiltless blood of innocents,
> Corrupt and tainted with a thousand vices,—
> Because you want the grace that others have,
> You judge it straight a thing impossible
> To compass wonders, but by help of devils.
> No, misconceiv'd! Joan of Arc hath been
> A virgin from her tender infancy,
> Chaste and immaculate in very thought—
> Whose maiden blood, thus rigorously effus'd,
> Will cry for vengeance at the gates of heaven.
> *York.* Ay, ay;——away with her to execution.
> *War.* And hark ye, sirs; because she is a maid,
> Spare for no fagots—let there be enough;
> Place barrels of pitch upon the fatal stake,
> That so her torture may be shortened.
> * * * * * * * * *
> *Puc.* Will nothing turn your unrelenting hearts?—
> Then, Joan, discover thine infirmity,
> That warranteth by law to be thy privilege:—
> I am with child, ye bloody homicides:
> Murder not then the fruit within my womb,
> Although ye hale me to a violent death.

LADY GREY.

Lady Elizabeth Grey, widow of Sir John Grey, and wife of Edward IV. of England, shares with Queen Margaret the sorrows of one tragedy, and, by her sufferings at the hands of the monster Duke of Gloster, constitutes a feature of melancholy interest in another.

She first appears as the widow Grey, pleading to King Edward for the restitution of certain lands which "were seized on by the conqueror," when her husband was slain at the battle of Saint Albans. In this interview the lady conducts herself with so much grace and discretion, that, notwithstanding the Earl of Warwick is negotiating for his sovereign at the French court, for the hand of the Lady Bona, sister of Louis XI., Edward falls in love with her, and makes the granting of her suit dependent on her acceptance of himself for a husband:

> *K. Edw.* Widow, we will consider of your suit;
> And come some other time to know our mind.
> *L. Grey.* Right gracious lord, I cannot brook delay;
> May it please your highness to resolve me now;
> And what your pleasure is shall satisfy me.
> *   *   *   *   *   *   *   *
> *K. Edw.* An easy task; 'tis but to love a king.

L. Grey. That's soon perform'd, because I am a subject.

* * * * * * * * *

K. Edw. Ay, but I fear me, in another sense.
What love, think'st thou, I sue so much to get?
L. Grey. My love till death, my humble thanks, my prayers:
That love which virtue begs and virtue grants.
K. Edw. No, by my troth, I did not mean such love.

* * * * * * * * *

L. Grey. My mind will never grant what I perceive
Your highness aims at, if I aim aright.

* * * * * * * * * *

K. Edw. Why, then thou shalt not have thy husband's lands.
L. Grey. Why, then mine honesty shall be my dower;
For by that loss I will not purchase them.
K. Edw. Therein thou wrong'st thy children mightily.
L. Grey. Herein your highness wrongs both them and me.
But, mighty lord, this merry inclination
Accords not with the sadness of my suit;
Please you dismiss me either with ay or no.
K. Edw. Ay; if thou wilt say ay to my request:
No; if thou dost say no to my demand.
L. Grey. Then no, my lord. My suit is at an end.
K. Edw. [*Aside.*] Her looks do argue her replete with modesty;
Her words do show her wit incomparable.
All her perfections challenge sovereignty:
One way or other she is for a king;
And she shall be my love, or else my queen.—
Say that King Edward take thee for his queen?
L. Grey. 'Tis better said than done, my gracious lord:
I am a subject fit to jest withal,
But far unfit to be a sovereign.
K. Edw. Sweet widow, by my state I swear to thee,
I speak no more than what my soul intends;

* * * * * * * *

Answer no more, for thou shalt be my queen.

And so the poor lady—a retiring, tender-hearted gentlewoman, fitted only for the secluded yet not undignified estate to which fortune had called her—becomes Edward's crowned queen, a very lamb tossed to the ravening wolves of that reign of terror. Where Margaret, of iron nerves, dauntless will, and almost equal ferocity, has been trodden under foot, what better fate can be hoped for this gentle mother and modest housewife, who has ignorantly dared to assume a position so perilous?

"Small joy," indeed, has she "in being England's queen"—"baited, scorn'd, and storm'd at," by her fierce brothers-in-law during her husband's life, and after his death their unspared victim. Not only does Richard usurp the throne, of which he is lord-protector during the minority of his nephew, but the royal youngling and his brother are, by his order, murdered in the Tower.

The wretched mother's farewell exhortation to the prison which contains her infant sons, from whom she is debarred, has been justly pronounced one of the most beautiful passages in the play:

> *Q. Eliz.* Stay yet; look back, with me, unto the Tower.—
> Pity, you ancient stones, those tender babes,
> Whom envy hath immured within your walls!
> Rough cradle for such little pretty ones!
> Rude ragged nurse! old sullen play-fellow
> For tender princes, use my babies well!
> So foolish sorrow bids your stones farewell.

Were the wooer any other than the arch-fiend Richard himself, we should protest against the possibility that even so weak a woman, as this queen in spite of herself, could consent to wed her daughter to the crook-backed villain; but there is no resisting his wily tongue—she falls into the snare with dreadful compliance; Heaven alone saved the helpless young girl from so fatal a consummation:

> *K. Rich.* Be not so hasty to confound my meaning;
> I mean that with my soul I love thy daughter,

And do intend to make her queen of England.

* * * * * * * * *

* * * * * * * * *

The king that calls your beauteous daughter wife,
Familiarly shall call thy Dorset brother;
Again shall you be mother to a king,
And all the ruins of distressful times
Repair'd with double riches of content.
What! we have many goodly days to see;
The liquid drops of tears that you have shed
Shall come again, transform'd to orient pearl,
Advantaging their loan with interest
Of ten times double gain of happiness.
Go, then, my mother—to thy daughter go;
Make bold her bashful years with your experience;
Prepare her ears to hear a wooer's tale;
Put in her tender heart the aspiring flame
Of golden sovereignty. * * * * *

* * * * * * * * * *

Q. Eliz. What were I best to say? her father's brother
Would be her lord? Or shall I say her uncle?
Or he that slew her brothers, and her uncles?
Under what title shall I woo for thee,
That God, the law, my honor, and her love
Can make seem pleasing to her tender years?

* * * * * * * *

K. Rich. As I intend to prosper, and repent!
So thrive I in my dangerous attempt
Of hostile arms! myself myself confound!
Heaven, and fortune, bar me happy hours!
Day, yield me not thy light; nor, night, thy rest!
Be opposite all planets of good luck
To my proceeding! if, with pure heart's love,
Immaculate devotion, holy thoughts,
I tender not thy beauteous princely daughter!

* * * * * * * * *

Therefore, dear mother, (I must call you so,)
Be the attorney of my love to her.
Plead what I will be, not what I have been;
Not my deserts, but what I will deserve;

Urge the necessity and state of times,
And be not peevish found in great designs.
Q. Eliz. Shall I be tempted of the devil thus?
*   *   *   *   *   *   *   *   *
Shall I go win my daughter to thy will?
K. Rich. And be a happy mother by the deed.
Q. Eliz. I go.—Write to me very shortly,
And you shall understand from me her mind.
K. Rich. Bear her my true love's kiss, and so farewell.
[*Kissing her.* *Exit* Q. ELIZABETH.
Relenting fool, and shallow, changing—woman!

LADY ANNE.

This lady, the eldest daughter of that renowned "setter up and plucker down of kings," the Earl of Warwick, was twice married—first to Edward, Prince of Wales, son of Henry VI., by Margaret of Anjou; and afterward to Richard, Duke of Gloster.

The scene in *King Richard III.*, where, even in the act of following the corse of her father-in-law to the grave, she is wooed and won by his murderer, who had also "cropp'd the golden prime of the sweet prince," her husband, leaves nothing to be desired as an exemplification of her character. That demonstrates her a woman, doubtless of good intentions and a sufficiently kind heart, but lamentably deficient in intellect and the plainest common sense—without any fixed principles or opinions, or the simply natural impulses of a saving pride. We grant the irresistible fascination, that would exist for such a woman as Anne, in the towering superiority, the flashing audacity of Richard—and he purposely makes a display of it by threatening the gentlemen who bear the body; but nothing is truer of her than that "in a less critical moment a far less subtle and audacious seducer would have sufficed."

She is an eminent example of weakness, the effects of which are scarcely less deplorable than those of deliberate criminality; nor do they differ from those materially. In her community of good and bad fellow-creatures she exists a negative abstraction, equally ready to be good or bad, as any one, for selfish purposes, may take the pains to influence her.

With Anne, Richard appeals to her personal vanity, her propensity to inspire passion, as, subsequently with Elizabeth, he tempts maternal ambition; but in both cases it is himself—his wily words, and, above all, his own implicit faith in the infallibility of his arguments—that constitutes the most dangerous snare·

Anne. What! do you tremble? are you all afraid?
Alas! I blame you not; for you are mortal,
And mortal eyes cannot endure the devil.—
Avaunt, thou dreadful minister of hell!
Thou hadst but power over his mortal body—
His soul thou canst not have; therefore, begone!
Glo. Sweet saint, for charity, be not so curst.
Anne. Foul devil! for God's sake, hence, and trouble us not;
For thou hast made the happy earth thy hell,
Fill'd it with cursing cries, and deep exclaims.
If thou delight to view thy heinous deeds,
Behold this pattern of thy butcheries:
* * * * * * * *
Glo. Lady, you know no rules of charity,
Which renders good for bad, blessings for curses.
Anne. Villain, thou know'st no law of God nor man;
No beast so fierce but knows some touch of pity.
Glo. But I know none, and therefore am no beast.
Anne. O wonderful, when devils tell the truth!
Glo. More wonderful, when angels are so angry.—
Vouchsafe, divine perfection of a woman,
Of these supposed evils to give me leave,
By circumstance, but to acquit myself.
* * * * * * * *
* * * * * * * *
Your beauty was the cause of that effect;
Your beauty, which did haunt me in my sleep

To undertake the death of all the world,
So I might live one hour in your sweet bosom.

* * * * * * * * *

I never su'd to friend nor enemy:
My tongue could never learn sweet soothing word;
But now thy beauty is propos'd my fee,
My proud heart sues, and prompts my tongue to speak.
[*She looks scornfully on him.*
Teach not thy lip such scorn; for it was made
For kissing, lady, not for such contempt.
If thy revengeful heart cannot forgive,
Lo! here I lend thee this sharp-pointed sword!
Which if thou please to hide in this true breast,
And let the soul forth that adoreth thee,
I lay it naked to the deadly stroke,
And humbly beg the death upon my knee.
[*He lays his breast open; she offers at it with his sword.*
Nay, do not pause; for I did kill King Henry;—
But 'twas thy beauty that provoked me.
Nay, now despatch; 'twas I that stabb'd young Edward:—
[*She again offers at his breast.*
But 'twas thy heavenly face that set me on.
[*She lets fall the sword.*
Take up the sword again, or take up me.
Anne. Arise, dissembler: though I wish thy death,
I will not be thy executioner.

* * * * * * *

I would I knew thy heart.
Glo. 'Tis figur'd in
My tongue.
Anne. I fear me both are false.
Glo. Then man
Was never true.
Anne. Well, well, put up your sword.
Glo. Say, then, my peace is made.
Anne. That shall you know
Hereafter.
Glo. But shall I live in hope?

Anne. All men,
I hope, live so.
Glo. Vouchsafe to wear this ring.
Anne. To take is not to give. [*She puts on the ring.*
Glo. Look, how this ring encompasseth thy finger,
Even so thy breast encloseth my poor heart;
Wear both of them, for both of them are thine.
And if thy poor devoted servant may
But beg one favor at thy gracious hand,
Thou dost confirm his happiness forever.

* * * * * * * * * *

Anne. With all my heart; and much it joys me, too,
To see you are become so penitent.—
Tressel and Berkley, go along with me.

With all our appreciation of the gentleness of this "gentle Lady Anne," "ay, too gentle," we cannot forbear ejaculating with Richard, himself:

Was ever woman in this humor woo'd?
Was ever woman in this humor won?
I'll have her,—but I will not keep her long.
What! I, that kill'd her husband, and his father,
To take her in her heart's extremest hate—
With curses in her mouth, tears in her eyes,
The bleeding witness of her hatred by—
With God, her conscience, and these bars against me,
And I no friends to back my suit withal,
But the plain devil, and dissembling looks,
And yet to win her?—all the world to nothing!

When we next meet her, she is summoned to her coronation; and it is a touching picture that she gives us of the grievous penance she has undergone for that blundering hour of flattered vanity:

Stan. * * * * * * *
Come, madam, you must straight to Westminster,

There to be crowned Richard's royal queen.

*   *   *   *   *   *   *   *   *   *

*   *   *   *   *   *   *   *   *   *

Anne. And I with all unwillingness will go.—
O, would to God that the inclusive verge
Of golden metal, that must round my brow,
Were red-hot steel, to sear me to the brain!
Anointed let me be with deadly venom—
And die, ere men can say God Save the Queen!

*   *   *   *   *   *   *   *   *

When he, that is my husband now,
Came to me, as I followed Henry's corse—
When scarce the blood was well wash'd from his hands,
Which issu'd from my other angel husband,
And that dead saint which then I weeping follow'd—
O, when, I say, I look'd on Richard's face,
This was my wish,—*Be thou*, quoth I, *accurs'd,*
For making me, so young, so old a widow!
And, when thou wed'st, let sorrow haunt thy bed;
And be thy wife (if any be so mad)
More miserable by the life of thee
Than thou hast made me by my dear lord's death!
Lo, ere I can repeat this curse again,
Even in so short a space, my woman's heart
Grossly grew captive to his honey words,
And prov'd the subject of mine own soul's curse,
Which ever since hath held mine eyes from rest;
For never yet one hour in his bed
Did I enjoy the golden dew of sleep,
But with his timorous dreams was still awak'd.
Besides, he hates me for my father Warwick;
And will, no doubt, shortly be rid of me.

And when, at last, poor Anne "has bid the world good-night," and Gloster is already promised another bride, her ghost appears to her guilty husband—to swell the horrors of his sleep before the battle in which he is doomed to fall, and like the rest of his supernatural visitants, victims of his cruelty, to pronounce a malediction:

The Ghost *of* QUEEN ANNE *rises.*

Ghost. Richard, thy wife, that wretched Anne thy wife,
That never slept a quiet hour with thee,
Now fills thy sleep with perturbations;
To-morrow in the battle think on me,
And fall thy edgeless sword. Despair, and die!

LADY PERCY.

Lady Katharine Percy, wife of young Harry Percy—surnamed Hotspur, for the fiery recklessness of his character—can scarcely be denominated the heroine of *King Henry IV.*, because, properly speaking, that play is constructed without one; but as she is the only female character in the serious part of the dramatic action, she may claim that honor without challenging invidious comparison.

King Henry IV., in its two parts, treats, on the one hand, of the revolts of discontented nobles against the king—being, so far, of the "drum and trumpet" type; and on the other, gives us the adventures of the mad-cap heir apparent, Prince Henry, in company with his boon companion, Sir John Falstaff.

The part of Lady Percy is a mere miniature sketch, noticeable only for its fidelity to every-day human nature, and contained in two or three short scenes in the domestic life of the spoilt-child wife of a hot-headed young warrior, who, his soul all alive with the blaze and din of battle-fields, is accustomed to pet her with good-natured contempt.

She is young, fond and proud of her gallant Hotspur, innocent and engaging; but she has no peculiar traits, mental or moral.

The nature of the conjugal relation between a pair so opposed, is best exemplified by the scene where Percy takes leave of his wife, before going to the wars:

Hot. * * * * * * * *
How now, Kate? I must leave you within these two hours.
Lady P. O, my good lord, why are you thus alone?
For what offence have I, this fortnight, been
A banish'd woman from my Harry's bed?
Tell me, sweet lord, what is't that takes from thee
Thy stomach, pleasure, and thy golden sleep?
Why dost thou bend thine eyes upon the earth,
And start so often when thou sitt'st alone?
Why hast thou lost the fresh blood in thy cheeks,
And given my treasures, and my rights of thee,
To thick-ey'd musing, and curs'd melancholy?
In thy faint slumbers I by thee have watch'd,
And heard thee murmur tales of iron wars,
Speak terms of manage to thy bounding steed,
Cry, *Courage!—to the field!* * * * *
* * * * * O, what portents are these?
Some heavy business hath my lord in hand,
And I must know it, else he loves me not—
* * * * * * * *
What is it carries you away?
Hot. My horse,
My love, my horse. * * * *
Away, away, you trifler! Love? I love thee not—
I care not for thee, Kate. * * *
* * * * * Gods me, my horse!
What say'st thou, Kate? what would'st thou have with me?
Lady P. Do you not love me? do you not, indeed?
* * * * * Do you not love me?
Nay, tell me, if you speak in jest or no.
Hot. Come, wilt thou see me ride?
And when I am o' horseback I will swear
I love thee infinitely. But hark you, Kate—
I must not have you henceforth question me
Whither I go, nor reason whereabout:
Whither I must, I must; and, to conclude,

This evening must I leave you, gentle Kate.
I know you wise—but yet no further wise
Than Harry Percy's wife; constant you are—
But yet a woman; and for secresy,
No lady closer—for I well believe
Thou wilt not utter what thou dost not know;
And so far will I trust thee, gentle Kate!

At the battle of Shrewsbury, the gallant Hotspur falls, mortally wounded by Prince Henry; and in the Second Part of *King Henry IV.*, we find, in dismal contrast to the playful, pouting, self-willed young wife, the subdued, grief-stricken widow. In her appeal to her Harry's father to "go not to these wars," she pronounces a beautiful eulogium on her dead soldier, replete with eloquent pathos:

O, yet, for God's sake, go not to these wars!
The time was, father, that you broke your word
When you were more endear'd to it than now—
When your own Percy, when my heart's dear Harry,
Threw many a northward look, to see his father
Bring up his powers; but he did long in vain.
Who then persuaded you to stay at home?
There were two honors lost—yours and your son's.
For yours—may heavenly glory brighten it!
For his, it stuck upon him, as the sun
In the gray vault of heaven; and by his light
Did all the chivalry of England move
To do brave acts; * * * * *
* * * * So that, in speech, in gait,
In diet, in affections of delight,
In military rules, humors of blood,
He was the mark and glass, copy and book,
That fashion'd others. * * * *
* * * * —let them alone:
The marshal and the archbishop are strong;
Had my sweet Harry had but half their numbers,
To-day might I, hanging on Hotspur's neck,
Have talk'd of Monmouth's grave.

THE PRINCESS KATHARINE.

The play of *King Henry V.*, which concludes with the marriage of the daughter of Charles VI. to the English monarch, Henry, commemorates the latter's extensive conquests in France, and though chiefly occupied with martial exploits, is not altogether devoid of the comic element. This is especially noticeable in Henry's broken-French wooing of the Princess Katharine, who is equally ignorant of English.

The princess, herself, is the familiar model of the *bien élevé* French demoiselle—shy, excessively circumspect, and very chary of words. She is quite overwhelmed by the tempestuous suit of the bluff "king of good fellows;" but is plainly flattered by the prospect of being queen of England.

Besides this scene with King Henry, she appears only once; and then, with admirable prescience of her coming good fortune, she takes a lesson in English from her lady-in-waiting. As for *character* in a demoiselle of gentle breeding, to be even suspected of having one "*devant ses noces*," that "is not be," in the words of the naive interpreter, "de fashion *pour les* ladies of France," any more than the granting of a kiss to a lover—a maxim of national etiquette, by the by, which King Hal expounds with practical cleverness:

K. Hen. Fair Katharine, and most fair!
Will you vouchsafe to teach a soldier terms,
Such as will enter at a lady's ear,
And plead his love-suit to her gentle heart?

Kath. Your majesty shall mock at me; I cannot speak your England.

K. Hen. O fair Katharine, if you will love me soundly with your French heart, I will be glad to hear you confess it brokenly with your English tongue. Do you like me, Kate?

Kath. Pardonnez moy, I cannot tell vat is—like me.

K. Hen. An angel is like you, Kate; and you are like an angel.

Kath. Que dit-il? que je suis semblable à les anges?

Alice. Ouy, vrayment, (sauf vostre grace,) ainsi dit-il.

K. Hen. I said so, dear Katharine; and I must not blush to affirm it.

Kath. O bon Dieu! les langues des hommes sont pleines des tromperies.

K. Hen. What says she, fair one? that the tongues of men are full of deceits?

Alice. Ouy; dat de tongues of de mans is be full of deceits: dat is de princess.

K. Hen. Marry, if you would put me to verses, or to dance for your sake, Kate, why you undid me; for I speak to thee plain soldier: If thou canst love me for this, take me; if not, to say to thee that I shall die, is true; but, for thy love—by the Lord, no; yet I love thee too. And while thou livest, dear Kate, take a fellow of plain and uncoined constancy; for he perforce must do thee right, because he hath not the gift to woo in other places; for these fellows of infinite tongue, that can rhyme themselves into ladies' favors,—they do always reason themselves out again. If thou would have such a one, take me; and take me, take a soldier; take a soldier, take a king: And what sayest thou then to my love? speak, my fair, and fairly, I pray thee.

Kath. Is it possible dat I should love de enemy of France?

K. Hen. No; it is not possible you should love the

enemy of France, Kate; but, in loving me, you should love the friend of France; for I love France so well, that I will not part with a village of it; I will have it all mine; and, Kate, when France is mine, and I am yours, then yours is France, and you are mine.

Kath. I cannot tell vat is dat.

K. Hen. Now fye upon my false French! By mine honor, in true English, I love thee, Kate; by which honor I dare not swear thou lovest me; yet my blood begins to flatter me that thou dost, notwithstanding the poor and untempering effect of my visage. And therefore tell me, most fair Katharine—will you have me? Put off your maiden blushes; avouch the thoughts of your heart with the looks of an empress; take me by the hand, and say—Harry of England, I am thine: which word thou shalt no sooner bless mine ear withal, but I will tell thee, aloud, England is thine, Ireland is thine, France is thine, and Henry Plantagenet is thine—who, though I speak it before his face, if he be not fellow with the best king, thou shalt find the best king of good fellows. Come, your answer in broken music—for thy voice is music, and thy English broken; therefore queen of all, Katharine, break thy mind to me in broken English: Wilt thou have me?

Kath. Dat is as it shall please de *roy mon pere*.

K. Hen. Nay, it will please him well, Kate; it shall please him, Kate.

Kath. Den it shall also content me.

K. Hen. Upon that I will kiss your hand, and I call you—my queen.

Kath. Laissez, mon seigneur, laissez, laissez! ma foy, je ne veux point que vous abbaissez vostre grandeur, en baisant la main d'une vostre indigne serviteure! excusez moy, je vous supplie, mon tres puissant seigneur.

K. Hen. Then I will kiss your lips, Kate.

Kath. Les dames, et damoiselles, pour estre baisées devant leur nopces, il n'est pas le coútume de France.

K. Hen. Madam my interpreter, what says she?

Alice. Dat it is not be de fashion *pour les* ladies of France,—I cannot tell what is, *baiser*, *en* English.

K. Hen. To kiss.

Alice. Your majesty *entendre* bettre *que moy.*

K. Hen. It is not the fashion for the maids in France to kiss before they are married, would she say?

Alice. Ouy, vrayment.

K. Hen. O Kate, nice customs curt'sy to great kings. Dear Kate, you and I cannot be confined within the weak list of a country's fashion: we are the makers of manners, Kate; and the liberty that follows our places, stops the mouths of all find-faults—as I will do yours, for upholding the nice fashion of your country, in denying me a kiss; therefore, patiently and yielding. [*Kissing her.*] You have witchcraft in your lips, Kate; there is more eloquence in a sugar touch of them than in the tongues of the French council; and they should sooner persuade Harry of England than a general petition of monarchs.

PORTIA.

This lady, daughter of Cato, and wife of Marcus Brutus, is introduced with grateful effect in the tragedy of *Julius Cæsar*, affording relief, by her truly feminine presence, to that painful record of "treason, stratagems," and foul conspiracy.

Portia is the just impersonation of a matron "after the high Roman fashion,"—carefully finished, and severely classic in its lightest touches. Full of sensibility, tenderness, and all the timid flutterings of her sex, she yet entertains lofty ideas of the heroic fortitude, severe virtues, and unflinching nerve that become "Cato's daughter," and "the woman that Lord Brutus took to wife;" and in her unavailing self-discipline to attain those stoical perfections, she presents one more example of the ineffectuality of the "schools" to divert the natural bent of the female character.

"For the picture of this wedded couple, at once august and tender," says Campbell, "human nature, and the dignity of conjugal faith, are indebted;" it is almost the only instance, among all of Shakspeare's married people, in which, long after the honeymoon has departed, the wife is neither the *master*, slave, nor pretty toy of her husband:

Bru. Portia, what mean you? Wherefore rise you now?
It is not for your health, thus to commit
Your weak condition to the raw-cold morning.

Por. Nor for yours neither. You have ungently, Brutus,
Stole from my bed. And yesternight, at supper,
You suddenly arose, and walked about,
Musing, and sighing, with your arms across;
And when I ask'd you what the matter was,
You star'd upon me with ungentle looks.
I urged you further; then you scratch'd your head,
And too impatiently stamp'd with your foot;
Yet I insisted, yet you answer'd not—
But, with an angry wafture of your hand,
Gave sign for me to leave you: So I did.
* * * * * * Dear my lord,
Make me acquainted with your cause of grief.

Bru. I am not well in health, and that is all.

Por. Brutus is wise; and, were he not in health,
He would embrace the means to come by it.

Bru. Why, so I do.—Good Portia, go to bed.

Por. * * * * * * *
* * * * * No, my Brutus;
You have some sick offence within your mind,
Which, by the right and virtue of my place,
I ought to know of: And, upon my knees,
I charm you, by my once commended beauty,
By all your vows of love, and that great vow
Which did incorporate and make us one,
That you unfold to me, yourself, your half,
Why you are heavy. * * * *
* * * * * * * *

Bru. Kneel not, gentle Portia.

Por. I should not need, if you were gentle Brutus.
Within the bond of marriage, tell me, Brutus,
Is it excepted I should know no secrets
That appertain to you? Am I yourself
But, as it were, in sort, or limitation—
To keep with you at meals, comfort your bed,
And talk to you sometimes? Dwell I but in the suburbs
Of your good pleasure? If it be no more,

Portia is Brutus' harlot, not his wife.
Bru. You are my true and honorable wife,
As dear to me as are the ruddy drops
That visit my sad heart.
Por. If this were true, then should I know this secret.
I grant I am a woman—but, withal,
A woman that Lord Brutus took to wife;
I grant I am a woman—but, withal,
A woman well reputed—Cato's daughter.
Think you I am no stronger than my sex,
Being so father'd, and so husbanded?
Tell me your counsels—I will not disclose them:
I have made strong proof of my constancy,
Giving myself a voluntary wound,
Here, in the thigh. Can I bear that with patience,
And not my husband's secrets?
Bru. O ye gods,
Render me worthy of this noble wife!—
Hark! hark! one knocks: Portia, go in awhile;
And by and by thy bosom shall partake
The secrets of my heart.
All my engagements I will construe to thee.

The scene where Portia, aware of the plot to kill Cæsar in the capitol, sends her page thither to gather tidings for her agonized suspense, is full of spirit; the natural excitability and weak tremors of the woman are portrayed to the life, and prove the worthlessness of her boasted philosophy to keep her heart down, when it starts up alarmed for her husband's safety:

Por. I pr'ythee, boy, run to the senate-house;
Stay not to answer me, but get thee gone—
Why dost thou stay?
Luc. To know my errand, madam.
Por. I would have had thee there, and here again,
Ere I can tell thee what thou should'st do there.—
O constancy, be strong upon my side!
Set a huge mountain 'tween my heart and tongue!
I have a man's mind, but a woman's might.

How hard it is for women to keep counsel!—
* * * * * * * * *
Bring me word, boy, if thy lord look well,
For he went sickly forth. And take good note
What Cæsar doth, what suitors press to him.
Hark, boy! what noise is that?
* * * * * * * *
* * * Ah me! how weak a thing
The heart of woman is! O Brutus!
The heavens speed thee in thine enterprise!
Sure, the boy heard me:—Brutus hath a suit
That Cæsar will not grant.—O, I grow faint:—
Run, Lucius, and commend me to my lord;
Say I am merry. Come to me again,
And bring me word what he doth say to thee.

But alas for this gentle lady of "a man's mind, but a woman's might!" these alternations of hope, fear, suspense, and heroic efforts at self-command, are too much for her delicate organization; in a fit of wild distraction she puts an end to her life. Her husband thus communicates the grievous tidings to his friend Cassius:

Bru. O Cassius, I am sick of many griefs.
Cas. Of your philosophy you make no use,
If you give place to accidental evils.
Bru. No man bears sorrow better:—Portia is dead.
Cas. Ha! Portia?
Bru. She is dead.
Cas. How scap'd I killing, when I cross'd you so?
O insupportable and touching loss!—
Upon what sickness?
Bru. Impatient of my absence,
And grief that young Octavius with Mark Antony
Have made themselves so strong;—for with her death
That tidings came. With this she fell distract;
And, her attendants absent, swallow'd fire.
Cas. And died so?
Bru. Even so.
Cas. O ye immortal gods!

VIRGILIA.

The Virgilia of *Coriolanus*, wife of the Roman hero, is a pleasing outline study of the patrician lady of that classic period. In her conjugal devotion, her "gracious silence," and her shrinking modesty—befitting a virgin, rather than the wife of the renowned Marcius, and the mother of his boy—she is strongly contrasted with her mother-in-law, Volumnia, whose grand patriotism, stately pride of intellect and blood, and lofty spirit, constitute her a representative matron of old Rome.

In the dramatic action, as well as in her domestic relations, Virgilia is entirely subordinate to Volumnia; Marcius is a tender husband, but his mother is the inspiration of his most famous achievements, and hers the only influence he acknowledges—Virgilia has neither the intellect, nor the desire, to control his haughty spirit.

After the departure of Marcius for the wars against the Volcians, whence he returns distinguished with the name of Coriolanus, these two ladies are discovered in a home scene, full of the charm of privacy and feminine ways, sitting on "low stools" at their "stitchery;" they are interrupted in their conversation by a call from the Lady Valeria, "the noble sister of Publicola, the moon of Rome."

The talk between the mother and her son's wife concerning their mutual idol, Marcius—the heroic love of glory in the one, opposed to the timid tenderness of the other—discriminates with much nicety their widely contrasted characters:

Vol. I pray you, daughter, sing; or express yourself in a more comfortable sort. If my son were my husband, I should freelier rejoice in that absence wherein he won honor.
* * * * * * * * * When yet he was but tender-bodied, and the only son of my womb; when youth with comeliness plucked all gaze his way; when, for a day of king's entreaties, a mother should not sell him an hour from her beholding—I, considering how honor would become such a person—that it was no better than picture-like, to hang by the wall, if renown made it not stir—was pleased to let him seek danger where he was like to find fame. To a cruel war I sent him; from whence he returned, his brows bound with oak. I tell thee, daughter, I sprang not more in joy at first hearing he was a man-child, than now in first seeing he had proved himself a man.

Vir. But had he died in the business, madam? how then?

Vol. Then his good report should have been my son; I therein would have found issue;

* * * * * * * * *

Methinks I hear hither your husband's drum—
See him pluck Aufidius down by the hair—
As children from a bear, the Volces shunning him;
Methinks I see him stamp thus, and call thus,—
Come on, you cowards! you were got in fear,
Though you were born in Rome. His bloody brow
With his mail'd hand then wiping, forth he goes—
Like to a harvest-man, that's task'd to mow
Or all, or lose his hire.

Vir. His bloody brow! O, Jupiter, no blood!

Vol. Away, you fool! it more becomes a man
Than gilt his trophy: The breasts of Hecuba,
When she did suckle Hector, look'd not lovelier
Than Hector's forehead when it spit forth blood
At Grecian swords' contending.—Tell Valeria
We are fit to bid her welcome.
Vir. Heavens bless my lord from fell Aufidius.
Vol. He'll beat Aufidius' head below his knee,
And tread upon his neck.

And yet, to a woman, who alone can appreciate the temptation, Virgilia's persistent resistance of her friend's and her mother's entreaties to "go forth with them," bespeaks a quiet firmness of purpose, for which, with her usual soft yielding, one would scarce give her credit:

Val. How do you both? you are manifest house-keepers. What! are you sewing here? A fine spot in good faith.

* * * * * * * * *

Come lay aside your stitchery; I must have you play the idle huswife with me this afternoon.

Vir. No, good madam; I will not out of doors.

Val. Not out of doors!

Vol. She shall, she shall.

Vir. Indeed, no, by your patience: I will not over the threshold, till my lord returns from the wars.

Val. Fye! you confine yourself most unreasonably.

* * * * * * * *

Vol. Why, I pray you?

Vir. 'Tis not to save labor, nor that I want love.

Val. You would be another Penelope; yet, they say, all the yarn she spun, in Ulysses' absence, did but fill Ithaca full of moths. Come; I would your cambric were as sensible as your finger, that you might leave pricking it for pity. Come, you shall go with us.

Vir. No, good madam—pardon me; indeed, I will not orth.

Vol. Let her alone, lady; as she is now, she will but disease our better mirth.

Val. In troth, I think she would:—Fare you well then.—Come, good sweet lady.—Pry'thee, Virgilia, turn thy solemness out o'door, and go along with us.

Vir. No—at a word, madam; indeed, I must not. I wish you much mirth.

Val. Well then, farewell.

The separate individualities of the two ladies are also clearly shown in their manner of receiving the tidings of their absent warrior; Volumnia proudly rejoices in that which fills the gentle soul of Virgilia with unqualified horror:

Vol. Honorable Menenius, my boy Marcius approaches; for the love of Juno, let's go.

Men. * * * * *

* * * * * Is he not wounded? he was wont to come home wounded.

Vir. O, no, no, no!

Vol. O, he is wounded—I thank the gods for't!

* * * * * * * * * *

Lo, on's brows, Menenius! he comes the third time home with the oaken garland.

So, too, their several receptions of him on his return from victory:

Cor. O!
You have, I know, petition'd all the gods
For my prosperity. [*Kneels.*
Vol. Nay, my good soldier, up!
My gentle Marcius, worthy Caius, and
By deed-achieving honor newly nam'd—
What is it? Coriolanus, must I call thee?
But O, thy wife——
Cor. My gracious silence, hail!
Would'st thou have laugh'd had I come coffin'd home,
That weep'st to see me triumph? Ah, my dear,
Such eyes the widows in Corioli wear,
And mothers that lack sons.

When Coriolanus is banished, Virgilia is overwhelmed with grief; it leaves her no words—only pitiful ejaculations; but Volumnia stuns the ears of her ungrateful countrymen with her curses, her accusations, her withering sarcasm.

And again, on the occasion of Volumnia's grand triumph over her son's headlong determination of revenge, this "most noble mother in the world" appeals to him in a torrent of immortal eloquence; Virgilia, with no other arguments than the tears in "those doves' eyes, which can make gods forsworn"—her hands raised to heaven, she kneeling, with her boy, in the dust.

LAVINIA.

Lavinia, daughter of Titus Andronicus, a Roman general, and wife of Bassianus, brother to the emperor, is the heroine of that revolting tragedy which bears her father's name.

"Gracious Lavinia, Rome's rich ornament," is described as the most dutiful of daughters, chastest of virgins, noblest of wives; and for the very reason, it would seem, that she is so spotless, is she, like Lucrece, doomed to be the victim of one of those crimes of tragic horror which foully blot the pages of classic story.

For Lavinia's history we beg leave to refer to the text; from the task of describing its terrible details, a woman's pen, however innocently bold, naturally revolts.

The lament of her uncle, Marcus Andronicus, over the fatal catastrophe of her wrongs and mutilation, affords us a few personal touches, suggestive of the accomplishments of this "martyr'd lady:"

> O, that delightful engine of her thoughts,
> That blabb'd them with such pleasing eloquence,
> Is torn from forth that pretty hollow cage;
> Where, like a sweet melodious bird, it sung
> Sweet varied notes, enchanting every ear!
> * * * * * * * * *
> * * * * * * * * *

Fair Philomela, she but lost her tongue,
And in a tedious sampler sew'd her mind;
But, lovely niece, that mean is cut from thee;
A craftier Tereus hast thou met withal,
And he hath cut those pretty fingers off,
That could have better sew'd than Philomel.
O, had the monster seen those lily hands
Tremble, like aspen leaves, upon a lute,
And make the silken strings delight to kiss them,
He would not then have touch'd them for his life;
Or had he heard the heavenly harmony
Which that sweet tongue hath made,
He would have dropp'd his knife, and fell asleep,
As Cerberus at the Thracian poet's feet.
Come, let us go, and make thy father blind;
For such a sight will blind a father's eye.
* * * * * * * * *

Mar. What means my niece Lavinia by these signs?
Tit. Fear her not, Lucius:—Somewhat doth she mean.
See, Lucius, see, how much she makes of thee!
Somewhither would she have thee go with her.
Ah, boy, Cornelia never with more care
Read to her sons, than she hath read to thee,
Sweet poetry, and Tully's Orator.

Tit. Lucius, what book is that she tosseth so?
Boy. Grandsire, 'tis Ovid's Metamorphoses;
My mother gave't me.
Mar. For love of her that's gone,
Perhaps she cull'd it from among the rest.
Tit. Soft! see, how busily she turns the leaves!
Help her:—
What would she find?—Lavinia, shall I read?
This is the tragic tale of Philomel,
And treats of Tereus's treason.

THE END.

www.ingramcontent.com/pod-product-compliance
Lightning Source LLC
Chambersburg PA
CBHW030858270326
41929CB00008B/471
* 9 7 8 3 3 3 7 0 3 2 1 1 1 *